MINUTES OF THE

VIENNA PSYCHOANALYTIC SOCIETY

VOLUME IV:

1912–1918

MINUTES OF THE
VIENNA PSYCHOANALYTIC SOCIETY

Volume IV: 1912–1918

EDITED BY

HERMAN NUNBERG
ERNST FEDERN

*Translated by M. Nunberg
in collaboration with
Harold Collins*

New York

INTERNATIONAL UNIVERSITIES PRESS, INC.

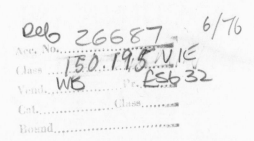
Copyright © 1975, International Universities Press, Inc.

Library of Congress Cataloging in Publication Data

Wiener Psychoanalytische Vereinigung.
  Minutes of the Vienna Psychoanalytic Society.

  Bibliographical footnotes.
  CONTENTS: v. 1. 1906–1908.—v. 2. 1908–1910.—v. 3. 1910–1911.—v. 4. 1912–1918.
    1. Psychoanalysis—Societies, etc. I. Nunberg, Herman, 1884–   ed. II. Federn, Ernst, ed.
  BF173.A2W5   150'.19'5   62-15591
  ISBN 0-8236-3402-7 (v. 4)

Manufactured in the United States of America

CONTENTS

REFERENCES
Key to Abbreviations

C.P. Sigmund Freud: *Collected Papers*, 5 Volumes. London: Hogarth Press, 1924–1950.

G.S. Sigmund Freud: *Gesammelte Schriften*, 13 Volumes. Vienna: Internationaler psychoanalytischer Verlag, 1924–1934.

G.W. Sigmund Freud: *Gesammelte Werke*, 17 Volumes. London: Imago Publishing Company, 1940–1952.

J. *International Journal of Psycho-Analysis*

Jb. *Jahrbuch für Psychoanalyse*

S.E. *The Standard Edition of the Complete Psychological Works of Sigmund Freud*, 24 Volumes. London: Hogarth Press, 1953–

Yb. *The Yearbook of Psychoanalysis*, 10 Volumes. New York: International Universities Press, 1945–1954.

Z. *Internationale Zeitschrift für Psychoanalyse*

Zb. *Zentralblatt für Psychoanalyse*

FOREWORD

As I noted in the Introduction to Volume I of these Minutes, in my editorial work I tried to remain as neutral as possible. When I added footnotes, I did so only in order to elucidate or to call attention to some passages that did not seem quite clear.

In the minutes of the final volume, one finds something that is quite puzzling—namely, that Freud's most devoted followers are beginning to minimize his achievements, and on certain occasions it almost looks as if there were a mutual understanding among them to do so, one in which even Tausk, Federn, Hitschmann, Sadger—those most devoted pupils of Freud—are taking part. At times, these men seem to have forgotten Freud's teachings.

One can only admire the patience with which Freud tried to show them their errors and wrestled with them for their recognition of the basic tenets of psychoanalysis, which formed the foundation for their own work.

H.N.

INTRODUCTION

It has taken a little over two decades to complete the publication of the four volumes of the *Minutes of the Vienna Psychoanalytic Society*. What is most regrettable about this long period—aside from the fact that it rendered unavailable, for longer than one would have wished, this invaluable material—is that the work came to an end almost three years after the death of one of the two co-editors who made such an unmatchable contribution to it—Dr. Herman Nunberg.

There were many difficult, sometimes unsolvable, problems all along the way. Transcribing the protocols from the Gothic longhand script in which they were recorded was itself an enormous task, and thanks, even if belatedly, must go to Mrs. Emmy Bloch for having carried it through. Innumerable references and allusions in the text—persons, places, and publications, among others—had to be identified, and that task fell to my late brother, Walter Federn, who brought to it his extraordinary scholarship. He, too, was not allowed to enjoy seeing the completed volumes.

Yet even these difficulties pale when considered side by side with the tasks of annotation and explanation, willed by my father, Paul Federn, to Dr. Nunberg. For many years he placed at their disposal his well-known clarity of thought and expression, together with his unsurpassed knowledge of Freud's work and of psychoanalytic theory as a whole. So great was Dr. Nunberg's devotion to these tasks that he even put to one side the writing of his own memoirs until he had completed the substantive footnotes that constitute such a valuable part of these three volumes.

Tremendous pitfalls lay in the path of the translator, Margarete Nunberg, who fortunately was able to surmount them.

For both Dr. and Mrs. Nunberg, as for others who contributed to the final product, this has been a labor of love. In their name, I am proud to commit it to the readers who have so long awaited its conclusion.

E.F.

TRANSLATOR'S NOTE

As translator of these four volumes, I would like to point out what was the greatest pitfall that had to be avoided throughout—namely, forgetting that the expositions in these minutes represent, at their best, the psychoanalytic thinking, not of the 1970's or of the 1930's, but of the pioneering years at the beginning of this century. One had continuously to be on guard against "smoothing out the rough edges" of positions that had not yet been fully worked out, or unwittingly smuggling into statements made more than six decades ago concepts and viewpoints that were not to become part of psychoanalytic thinking until 15 to 25 years later. That this did not happen is owing to Dr. Nunberg's careful supervision and his insistence on historical accuracy.

M.N.

ADDITIONAL BIOGRAPHICAL NOTES
ON THE MEMBERS

THEODOR REIK, Ph.D.,* 1888–1969, was born in Vienna, and studied psychology as well as German and French literature at the University of Vienna. He met Freud in 1910, joining the Society in the following year. He went to Berlin for analysis with Karl Abraham and, after serving in World War I as an officer in the Austrian army, returned to Vienna and psychoanalytic work. He succeeded Rank as secretary of the Vienna Society, fulfilling this function until his departure for Berlin in 1928. He moved to The Hague in 1934 and emigrated to the United States four years later. He established himself in New York City, where he founded the National Psychological Association for Psychoanalysis and taught and trained lay psychoanalysts.

Reik was a prolific writer, particularly in applied analysis. Some of the books for which he became well known are: *Psychological Problems of Religion* (1919); *Masochism in Modern Man* (1941); *Listening With the Third Ear* (1948); and *The Compulsion to Confess* (1959).

HANNS SACHS, LL.D.,* 1881–1947, was born in Vienna and studied law there. A highly cultured man with profound artistic and literary interests, he became acquainted with and fascinated by psychoanalysis, joining Freud's group in 1909. He co-edited the *Imago* with Rank and took over the editorship when Rank left. In 1920, Sachs gave up the practice of law and devoted himself entirely to psychoanalysis. He was invited to become a training analyst at the newly founded Psychoanalytic Institute in Berlin. He worked there and practiced psychoanalysis until 1932, when he left for Boston to become a teacher at the Boston Psychoanalytic Society. He was the founder of *American Imago*.

---

* The information comes from *Psychoanalytic Pioneers* (1966), ed. F. Alexander, S. Eisenstein & M. Grotjahn. New York/London: Basic Books.

Hanns Sachs wrote numerous essays in the field of applied psychoanalysis, as well as articles on theory and technique. Among his better-known books are *Day Dreams in Common* (1924); *The Creative Unconscious, Studies in the Psychoanalysis of Art* (1942); and *Freud, Master and Friend* (1944).

RICHARD WAGNER, M.D., born 1887 in Vienna, was an active member of the Society 1910–1912. As he became increasingly interested in biochemistry and pediatrics, he resigned his membership in the Society and moved to Strasbourg for further study in his main field of interest. After World War I he worked at the Vienna Children's Clinic under the great Pirquet, whose biography he recently published. When Hitler overrode Austria, Wagner moved to Boston where he has been living ever since. He was Clinical Professor at Tuft's University Medical School.

156

SCIENTIFIC MEETING *on January 3, 1912*

Present: Dattner, Federn, Freud, Friedjung, Hitschmann, Nepallek, Rank, Reitler, Reik, Rosenstein, Sachs, Sadger, Stekel, Tausk, Wagner, Winterstein.
Guests: Marcinowski, Krauss, Kelsen.

PRESENTATION

From Hebbel's Childhood [1]

SPEAKER: DR. J. SADGER

Because the speaker's presentation is to be published complete in book form, these minutes will be limited to an indication of their content. On the basis of the poet's account of his childhood, as set down by himself (which shows a rare continuity of recollections from the second year onward), Hebbel's childhood relationship to his parents is discussed, along with his early intense falling in love, as well as the relationship, which he himself describes, of his religious ideas

---

[1] Sadger published an article "Über das Unbewusste und die Träume bei Hebbel" [On the Unconscious and the Dreams of Hebbel] in *Imago*, 1913, 2:336–356; an essay, "Freud'sche Mechanismen bei Hebbel" [Freudian Mechanisms in Hebbel] in Z. (1913), 1:165–168; and a book *Friedrich Hebbel, ein psychoanalytischer Versuch* [Friedrich Hebbel, A Psychoanalytic Study], which appeared as late as 1920 (Vienna: Deuticke).

to the father complex. All of this fully confirms the psychoanalytic views about the development of and conflicts within a child's soul.

Further, attention is called to the intimate connection between his vivid imagination and his erotism, which had been awakened at an early age, as well as to his infantile states of anxiety, which had also resulted therefrom. The incidental comment is made that the reason why children tolerate religious dogmas so well and without revolting [Anstoss], is that these dogmas meet the unconscious complexes halfway.

In conclusion, the speaker remarks that the poet was able to write these memoirs only while in a feverish condition, as was often the case with his poetic writings. Since there are similar reports about other poets—Grillparzer, for instance—this may perhaps provide some insight into the process of poetic writing in general, especially if we consider Hebbel's remark that in these states the grotesque faces of old re-emerge—the same faces that in his childhood used to torment him before he fell asleep and which he had not seen since then.

DISCUSSION

STEKEL wishes to object to the discussion of widely known poetic works, and would caution against bringing out once again the mother complex in a poet, since we already know that this complex is operative in everyone. He has not found it to be true that religious dogmas make no impression on children; on the contrary, he feels compelled to ascribe to these dogmas a pathological effect in the emergence of the neurosis, even though it is often an effect that may become apparent only after many years. In one's feelings, the old childhood belief continues to exist forever.

The peculiar precondition for poetic writing is explained by the fact that in a fevered state a breakthrough of the unconscious occurs.

REIK remarks that the suggestions offered by the speaker may be gratefully received as an attempt to discover the basic relation-

2

ships between poetry and childhood experience. In connection with the relationship between illness and poetic production, Goethe's severe illness after his stay in Strasbourg is touched upon, as well as the conception of *Werther*. Schiller said that he was able to write poetry only while in a sort of pathological state.

TAUSK is almost inclined to join with Stekel in his cautioning against the mother complex. What one looks forward to is a psychology of creation. The effect of a feverish state is explained, in terms of Stekel's thinking, as a breakthrough of the unconscious. To this is added the fantasy young people frequently have of longing to be seriously ill in order to be able to create. Actually, this is in order to experience strong infantile affects—that is, in order to bring their infantility to a breakthrough.

SACHS, in contrast to Stekel, would emphasize the value of such inquiries, which for the time being offer us the only possibility for showing that psychoanalysis is a psychology of the normal individual as well. The fact that everyone has a parental complex does not in the least alter the interesting fact that the poet tells us about it, whereas the average person does not. Such a presentation of childhood, however, is by no means unique; we need only call back to mind Rousseau, "Green Henry," and other autobiographies.

ROSENSTEIN does not understand why Hebbel's violent rage is regarded as a symptom of hereditary encumbrance and why no attempt has been made to explain it psychologically (sadism). As against Sachs, one can say that the poet is just as far from being normal as is the neurotic. The explanation of the state of fever seems to be less a psychological matter than an organic one; a toxic effect seems to be involved. Nor does the emergence of the unconscious explain everything; a specific qualitative spiritual endowment is necessary as well.

HITSCHMANN considers it quite understandable that Hebbel, who put down in his diary so many judicious and striking thoughts about the dream and unconscious creation, should have become subject to such a psychoanalytical inquiry, but Sadger's broad exposition does not appeal to him. Sadger did not express the slightest doubt about whether such childhood recollections, brought forth so late, can be taken all that objectively, and whether any psychoanalytic value can be attributed to them. On the whole, it seems that the works of the greater and more conscious poets are less suitable for consideration. Hitschmann would like to offer for discussion the question of how the ideal love object comes into being in very early childhood, and whether the infantile object choice continues later on—side by side with the recollection of the mother—to be an effective model. It may be that a love object does exist even before the incestuous object; but how does it come about that, at that early period, an erotic object choice is possible, alongside that love for adults which is based on *caritas?*

PROF. FREUD, referring to the last remark, mentions that Sanford Bell [2] observed such an early object choice, which had all the psychological signs of being in love, in more than 800 cases (between the ages of three and eight). Object choice takes place at two initial points: the first occurs during infantile life (between the ages of three and four); then follows, after a latency period, the second stormy onset at puberty. This dual onset has certain consequences, inasmuch as children vary in how far they progress beyond the first start. Those who are precocious mentally and sexually fall sexually in love before their time (Byron, Dante); and if a poet spends his life singing of love, we should not be surprised to discover that in his childhood years he was already capable of intensive love for an object. Children's relationship to religion is probably a complicated matter; one finds the positive side of the situation tending to be beneficial, just as the negative side tends to be inhibitory.

In connection with the theme of "illness and creating," FEDERN mentions Heine's poem: *Ich glaube, dass der tiefste Grund/des Schaffens Krankheit ist gewesen,/nur schaffend wurde ich gesund,/nur schaffend konnte ich genesen* [I think that the deepest roots of my creating have lain in illness; it was only by creating that I became well, only by creating that I could recover]. Considering, in this

[2] The reference is probably to Sanford Bell: "A Preliminary Study of the Emotion of Love between the Sexes." *American Journal of Psychology*, 1902, 13.

context, that Hebbel was frequently unable to produce for a long time, one has to say that poets of this sort need specific grounds for being able to create at all. The toxic symptoms of an illness may be just as effective in this regard as is on other occasions some experience of love life. Lying in bed in and of itself creates an infantile attitude in an individual (in bed, one has the self-image of being small), and the transference from mother to the nurse is particularly obvious in this situation. These are occasions that cause childhood recollections to be awakened. Hebbel is one of those neurotic people whom disappointment often renders incapable of working; the illness then excited him to such an extent that despite his inhibitions he became able to produce.

The topic is part of the whole question of the extent to which a poet is normal. Finally, the discussant definitely objects to the publication of the work as well as to the concept of hereditary encumbrance, which can be reduced to the fact that all outstanding men were at an early age intensely sexual and sadistic and therefore showed all those reactions early that in others make their appearance only later and without such intensity.

PROF. FREUD, in connection with the topic of "creativity and illness," mentions that with a prolonged illness there is usually linked the factor of abstinence, and therefore also the tendency toward introjection of the libido.

FRIEDJUNG, as a counterpart to this, draws on his observations of children, in which he finds that the convalescent child misses the increased affection that was lavished upon him during his illness; this brings about similar neurotic symptoms of abstention.

STEKEL adds that the poet flies into raptures of creation when he has recovered from a serious illness. People who are faced with death want to conquer mortality by way of immortality. In all, the psychology of illness should be discussed further; how significant it is for the individual is shown us by the neurotic. Hebbel presents another interesting psychological problem: his writing lies constantly under the shadow of inhibition and never reaches the height aspired to; it often remains far beneath what his subtle and deep psychological comments lead one to expect.

5

MARCINOWSKI, too, is inclined to regard production while feverish as a physiological problem. Inhibitions fall away, as in states of alcoholism or mania. Marcinowski opposes the view that a religious education does not harm the child; he would assert precisely the opposite. In the very frequent blasphemous utterances of children a spite and rebellion is expressed that is actually meant only for the father. The term object *"choice"* may perhaps be misleading, since we do not actively choose but are under a compulsion to choose.

DOZENT KELSEN finds it quite understandable that children fall in love at an early age; he himself remembers several such cases. He did not clearly understand the connection the speaker said existed between every child's aversion to nail cutting and "skin erotism."

SADGER, in his concluding remarks, thanks Prof. Freud for his illumination and Dr. Sachs for having come to his defense, and he replies to Stekel's attacks.

He adds as another noteworthy fact that Hebbel, despite his fantastic memory, was incapable of learning Latin declensions—which may be connected with his early sexual development. These poets probably have erotic fantasies at an early age, and their fantasies become active in every feverish state. The mental precocity which runs parallel to precocious sexual development may be a precondition for artistic production.

157

Present: Dattner, Federn, Freud, Hitschmann, Rank, Rosenstein, Sadger, Steiner, Stekel, Tausk.
Guest: Dr. Krauss.

PRESENTATION

Drawings of Dreams[1]

SPEAKER: DR. MARCINOWSKI

The speaker presents a number of dreams which are accompanied by illustrations drawn by the dreamers, who were just as unaware of the concealed symbolic meaning of these drawings as they were of the actual meaning of the dreams themselves. As a result of the analyses of these dreams and illustrations, three theses are set forth:

(1) All landscapes and localities are symbolic reinterpretations of human bodies. (2) These body representations are in the last analysis fantasies about the mother's womb and about the father's "womb,"

---

[1] Marcinowski was the owner of a sanitarium in Pomerania. The present paper was published in *Zb.* (1911–1912), 2: 490–518 under the title "Gezeichnete Träume" [Dreams Put Down in Drawings].

7

onto which are piled by way of condensation the dreamer's own erotic experiences. For this reason, and as a result of the child-parent relationship, (3) religious ideas play an important role in all these fantasies.

We live in conflicts: each conflict comprises right and wrong, God being the judge thereof.

The speaker then discusses the intimate linking of religion and erotism, explaining it from the standpoint of: (1) developmental history, by way of fusion of the primordial fear of natural forces with the worship of sexual life. This took shape in the deities that thereby evolved out of fear and love in the dying God-Savior, for instance, who is resurrected, a personification of the collapsing phallus which then becomes once again erect; (2) the individual, by reference to his emotional attitude to his parents during childhood. A schema is outlined for the two sexes: from the woman's parental complex, the speaker draws the inference that her prospects for piety are greater; the man suffers from the process of repression. The woman's libido is rather freer and less subject to odium (homosexuality in women, for instance, is not legally forbidden).

DISCUSSION

FEDERN knows only one patient who had the habit of illustrating his dreams by drawings. Once he drew—quite without knowing it—a urinary bladder: he had the theory that he had come into the world out of the urinary bladder. Federn would not, to begin with, believe that every landscape must necessarily represent a human body. Those patients who spontaneously feel compelled to draw will certainly always put in their drawings something obscene which they are concealing from themselves. In the case of Dr. Marcinowski's dreamer, too, his deeply hidden homosexuality was revealed only through his drawing.

HITSCHMANN calls attention to the fact that last year he presented to us a dream-drawing by a girl who drew a cave surrounded by bushes, giving it the unmistakable shape of genitals; thus, also landscape as genitals. The premise of today's paper—that such drawings are conceived unconsciously—is a matter of course.

8

The objection of an opponent of psychoanalysis rested on his assertion that his dreams were not sexual at all, that invariably what he dreamed about was only landscapes. Particularly in this man, however, the mother complex is very marked, as became evident from other utterances of his.

Dr. Marcinowski applied the concept of the fantasy about the mother's womb to the entire body of the mother, and not, as we have been accustomed to doing, only to the genitals.

TAUSK found especially well executed, in this quite excellent paper, the representation of phrases and verbal bridges, something that is usually difficult to achieve. Also worthy of praise is the courage with which everything that is in the dreamer himself was brought out within the framework of the dream. The matter of the landscapes does not always seem to be so unambiguous and simple.

STEKEL praises the formal perfection of the paper, adding the observation that among the poets' dreams he has collected, those that are about specific landscapes have the strongest emotional stress. Freud has already pointed out that all representations of landscapes are mother symbols. Dr. Stekel adds some points to the interpretation of some of the dreams (or shows an overinterpretation), remarking that a crowd of people in dreams often symbolizes an immense number of sperm. Like Dr. Marcinowski, he has to emphasize that all these sexual symbols are at the same time religious symbols.

The reason why women are more devout is not their family complex, but the fact that their apperception is based on their emotions, rather than on their intellect.

RANK calls attention to a counterpart in the realm of the psychology of peoples to the symbolic interpretation of the landscape: the earth, among almost all peoples, is identified with the mother. Gradually we have come to perceive that every dream, in addition to its psychoanalytic meaning and its functional meaning, probably has a third meaning. This is more or less identical with what is implied in Scherner's[2] view of body symbolization.

[2] R. A. Scherner, *Das Leben des Traumes* [*The Life of the Dream*], Berlin, 1861.

9

PROF. FREUD would like to refer to two analogies that confirm the speaker's statements. Pfister[3] has expressed the view that unconscious drawing occurs along the lines of the *Vexierbild* [find-the-figure picture-puzzles] (Leonardo's vulture on Saint Ann[4]). Furthermore, among Marcinowski's introductory statements, there were two that coincide with ideas that he himself will attempt to prove, in a series of writings in the field of the history of religion.

(1) Religion is created from the viewpoint of the son; this is in contrast to law, which stems from the father. In this sense, it is instructive to investigate further how the family complex influences all our psychic productions.

(2) The second point has to do with woman's attitude to religion. The gods are all created by men and worshipped by women. Among those primitive peoples who do not yet till the soil, neither the forces of nature nor the heavenly bodies play any role. In the beginning, animals are worshipped. Later, it is true, the worship of natural forces and of the forces of procreation became fused; this fusion has indeed left clear traces in our language, since all our classical expressions for sexual life stem from a comparison with vegetation. It was at the time when men began to cultivate the soil that this analogizing took place. Along with the right to work mother earth, a tremendous liberation of the libido occurs; a large number of things that were previously forbidden—primitive peoples impose severe sexual restrictions upon themselves—are now permitted. Representatives of that fusion are all those short-lived gods who are certainly gods of vegetation, but also phallic demons (the dying and resurrected God). The progress of civilization will explain—with the help of our psychoanalytical insights—the increasing complexity of these symbols.

That all landscapes and buildings symbolize the human body, and the genitals in particular, can hardly be regarded as doubtful any longer; of course, the plasticity of psychic material does admit of

---

[3] O. Pfister, *"Die psychologische Enträtselung der religiösen Glossolalie und der automatischen Kryptographie"* [*The Psychological Explanation for Religious Glossolalia and Automatic Cryptography*]. Leipzig, Vienna: Deuticke, 1912.

[4] Freud, "Leonardo da Vinci and a Memory of his Childhood." *S.E.*, 11: 59–137.

exceptions. What Tausk praised as an achievement on the part of the interpreter is really due to the dreamer and is absolutely individual.

In all likelihood, only educated persons or physicians will dream of large crowds as symbols for semen. As to the religious symbolism in dreams, the speaker has made an announcement rather than offered a proof.

STEKEL announces a paper on religious symbolism in dreams; it plays a role everywhere because all of us suffer from the religious complex. With regard to the various stages of religion, men always worship that on which they feed (animal, soil).

The "grave misfortune" that often occurs in dreams is birth, which is conceived of in a pessimistic fashion.

TAUSK asks [Freud] what the limitations of libido among the primitives consist of, and receives [from Freud] intimations of a work in progress on the prevention of incest.[5]

Tausk then expresses the opinion that it must be connected with the differentiation of the sexual instinct, which becomes detached from the state of being "in heat."

FEDERN, referring to the religious complex, mentions that the frequent preference given to the youngest sons in the Old Testament (Benjamin, Joseph) might indicate that these tales were composed by youngest sons who wished to possess their father's love with as little limitation and for as long a time as possible. Arguing against Stekel, Federn remarks that the religion people receive and accept as it is, does no harm; it is those who, from the very beginning, founder on the parental complex, and who must therefore recreate their religion on the basis of this complex, that do suffer severely from it.

SADGER gives two examples of dream representations in which a halo [Heiligenschein] proved to symbolize a hypocrite [Scheinheiliger] and the Mariahilferstrasse [street of Mary's help] stood for flight to the mother.

---

[5] Totem and Taboo made its appearance first in the form of a series of articles in Imago 1 and 2 before being published as a book.

KRAUSS calls attention to a little-known brochure by Rosskoff [6] about the religion of primitive peoples.

MARCINOWSKI in his concluding remarks asserts that he has inferred the religious symbolism less from details than from the entire affective attitude of the individuals concerned.

The earlier material of religious images was known to him, indeed; but in consideration of the topic under discussion he did not include it in his presentation.

Finally, he expresses his warmest gratitude to Prof. Freud and accounts for his staying out of the Psychoanalytic Society, by way of a personal complex.

[6] G. Rosskoff, *Das Religionswesen der rohesten Naturvölker* [*Religion of the most primitive peoples*], Leipzig, 1880.

12

158

Present: Dattner, Federn, Freud, Friedjung, Heller, Hitschmann, Nepallek, Rank, Reitler, Sadger, Steiner, Stekel, Reinhold, Sachs, Rosenstein, Tausk.
Guests: Drs. Kerner,[1] Krauss, Marcinowski.

PRESENTATION

From Hebbel's Boyhood

SPEAKER: DR. SADGER

Following up on his earlier presentation, the speaker discusses, on the basis of the biographical material, the poet's later attitude to his parents and siblings. It is characterized above all by an exacerbation of his relationship to his father and a closer attachment to his mother. Hebbel confesses that it was owing to his mother alone that he was able to elude the strong pressure by his father, who had early wanted to force him to enter a profession that ran counter to his entire nature. Although the mother quite obviously in fact preferred

---

[1] Dr. Kerner's identity could not be established.

her oldest son, the poet, nevertheless, in a recently published poem (composed in his puberty), and in the fairy tale "The Lonely Children," [2] the poet expressed the feeling that the mother preferred the younger brother.

The speaker resolves this striking contradiction by locating the feeling back in early childhood, when the mother probably did really favor the newborn, helpless younger brother. This fairy tale shows the author's dislike for his brother, just as does another poetic work of his puberty, "Fratricide".[3] Hatred of the father, grounded in the Oedipus complex, is expressed in *Patricide*,[4] a work of the same period. The insatiability of the child's neurotic need for love may also have contributed to his viewing his brother as a preferred rival. One may possibly infer anthropophagic ideas from the fairy tale, as well as from the vehement impression [made] upon Hebbel by the passage in Jeremiah,[5] in which the mothers slaughter their children.

Next to the family complex, the religious complex plays the chief role in the poet's psychic life. Hebbel discloses to us two roots of religious feeling: (1) fear; (2) becoming aware of a power superior to that of one's parents. The reason why the child accepts religious dogmas which he does not understand is that, as Hebbel's notes make clear, these dogmas meet his unconscious halfway and match it in mysteriousness.

From all this the speaker draws the conclusion that we are dealing here with a case of infantile obsessional neurosis, with brooding and doubting mania (tormented by thoughts about nothingness). Throughout his life, the poet had experienced—as the figures in his dramas also show—an urge for self-justification.

Then the speaker attempts to prove that as early as in his first or second year Hebbel must have overheard parental intercourse.

[2] Friedrich Hebbel, *Meine Kindheit. Die einsamen Kinder. Geschichte.* Auswahl von Gustav Falké. [*My Childhood. The Lonely Children. Poems.* Selected by Gustav Falke]. 1906.

[3] *Der Brudermord* (1831). *Sämtliche Werke*, VIII.

[4] *Der Vatermord. Ein dramatisches, Nachtgemälde* [*Patricide. A Dramatic Night-painting*].

[5] *Die Klagelieder des Jeremias* [*The Lamentations of Jeremiah*]. In *Aufzeichungen aus meinem Leben* [*Notes from My Life*], Hebbel writes: "I still remember what horror filled me when I heard those words, perhaps because I did not know whether they were referring to the past or the future, to Jerusalem or to Wesselburen, and because I was a child myself and had a mother."

This brought about the entire oedipal attitude as revealed in his poems of puberty; its influence can be followed even as far as *Judith.*

As with every obsessional neurotic, we also find in him a strong sadistic component as well as, of course, the masochistic vein.

The poet's development was decisively influenced by his father's death, which occurred when the boy was in his fifteenth year; he blamed himself for it.

Finally a dream of the four- or five-year-old boy is related: he is being rocked by his father and has anxious feelings. The dream is interpreted as an expression of repressed libido (anxiety), and of the death wish directed against the father.

DISCUSSION

SACHS, on the basis of three notes in Hebbel's diary, would like to support the supposition that as a small child the poet overheard his parents' sexual intercourse. There are two dreams, one of which unambiguously symbolizes his overhearing sexual intercourse, and there is also a slip in writing (*"Noah's"* daughters who committed incest with their father, instead of *Lot's* daughters; on the other hand, Noah's sons saw their father naked). An interesting parallel to these dreams of having overheard something is mentioned from Wassermann's[6] first novel *Mother, Are You Sleeping?* However, in that novel, this complex has already been built into the later family romance.

STEKEL is better satisfied with today's presentation. He himself has made a collection of Hebbel's dreams, many of which refer to the mother's womb. It is in that sense that Stekel would also interpret the dream of the four-year-old. Not only does it contain the inversion of actual criminal ideas into anxiety; it also contains the fantasy that the child in the mother's womb takes part in parental intercourse.

REINHOLD would also interpret the dream along the same lines as Stekel: the child wants to be taken along to intercourse.

[6] Jacob Wassermann (1873–1934), an important German writer.

FEDERN first criticizes some deficiencies in style, and objects in general to the form of the presentation; the contents are for the most part correct, but they are not acceptable in the way they are presented. It won't do, for instance, in this context and in this fashion, to toss in—in passing, as though it were a matter of course —the interpretation of the Resurrection as erection. That is surely correct for a certain psychic and cultural stratum, but certainly it does not correspond to the intentions of those with whom this view originated to present it in this fashion. It discredits their conception.

The child accepts religion because he does not exercise any criticism. He does not have to be an obsessional neurotic for this, just as he does not have to be an obsessional neurotic to identify with Christ—something that any believing Catholic can achieve. The real problem of sadism was not broached: the problem of whether it originates in the fact that the child has been ill treated, or goes back to an independent *Anlage*. As an etiological factor, one often encounters an early combination of precocious sexual sensations with corporal punishment, even if it was not these persons themselves who were beaten. In one case in which this influence had not existed, anthropophagic tendencies, which Sadger also mentioned, proved to be present. In all individuals who are in some way out-standing, the strongest and oldest instinctual drives of mankind are present in greater intensity and with more effectiveness than they are in the average man.

PROF. FREUD, in a more general critique, attempts to explain why Sadger consistently encounters opposition: he has too harsh a way of approaching delicate problems. Above all, however, he in-variably neglects the whole superstructure and presents things as though the psychosexual factors which are at the deepest roots were the solutions that offered themselves at the start. In the second place, Sadger ignores the fact that all these things are constituent parts of every human soul. Even without analysis we know that poets, like other human beings, have had parents and therefore also a parental complex; what we want to see is what has become of this complex in the case of the poet, which attitude in his later life we can perhaps trace back to a specific constellation of that complex.

16

On the basis of the material, it appears wrong to call Hebbel a severe obsessional neurotic; [those traits] must still be ascribed to character formation.

What Sadger has said about religion is not valid; if religion were to be used as proof for the existence of the unconscious, animals, who work almost exclusively with the unconscious, would have to be more religious than men. The connection between the fear of the nutcracker and the father seems rather obvious, in view of the fact that the predilection many people have for the ugly and for caricature would permit us to suspect that they have an (unconscious) criticizing attitude toward the father. The dream of the four-year-old Hebbel cannot be interpreted in the way Stekel did, because in order to do so one must first introduce the mother's womb into the dream.

There is no objection to Sadger's interpretation, aside from the fact that it is incomplete. True, he mentioned it in connection with overhearing parental intercourse, but he did not find that meaning in the dream. The dream, which above all has the rhythm of sexual intercourse, is exquisitely a dream of overhearing [parental intercourse], with a special turn. For the child reacts to this trauma in a twofold manner (ambivalently): (1) he would like to be in his father's place (with all the consequences of the Oedipus complex); (2) he would, on the other hand, also like to be in his mother's place (passive attitude). Hebbel's dream is the sort of dream that expresses the homosexual attitude toward the father: he wants to be used by him in sexual intercourse. In this context, Freud adds the general remark that the fragmentary dreams often reported by patients are in most cases more complete than we think: it is only that they contain the situation as such, along with the symbols of the situation.

TAUSK turns first to an aesthetic critique, expressing in particular his wish to see eliminated the phrase "wee Frederic." He, too, finds that the speaker says only the most primitive and "final" things, but also that he is correct only where he does say these things, and not otherwise. Tausk objects to the assertion that the capacity to remember indicates the *poet*; it indicates any kind of intellectual power. The meaning of caricature along the lines of

17

Freud's interpretation is confirmed by means of one case. In another case the burial fantasies represented the love for the mother in its inversion into hatred; many burial fantasies are castration fantasies. The "torments of nothingness" are connected with: (1) the sensation of feeling everything in one primordial emotion; (2) the poet's love for the old book; (3) weeping for himself. Aside from the fact that this appears in relation to anxiety, it is a notion that signifies a long-lasting and severe disappointment, a period of detaching oneself, during which period one no longer has any dealings with the past and none, as yet, with the future. In this period, the affect must work to take the man away from himself. This is the peculiar *post coitum triste*, no matter when it may appear. The old book shows the poet's love for the past; his weeping for himself shows how miserable he is.[7]

HITSCHMANN points out that the murder of the squirrel (brother) as described in the fairy tale written in Hebbel's puberty, leads one to regard his subsequent exaggerated affection for his squirrel as a reaction to his infantile impressions. The [four-year-old] boy's dream is in its contents a kind of flying dream.

It is correct that an unusual power of recollection characterizes a poet.

Man's jealousy in later years certainly derives its main strength from the infantile sibling jealousy.

We should pay attention to the way in which certain complexes present themselves; we should, for instance, attempt to define specific mother complexes—for example, how development looks on the part of someone who lost his mother at an early age (Segantini, Wassermann).

RANK, in reference to the sadomasochistic complex, mentions a puzzling action that occurred in Hebbel's early years when he was very miserable. (It is recorded in his diary.) He would hold his breath as long as possible and until it caused him pain, for the sole purpose of achieving an awareness of his self (Tausk's "torments of nothingness").

---

[7] This discussion is very difficult to understand, probably because of the overcondensation by Rank.

18

MARCINOWSKI mentions, in connection with the meaning of caricatures and grimaces, a woman patient who would show herself to be inhibited by her father complex whenever the physician's face revealed an angry or sullen expression. He, too, objects to the diagnosis of an obsessional neurosis in Hebbel; it is an arbitrary generalization to describe as "obsessional neurosis" every psychic constellation that excludes voluntary action.

SADGER, in his concluding remarks, stresses that he evaluated the significance of religion solely on the basis of the poet's own words. He replies to Federn that he had not regarded those features to which Federn had objected as the result of obsessional neurosis (identification with Christ, etc.). During the course of his broad activity as a writer of many years, his style has never so far caused offense anywhere. As far as the singularly emotional rejection by this group of "hereditary taint" is concerned—the symptoms of which are confirmed over and over again—this notion seems to be disagreeable to many for the reason that it touches upon personal complexes. The one-sidedness of his presentation, with which fault was found, is due to the fact that he had omitted from his paper those points that are taken for granted in this circle; but he had dealt adequately with them in publication.

159

SCIENTIFIC MEETING *on January 24, 1912*

Present: Dattner, Federn, Freud, Friedjung, Hitschmann, Nepallek, Rank, Reik, Reitler, Rosenstein, Sachs, Sadger, Silberer, Spielrein, Steiner, Stekel, Tausk, Wagner.
Guests: Dr. Krauss, Dr. Schmelz, Dr. Reinhard, Egon Popper.

FOURTH DISCUSSION ON MASTURBATION

SPEAKERS: FRIEDJUNG, FERENCZI

FRIEDJUNG presents data collected during the course of the past year-and-a-half and stresses the difficulties encountered in obtaining such material. He mentions in particular the fact that mothers and nurses with intelligence do not say anything about these things, even if they are aware of them. The observations have to do with 35 children: 18 boys and 17 girls; there is thus an even distribution of the sexes.

As early as at the age of three to four months, when children are already lying uncovered for a while, one can see them touching their genitals with clearly pleasurable sensations—the boys, in most cases, without erection; the girls, without conspicuous psychic concomitants. In some children, these manipulations bring about orgasm as early as in the first year of life. (Some of these acts last for as long as a quarter of an hour). These things occur until about the fourth half-year without any sign of shame. Obviously it is the cleansing process that draws the child's attention to the genital as a source of pleasure.

In both sexes, hand and finger are most frequently employed for that purpose; pressure of the thighs is used, and not only by the female sex; objects too are resorted to. Besides, contrary to Sadger's assumption, children are able to use these methods interchangeably.

The thrust of repression around the second year, induced by way of training, can be clearly recognized in some cases. In later years, it is often an external cause (balanitis) that leads boys to masturbate between the ages of five and 12. Orgasm occurs less frequently at this later period or it occurs only in disguised form. The fact that masturbation flares up once again during the period after the first thrust of repression is often traceable to seduction by older persons. Extragenital masturbation is not infrequent either (at the navel; sucking: Lindner-Freud).[1]

The observations took in children belonging to different strata of the population and to different races; what was seen is probably true of all children in the first two years of life, and is tolerated well by them.

As far as psychic concomitants in the later years of childhood are concerned, no fantasies in Freud's sense could be observed—at least no conscious ones; if nothing else, there existed a split of the personality, since the boys were able, side by side with their ample and varied masturbatory activity, to function irreproachably as pupils. Boys succeed most easily in achieving the transition to normal sexual intercourse if while masturbating they have had a so-called "normal fantasy" about woman. The factor that turns normal masturbation into a pathological phenomenon seems to lie in the realm of the psyche.

[1] See Freud, "Three Essays on the Theory of Sexuality," *S. E.*, 7: 125–243.

DISCUSSION

SADGER finds his analytic conclusion confirmed by the speaker's observations—namely, that masturbation arises out of the stimulation provided by parents during bodily care of the infant. In touching their genitals, children merely repeat the experience they had while being cleaned. Pressing together the thighs, on the other hand, seems to go back to the pleasurable sensation evoked by swaddling. It is only from parents who are psychoanalytically trained that one can learn anything about the masturbatory fantasies of childhood.

FEDERN mentions that in the *Theory of Sexuality* Freud already pointed out the connection between a suckling's masturbation and his bodily care, adding that neglect in this care also makes for the child's early acquaintance with this erotogenic zone.

Federn has observed infants who had erections as early as during the first four weeks. The question is whether a sexual fantasy is linked with every act of masturbating. Children also have sexual discharges with processes that have nothing to do with sexuality, and individuals may well have similar fantasies while masturbating. On the other hand, it is unquestionably true that children do have a number of sexual fantasies, and there is no basic difference whether these fantasies are consciously evoked to accompany the act or are merely unconsciously nourished by it.

STEKEL values the presentation very highly, yet he would like to give voice to some differences of opinion. In his article on "Intercourse in Childhood," [2] he mentioned that Henoch [3] knew of infant-masturbation. Masturbation does not start in the fourth month, but it does start in the very earliest period of life. It is true, though, that it is not always performed on the penis, but just as frequently at the anus. Boys usually acquire balanitis because they masturbate, just as in most instances vaginal discharge is a consequence of masturbation. Orgasm in children consists of an intense tickling sensation, which in rare instances terminates in a urinary discharge. Emission hardly ever occurs before the age of 12. The going over to

[2] "Koitus im Kindesalter."
[3] E. H. Henoch (1820–1910), German pediatrician. It could not be established to what article Stekel was referring.

22

the woman appears to be somewhat more complicated. There is no doubt that infants have no fantasies; these appear only later as mental superstructure, and with them the feeling of guilt also sets in.[4]

TAUSK also stresses the value of empirical observations as a supplement to material disclosed by psychoanalysis.

Two kinds of fantasies must be distinguished: (1) fantasies that are immanent, and (2) fantasies that run parallel to the act. The former are those that are truly unconscious and cannot simultaneously (with the masturbatory act) be transformed into images. The child behaves "as if." The masturbatory act corresponds to a fantasy; later on, the image is carried into it, and the fantasy may become pathogenic.

PROF. FREUD, replying to Stekel, interposes that the question was not whether infants masturbate with or without fantasies; that question has to do with a later period of childhood.

DR. ROSENTHAL (Mrs.), drawing on the analysis of a 35-year-old woman, relates symptoms of psychic masturbation, which consisted in imagining sexual intercourse with a man (the hero of a novel). The analysis disclosed that at the age of three the patient had practiced physical masturbation, which was then forbidden by her mother. As a result, psychic masturbation set in when the patient was five or six years old; its hero, a fairy-tale prince, proved to be a displacement from an affectionate uncle.

HITSCHMANN also thinks that the frequency of anal masturbation has not been stressed sufficiently; it is extremely common, yet just as commonly it escapes notice because it is not regarded as masturbation. (Case of a decidedly anal-erotic girl; moving back and forth on a seat.)

ROSENSTEIN remarks that the question about fantasies is connected with the question of autoerotism; if the fantasies are related to another person, masturbation is no longer purely autoerotic. In

---

[4] It is immaterial whether small children do or do not have fantasies; it is almost impossible, in any event, for the adult observer to ascertain whether they do or do not. There is just as much justification for characterizing the small child's psychic life as conscious as there is for characterizing it as unconscious. If one cannot establish the presence of fantasies, however, that does not mean that these children actually do not have any fantasies.

his conception of unconscious fantasies, Federn sees in the unconscious not merely the repressed but also the innate component part of the psyche.

That recollections of infancy could have been ascertained by means of psychoanalysis seems to Rosenstein to be impossible.

PROF. FREUD appreciates the value of these independent observations, but assures Mr. Rosenstein that analysis does reach back into the first and second years of life. Often, however, what is disclosed during the course of an analysis is merely circumstantial evidence, which the patient can usually confirm at the end of his treatment by way of recollection. The negative value of information provided by adults, which Friedjung emphasized, can also be recognized in analysis; it is for this reason that one should never try to corroborate the results of an analysis by means of such information.

It would be of great value if the speaker were also able to relate to us his observations about how often the castration threat (or a threat analogous to it—for example, the threat of death), which plays an enormous role in analyses, was actually brought forward under these circumstances in childhood. Then we would be better able to discern whether the impact of this threat rests on purely individual experience, or whether for a full understanding of it we would have to go back to the ancient traditions of mankind.

Since childhood masturbation is such a general occurrence and is at the same time so poorly remembered, it must have an equivalent in psychic life. And, in fact, it is found in the fantasy encountered in most female patients—namely, that the father seduced her in childhood. This is the later reworking which is designed to cover up the recollection of infantile sexual activity and represents an excuse and an extenuation thereof. The grain of truth contained in this fantasy lies in the fact that the father, by way of his innocent caresses in earliest childhood, has actually awakened the little girl's sexuality (the same thing applies to the little boy and his mother). It is these same affectionate fathers that are the ones who then endeavor to break the child of the habit of masturbation, of which they themselves had by that time become the unwitting cause. And thus the motifs mingle in the most successful fashion to form this fantasy, which often dominates a woman's entire life (seduction fantasy):

24

one part truth, one part gratification of love, and one part revenge.

In reply to Rosenstein, Freud states that as a rule we characterize as "autoerotic" only the first two years of life; the masturbation of the subsequent period, with its fantasies about other persons, is no longer purely autoerotic, but constitutes an intermediate stage between autoerotism and object love. It remains to be determined precisely what role the fantasies play in this transition.

STEKEL has a different point of view with regard to the castration fantasy; he believes that originally, out of envy, it is directed against the father, and that only later on, with the process of repression, it becomes transferred in the form of expiation onto the subject's own person. This plays an important role in the genesis of some cases of impotence. The second root lies in the tendency to work out the feminine aspect of the subject's nature. In the case of the Scoptics,[5] one sees how this father complex merges with the religious complex: they sacrifice the phallus out of feelings of guilt, because of their envy of the father.

The seduction fantasy mentioned by Freud occurs also in a very large number of men who insist on their having been seduced by a woman; what is sought for in this fantasy, as well as in the female seduction fantasy, is pleasure without guilt. The castration fantasy directed against the father is analogous to the girl's wish for sterility, which is directed against the mother. (FREUD: Little girls also imagine that one becomes a woman through castration).

SPIELREIN, referring to the question of psychic masturbation, remarks that a woman in love imagines herself in her lover's place, and thereby becomes excited; the transition from this psychic masturbation to physical masturbation takes place as the result of the fact that the woman then imitates this. A special form of female masturbation: sucking at her own breasts while imagining herself as both mother and child.

FRIEDJUNG has rarely seen anal masturbation in the first year of life. Certainly, the beginning of masturbation varies with the

[5] Skoptsi, a Russian religious sect, which was first discovered in 1771 when 14 Russian peasants had themselves castrated. In later years, this sect was satisfied with practicing sexual abstinence.

individual, but its appearance during the fourth week (Federn, Stekel) definitely belongs among the exceptions. Only in very few instances is *fluor* a consequence of masturbation; in 99 per cent of the cases, one finds gonococci.

STEKEL considers this a dubious point, since these gonococci have not been demonstrated to be infectious; nor do these children display any serious and general symptoms, such as those of gonorrhea.

STEINER, although not identifying himself with Stekel's view, mentions that undoubtedly nongonorrheic urethritis occurs in both sexes, and just as frequently one encounters nongonorrheic discharge (the so-called "anemic *fluor*").

HITSCHMANN shares Friedjung's opinion that crude discharge which has been caused by masturbation may also exist.

FEDERN remarks that on the basis of Friedjung's assertion the circumstantial evidence for masturbation by sucklings is very limited; it would seem that masturbation generates discharge, but that, on the other hand, discharge also stimulates masturbation.

FERENCZI, having excluded from his discussion some of the psychic disturbances caused by masturbation, because they are secondary and stem from fear (infantile fear of castration, as well as juvenile fear of incest), refers (and also goes into various particulars on the question) to the fact that masturbation is also capable of directly evoking certain nervous and psychic disturbances. In many cases he found, in addition to the psychosexual dreams and repressions—which play the far more significant role—a "one-day-neurasthenia," which may later on turn into genuine sexual neurasthenia in the Freudian sense.

Having given recognition to the significance of the psychic factor in *ejaculatio praecox*, the speaker points out that the genesis of the symbolism of tooth-pulling, which in dreams usually represents masturbation, probably lies in its connection with castration (the punishment for masturbation).

DISCUSSION

TAUSK establishes the similarity of Ferenczi's discussion to his own exposition, in which the harm done by masturbation was also traced back to the fact that the perversions do not come into the foreplay.

HITSCHMANN welcomes the fact that someone has laid stress, in the discussion, on the *physiological* harm done by masturbation. As to the relation between *ejaculatio praecox* and masturbation, he has found it to lie in the undischarged excitations (of the so called psychic masturbation).

REITLER remarks that, in his experience, the harm done by masturbation also makes its appearance with mutual masturbation between man and woman—that is to say, in a situation in which everything is available that is available in intercourse. This experience speaks against Ferenczi and Tausk.

STEKEL considers most of Ferenczi's exposition (one-day neurasthenia; morning libido) to be beside the point and incorrect; in his own report, he will come back to this. Nor does tooth neurosis have anything to do with masturbation; the fact of the matter is that the mouth as erotogenic zone is identified with the genital.

STEINER considers most of Ferenczi's exposition to be absolutely correct and to the point; in his own report, he will come back to this.

PROF. FREUD mentions a parallel to the tooth-pulling castration fantasy from the puberty rites of Australian primitives.

160

Present: Dattner, Federn, Freud, Friedjung, Hitschmann, Rank, Reik, Reinhold, Reitler, Rosenstein, Sachs, Sadger, Silberer, Spielrein, Steiner, Tausk, Wagner.

Guests: Krauss, Bardach, Kelsen, Rosenthal.

PRESENTATION

On the Sensation of Flying in Dreams[1]

SPEAKER: DR. PAUL FEDERN

The speaker first takes issue with Tausk's thesis that the psyche in sleep is identical with the psyche in the waking state; at most, the speaker would grant this in its negative form. The psyche of a person who is awake contains no ideational element that could not also make its appearance in a dream; but the dream contains

[1] Federn's paper "Über den Flugtraum" [On dreams of flying], was published as the third section of an article "Über zwei typische Traumsensationen" [On two typical dream sensations] in *Jb.* (1914), 6: 111–134. An excerpt appeared in *The Psychoanalytic Reader*, edited by R. Fliess, New York: International Universities Press, 1948, pp. 352–356.

elements that are completely alien to the healthy psyche in the waking state, elements that we encounter only in abnormal psychic phenomena.

One such element which is unknown to the waking state is the sensation of flying; Freud[2] has pointed out that dreams in which this occurs invariably reproduce a sexual content; and he has also dealt with the hitherto existing organ theories.

These organ theories (of which the speaker briefly outlines and discusses six) are also valid. However, they are invariably able to explain only particular types of dreams of flying or individual elements in these dreams; for instance, the dream-state perception of breathing (thoracic sensation) can explain only the dreamer's rhythmic movements. Other dreams of flying are codetermined by somatic elements.

The speaker believes that the lowering of skin sensitivity during sleep has a particular bearing on the sensation of rising into the air. In support of this opinion, the speaker adduces his own hypnagogic observation, and also refers to the flights of witches, with their sexual elements.

The speaker is inclined to distinguish, even in simple dream-sensations, between manifest content and dream source: that is, between the sense organ with which one feels the sensation and the one from which the stimulus emanates. If we wish to know via what sense organ the element that is common to all dreams of flying is felt, we must ask ourselves: on what other occasion do we have the feeling of moving, when in fact we are not? It is the case in *vertigo.*

The transformation of some dreams of flying into dreams of falling is also understandable in terms of the sensation of dizziness. Freud has pointed out the connection of dizziness with the wild games of childhood—being tossed up in the air and then dropped. The desire to do without the help of grown-ups is one of the roots of pride in flying: in dreams, this is invariably a personal skill. The organ with which the dream receives the sensation is the static organ, and the sensation of flying occurs by way of regression

[2] Presumably in his "Theory of Dreams," *Amer. J. Psych.* 1910, XXI, pp. 283–308.

to that organ. Establishing this does not, of course, say anything about either the psychic elements or material from organs elsewhere.

Another source of dreams of flying is the erection, which strikes man as being an abolition of the pull of gravity. In this, the representation of the erect penis must be distinguished from that of the process of erection. There are of course various ways of working up this sexual process in the dream; the theme of erection is often the determinant for the entire dimensional organization of the dream (this applies also to the female erection of the clitoris).

In view of the general conception among almost all peoples of the male membrum as a bird, and considering the winged phalli of antiquity, we may say: the dreamer flies because he is representing the flight of the phallus. The element of exhibitionism makes its appearance in every dream of flying. The termination of the erection often causes a sudden transformation of the flying dream into a dream of falling; the feeling of anxiety that, according to organ theories, is supposed to derive from heavy breathing, is here explained as ungratified libido. Flying downward is an inhibited sexual dream and corresponds to an erection that misfired. The speaker briefly mentions additional sources of the flying dream: a desire to ''outfly''; the connection with flatulence and with traveling, as pointed out by Jones; the utilization of the dream of flying as a symbol of dying (Freud, Stekel). These various sources do not contradict one another, but rather correspond to the fact that dreams have many determinants. Erection seems to be the essential one.

The speaker remarks that regression from sensation to the apparatus of thinking does not run parallel to the historical regression to infantile memories; we therefore encounter an ever more universal symbolism, in the analysis of which infantile material proves useless.

In conclusion, the speaker illustrates by a case of neurosis the identity of the dream of flying with the symptoms of dizziness; on the basis of his understanding of the bodily sensations in the dream, he sheds some light on the conversion. Dreams of flying are based on a sensation that they all have in common and, therefore, also on a common fantasy, which in other instances is expressed in hysterical conversion. Conversion is a specific process in which, out of a fantasy of that sort, there arises a somatic phenomenon, quite the other way round from the emergence of a psychic phenomenon out of a bodily stimulus. Yet the feeling of dizziness is not identical with the sensation of flying; consequently, the assertion that the psyches of the sleeping and the waking person are identical is not valid.

DISCUSSION

KRAUSS relates a report by the ethnologist Steinen:[3] on his South American trip, he had frequent flight dreams connected with daytime thoughts of his faraway fiancée.

REINHOLD would like to defend Tausk's assertion by pointing out that it is images of flying that we have in dreams, and not sensations of flying. As a matter of principle, it has to be explained how we get vestibular sensations in dreams at all; in neurotics an organic defect may perhaps be involved.

The direction in which one feels oneself spinning cannot be altered at will. The discussant has himself observed that dreams of falling occur to him when he is lying on his left side.

TAUSK identifies himself completely with the corrections and objections voiced by the preceding discussant and adds that the *image* of flying could have been present in the dreamer's thoughts even while he was awake. The regression derives, in Freud's sense, ontogenetically from individual experiences.

Flying downward as a symbol of inhibited erection? An inhibited erection is indeed no erection at all. Finally, Tausk refers to a dream that does not fit in with the schema set up by Federn: it begins with anxiety, and besides the dreamer feels too heavy.

FEDERN refers briefly to the objections raised: if the feeling of vertigo and the sensation of flying are not identical, then his assertion is valid. Flying is a sensation; the consciousness of it makes its

[3] Karl von den Steinen, 1855–1929: *Unter den Naturvölkern Zentral Brasiliens. Reiseschilderung und Ergebnisse der zweiten Schingu Expedition 1887–88.* [*With the Primitive Peoples of Central Brazil. Itinerary and Results of the Second Schingu Expedition, 1887–88.*] Berlin: 1894.

appearance, of course, in the form of an image. He has explained how it is that vestibular sensations emerge: we have certain conceptions of the *vestibularis,* and by way of regression the vestibular apparatus is again stimulated centrifugally. Persons who know that they are impotent may very well, in dreams, fall downward as a way of expressing an imperfect erection.

SPIELREIN refers to a special type of flying dream that is patterned after the model of childhood games (tossing a child in the air, spinning him, throwing him upside down, etc.).

RANK relates the flying dream of a healthy man which shows most clearly the exhibitionistic and anal factors in conjunction with the sexual factor (potency).

DR. (MRS.) ROSENTHAL discusses the relation of the dream of flying to conversion; she thinks that somatic compliance plays a role only at the moment of the appearance of the symptom, while conversion as such is something stabilized. Over and over again we see that the motor symptom of the conversion emerges on the basis of an image; we can dispense altogether with explanation in terms of sensations.

SACHS, referring to the dream related by Rank, comments that the great number of spectators probably represents, by means of the opposite, the single concealed female spectator, who is hinted at later on. The dreamer's pride is then the pride of the boy who exhibits his penis in front of that person (his sister) who does not possess one.

SILBERER finds much in the presentation that is to the point and, in particular, finds the hypnagogic phenomena to be very nicely observed; he calls attention to the significant individual variations of these phenomena. He then discusses the relation between flying dreams and staircase dreams, a relationship also alluded to by the speaker, and explains it by the fact that both types of dreams have exquisitely sexual contents. Finally, Silberer relates a dream of flying that he himself had last night, which shows almost all the conditions and characteristics mentioned by the speaker.

32

FEDERN mentions that the sensation of being carried, which stems from childhood and which Stekel showed to be present in wet-nurse dreams, may well supply material also for flying dreams. As to the question of conversion, there is a misunderstanding on the part of Dr. Rosenthal: somatic compliance is a permanent condition and has nothing to do with the *mechanism* of conversion.

ROSENSTEIN establishes that the speaker was not concerned with the interpretation of these dreams, but with determining and explaining certain elements in terms of sensations. In the Tausk-Federn controversy, Rosenstein sides with Federn. It is not absolutely necessary *a priori* for every dream element to go back to an infantile wish. The sharp distinction made between the sensation of a movement and its image is not justified; sensory and motor processes flow into each other.

PROF. FREUD is in considerable agreement with many of the speaker's statements and cannot take issue with others. In linking two inquiries that have nothing to do with each other, the speaker has blotted out one of the distinctions we have painstakingly established. The following are two totally different questions: what it is that a thing represents? what material it is made of? The question of what are the dream stimuli that produce a flying dream becomes interesting for us only where it is shown that a stimulus leading to erection is involved—a stimulus that is worked up psychically and then achieves representation in the dream.

The relation that conversion bears to the flying dream is the most interesting part of the paper. As a rule, one can represent regressively only what is visually present as a childhood memory. Formal and temporal regression usually coincide. By way of the fact that the stimulus of erection is reworked into flying, the latter feeling becomes sexualized; carrying it back into childhood simply serves the purpose of rendering it harmless.

Somatic compliance is a borderline position between the realms of the psychic and the organic; the essential factor is the erotogenic disposition of the organ. In conversion, it is probable that conditions of stimulation play a role. In the physiological phenomenon of paralysis, it is possible to pursue the share of the psychic factors rather far. Hysterical paralyses come about in the following way: first a particular organ becomes closely tied in with unconscious complexes. This has as its consequence changes of innervation, as well as changes in the proportions of sensitivity. It is in this physiological factor that somatic compliance lies; there are paths leading from the unconscious into the somatic. We can never derive from psychological factors the onesidedness of somatic symptoms.

With regard to the spontaneous recoveries mentioned by the speaker, transference is not the only path that leads to them; just as often they come about through cessation of the nosological gain. The peculiar pride is reminiscent of the fantasies about skills one finds among those who are ill; these skills invariably refer, in an infantile sense, to the sexual, to having intercourse. Relieving oneself in public in the dreams related by Rank represents a secret.[4]

TAUSK mentions in this context that the little child is taught to be proud of his stool. He [Tausk] thinks that the relief felt with defecation may also be one of the sources of the dream of flying.

FEDERN, in his concluding remarks, takes exception to the reproach that he has blotted out a line of division. He merely wanted at that point to show the connection with previous authors and to demonstrate how, in the light of psychoanalysis, old things take on new meaning and achieve new understanding on our part.

---

[4] At first, Freud was not convinced that Federn's interpretation was correct; however, he considered it significant enough to devote to it a paragraph in the third edition of *The Interpretation of Dreams*, 1911, which begins as follows: *Dr. Paul Federn hat die bestechende Vermutung ausgesprochen* . . . [Dr. P. Federn has put forward the attractive theory . . .] (*S.E.*, 5, p. 394). There is another reference to that interpretation in a footnote in the second edition of Freud's paper on Leonardo da Vinci, 1919 (*S.E.*, 11, p. 126).

In 1917, in *The Introductory Lectures*, Freud (*S.E.*, 15: 155) speaks of Federn's interpretation as "being established beyond any doubt"—an example of Freud's method of working, as well as of his attitude toward original contributions by his pupils.

161

SCIENTIFIC MEETING *on February 7, 1912*

Present: Dattner, Federn, Freud, Friedjung, Hitschmann, Rank, Reik, Reinhold, Reitler, Rosenstein, Sachs, Sadger, Spielrein, Steiner, Stekel, Tausk, Wagner.
Guests: Dr. (Mrs.) Rosenthal, Krauss, Marcus.

FIFTH DISCUSSION ON MASTURBATION

SPEAKERS: REITLER, STEKEL

REITLER intends to discuss only the reason why masturbation is harmful in certain cases. Before taking up his topic, he criticizes Stekel's assertion that neurasthenia is a psychogenic illness, pointing out that not everything that can be influenced by psychological means must for that reason be psychogenic.

The great differences in the psychological effects of masturbation on different individuals are explained, to begin with, by the differences in their psychosexual constitutions, as well as by the fact that a great variety of things is subsumed under the concept of masturbation. The speaker, in agreement with Löwenfeld,[1] doubts whether one is justified in inferring the sexual development of normal persons from that of neurotics. If we could set aside all the processes in neurotic sexual development that do not serve the goal and even run counter to it, then we might have some prospects of getting to know about normal sexual development. We should subsume under normal sexual development the suckling's masturbation at the erotogenic zones because it is purposeful and in the interests of the preservation of life. On the other hand, masturbation at the genital tract in prepuberty serves no purpose and is therefore not normal. The normal individual masturbates before puberty exclusively at the erotogenic zones, whereas an individual who before puberty already has an abnormal sexual constitution masturbates at the genitals and represses the pleasure-gain at other zones. Later on this causes the "hysterical negative" to develop in these zones.

STEKEL characterizes as masturbation any sexual activity that is performed without the cooperation of another person and would regard it as being, quite apart from the fantasies, autoerotic (so-called mutual masturbation is not an autoerotic activity). If in addition to genital masturbation one takes into consideration masturbation at the erotogenic zones, as well as the masked forms (those that endeavor to prevent orgasm altogether or to fractionate it) and the "rational" [?] forms of masturbation (with feces, urine, thumb-sucking, and the like), then one has to assert that everybody has masturbated. Aside from certain harmful forms of masturbation which result in disturbances of body chemistry (*Onania prolongata, interrupta, sine ejaculatione*), all masturbatory activity is completely harmless and uninjurious; indeed, it often has a directly salutary effect.

The typical image of the masturbator as mentally and physically deteriorated is a product only of outside influence, designed to

[1] Dr. L. Löwenfeld: *Über die sexuelle Konstitution und andere Sexual-probleme* [*On the Sexual Constitution and Other Sex Problems*]. Wiesbaden: Bergmann, 1911. According to a review of this book in *Zb.* 2 by Rosenstein, Löwenfeld criticizes Freud's assertions, insofar as he does not deem to be *a priori* admissible the inferences that have been drawn from the sexuality of neurotics as to the sexuality of those who have remained healthy.

frighten. Neurasthenia does not exist; behind it are hidden psycho-neurotic symptoms. According to Freud, anxiety neurosis comes into existence only when masturbation is being given up; usually, nocturnal emissions then appear which in the majority of cases are masturbatory acts, on the principle of "pleasure without guilt." Soon, however, patients come to recognize that emissions too are harmful; yet the psychological relief is sufficient for their recovery.

One does not always succeed in inducing patients to give up masturbating, but even in those cases in which one is successful, more often than not one has done harm thereby. It is the satisfaction that is adequate for an individual that is precisely his "normal" satisfaction. The homosexual, for instance, has no other means for giving vent to and fully satisfying his needs than masturbation; similarly, criminal fantasies often end in masturbation.

The diverse effects of masturbation can be understood in terms of the fact that those who have masturbated to the accompaniment of fantasies about women easily find the way to women, whereas it is otherwise with those to whom masturbation is a substitute for perverse fantasies. The disproportion between masturbation and the sense of guilt is explained by the fact that masturbation is utilized as a reservoir for a great variety of feelings of guilt. The reason for this lies on the one hand in the teleological point of view, and on the other in the fact that in his feeling of guilt, man creates an artificial resistance for the purpose of increasing plea-sure. At this point, we come upon a connection with religion. It is not Christianity that has burdened sexuality with the sense of guilt; it is the sense of guilt that has created Christianity. In this, the attitude toward the father must, of course, be taken into account.

DISCUSSION

FRIEDJUNG finds Reitler's criticism clear, to be sure, but still only theoretically conceived, and he considers Reitler's objec-tions at least as speculative as is what he disputes—the more so since, with the objective observation of children, Freud's statements have stood their ground.

SACHS objects to the introduction of the teleological point of view in Reitler's comments. As to Stekel's presentation, it has remained very doubtful why it should be precisely masturbation, which is in and of itself quite harmless, that should become the reservoir for all feelings of guilt.

ROSENSTEIN finds Stekel's statements plausible. As far as the much maligned teleological principle is concerned, it still seems that neurasthenia, if there is such an illness, can be understood only in terms of teleology. Even if, as Stekel thinks, most neurasthenic symptoms are the result of external influences, nevertheless, someone must have introduced this opinion, which must therefore have developed organically in some way.[2]

TAUSK refers to Reitler's remark that toothache and intoxication, even though they are organic phenomena, can be influenced by psychological means. Pain becomes pain only when it is perceived by consciousness. If consciousness is only a sense organ, then we can understand why, for instance, a toothache disappears as a result of psychic influence. Tausk himself has never clearly understood the primacy of the genital zone; for the rest, however, he does not concur with Reitler's views.

In Stekel's statements, it is correct that masturbation is used as a reservoir, and correct that in it instinctual drive and inhibition are clearly seen to be struggling with each other. If Stekel says, correctly: "It is the sense of guilt that has created Christianity," then he must add at this point his second sentence: "Because the sense of guilt is an artificial resistance that had to be 'cut in' in order to counteract the sexual way of living." Tausk would dispute the assertion that nocturnal emission tends to gain pleasure without guilt; wet dreams are simple intercourse dreams which apparently work by way of reflex.

PROF. FREUD is inclined to subscribe to Reitler's statements about neurasthenia, for he still holds to his earlier view. The

---

[2] Obviously, this sentence is garbled. The recorder seems to have contracted several thoughts into one; the idea is apparently the following: when neurasthenia was first described as an organic illness, someone who described it must have seen the syndrome; therefore, it may well be that there is a sound basis for Freud's opinion.

38

symptoms of genuine neurasthenia cannot be influenced by psychological means; they are the physiological expression of an intoxication. Even though he rarely sees neurasthenics, he still clearly sees the neurasthenic factor in his neurotics.

As far as the theory of sexuality is concerned, it is mainly from the dreams of healthy persons that he derived the justification for inferring that the sexuality of those children who become normal adults does not differ essentially from that of those who later become neurotics. This conclusion found additional support in the general insight that it is only in terms of quantity and not in terms of quality that differences exist between the normal and the neurotic individual.

Although we may consider nature in general from the teleological point of view, this approach fails us when it is applied to individual details, and we therefore have to reject it as a basis for a decision. Nocturnal emission is precisely the point at which the feeling of guilt can be tested. There is no blame attached to having nocturnal emissions, and yet the man who has emissions is just as miserable. The sense of guilt may not have been taken quite seriously enough, after all; Rank has made the most correct statements about it up to now. If we consider infantile sexuality to be the pathogenic[3] factor in the neuroses, then we cannot say that masturbation is harmless, because it is, indeed, nothing but the outflow of infantile sexuality.

RANK takes issue with two points in Stekel's exposition: (1) The overestimation of the external influences of threats and intimidation; as experience has shown, these influences play but a secondary and minor role. (2) Rank finds extremely inadequate the reasons given for the fact that it is precisely masturbation that is made into the reservoir for the feelings of guilt—that is, so long as we do not assume that from masturbation as such, what develops organically and in accordance with Freud's mechanism is anxiety, which then takes on the disguise of a feeling of guilt and becomes capable of attracting other feelings of guilt.

[3] The original has *pathologische*, but that would seem to have been an error in note-taking.

FEDERN: The inferences drawn from the sexuality of neurotics to the sexuality of normal individuals are fully vindicated by observation. If infantile sexuality is equated with masturbation this will not do, because one can not equate an effect with its cause. Infantile sexuality is the same in the sick person as it is in the healthy one; but not so masturbation, and Reitler was right in stressing that.

With regard to Stekel's standpoint, one must distinguish in neurasthenia between that which is the effect of masturbation and that which is the result of various forms of frustrated excitation. Federn is convinced that masturbation can bring about the actual-neurosis of neurasthenia. Stekel's argument is inadequate. Also, the derivation of the feeling of guilt from threats is untenable; on the other hand, feelings of guilt do not, as Rank thinks, originate in anxiety, either.

SPIELREIN believes that all children go through a period of neurosis. In some cases the neurosis remains latent in its course; in others it breaks through. Almost all children have anxieties. Besides, there is a period when the child is at an in-between age that usually coincides with that of religiosity. If it is generally believed that masturbation is harmful, one may expect there to be some reason for this belief. Some patients show a clear need for guilt and expiation—a trait connected with the destructive component.

HITSCHMANN thinks no sense of guilt would arise if, for instance, a boy were to see his father masturbating.

Not every popular belief is true. A great part of civilization seems to rest on the suppression of masturbation. The sense of guilt may perhaps start with masturbation because it is an action; this is not true, to the same degree, of exhibition and other infantile sexual activities. Adler's feeling of inferiority seems to correspond to the feeling of guilt connected with masturbation. If Stekel discovers a psychic conflict in neurasthenics, that does not prove anything at all; one encounters it in every human being. The difficulty in giving up the habit does not have to do only with perverse fantasies (homosexuality); it arises just as much in those cases in which masturbation is used, for instance, to induce sleep.

40

DATTNER would not equate extragenital masturbation with genital masturbation, which is much more easily linked up with fantasies.

REINHOLD: How inappropriate it is to apply the concept of purposiveness to questions of pleasure is evidenced by Reitler's exposition; for the *sexual* activity at the erotogenic zones does not serve their purpose either. A masturbatory act will in general not be harmful if it represents an adequate satisfaction. With regard to the concentration of all feelings of guilt in masturbation, one should refer to melancholia, during the last stages of which patients often masturbate excessively.

TAUSK thinks that masturbation is utilized only later on as a reservoir for feelings of guilt. Rank's view was once expressed by Freud in a casual remark, in which he indicated that the sense of guilt is anxiety that has been bound. Sexuality is never capable of giving complete satisfaction because it does not have to do with one individual alone. Under certain conditions, then, masturbation evokes anxiety, and this anxiety becomes attached to an object. First it is the father, and from there a direct path leads into religion; in Christianity, this is fully realized [in the philosophical sense].

ROSENSTEIN poses the question of why it is that masturbation [in adults] results in an actual neurosis, yet does not cause one in children. What are the truly harmful factors in masturbation—inasmuch as they also make their appearance in mutual masturbation, which is carried out with an object? In many cases nocturnal emission is brought about, more or less unconsciously, by actions, and is accompanied by a sense of guilt.

PROF. FREUD replies to Federn that although from the dreams of normal persons one can learn about the sexual component, one cannot learn in that same way whether they have masturbated. The opinion that masturbation is harmful finds support in observations made by an absolutely objective critic who traced back the later stultification of Arab youths to their masturbation, which was excessive and totally uninhibited. The sense of guilt has a special

41

relationship to infantile sexuality, since it does not make its appearance with other trespasses for which children are just as severely threatened and punished (all sorts of mischievous tricks), but only with regard to sexual matters. The concept of adequate sexual satisfaction was introduced in the first article on the anxiety neurosis. Christianity had its origins not only in the moral reaction of the Jewish community; other sources include heathen religions, which propagate themselves in the Mysteries. The tendencies of Christianity have their origin in the Mysteries; Judaism is merely the screen fantasy. One must agree with Rosenstein in his assertion that, if neurasthenia exists, there must also exist a physiologic-toxic mechanism thereof. This mechanism is not known as yet; a suggestion about it can be found in the *Theory of Sexuality*.

ROSENTHAL comments that children do not fall ill as a result of masturbation precisely because it is the expression of their sexuality. The conflicts arise only with the turn toward object love; prolonged masturbation renders an individual unfit for normal sexual intercourse. Incest fantasies play a major role in this.

STEKEL points out that Freud drew an incorrect conclusion in thinking that if infantile sexuality is harmful, masturbation, too, must be. In that case, thumb-sucking would also have to be harmful. It is not infantile sexuality that is harmful, but our attitude to it; if a feeling of guilt combines with this attitude, then a neurosis arises. Masturbation becomes the symbol of that which is forbidden, because all neurotics show fear of pleasure; they tell themselves: "you do not deserve to have that." This anxiety was created because otherwise it would not have been possible to govern mankind.

STEINER remarks that the problem of why one individual becomes a neurasthenic as a result of masturbation while another does not, can be solved only in terms of physiology; this Reitler certainly tried to do. As far as the feeling of guilt is concerned, there too the organic factor plays an important role, for there are persons who are not affected by any prohibitions; they simply show a tolerance for masturbation, just as others do for alcohol.

42

162

SCIENTIFIC MEETING on *February 14, 1912*

Present: Dattner, Federn, Freud, Friedjung, Hitschmann, Rank, Reik, Reinhold, Reitler, Rosenstein, Sachs, Sadger, Silberer, Spielrein, Stekel, Tausk.
Guests: Dr. Jokl,[1] Dr. Krauss, Dr. Popper, Dr. Rosenthal, Dr. Sachs (Mrs.), Dr. Schrötter, Dr. Spitzer.

PRESENTATION

Experimental Dreams[2]

SPEAKER: DR. KARL SCHRÖTTER[3]

To start off, the speaker remarks that at Swoboua's suggestion he has concerned himself with dream synthesis, in contrast to dream analysis, without drawing from his investigation any theoretical conclusions. His experiments made use of hypnosis, by means of

[1] This Dr. Jokl was a woman physician unrelated to Dr. Hans Jokl, who did not appear on the membership roster until 1922.
[2] Schrötter's paper "Experimentelle Träume" appeared first among the "Vorläufige Mitteilungen" ("Preliminary communications") in *Zb.* (1912), 2: 638–646. It was published in English by David Rappaport in *Organization and Pathology of Thought*, New York, Columbia University Press, 1961.
[3] Karl Schrötter, Ph.D., was a brilliant young philosopher who committed suicide in 1913. He was one of the first to experiment with dreams. It was subsequently that Otto Pötzl, Professor of Psychiatry at the University of Vienna, performed his famous experiments. At present, a number of researchers, such as Charles Fisher of New York, are experimenting with dreams, some of them trying to test psychoanalytic findings.

which he put his experimental persons into a deep hypnotic sleep with total amnesia and loss of consciousness. Dreams occurred during hypnosis or during the following night's sleep. The dreams during hypnosis did not differ essentially from those occurring during the normal state of sleep. The speaker then gives some detailed information about the persons upon whom he experimented—a girl of 20 and a young man of 22, both of whom had put themselves at his disposal because of their scientific interest. Then he characterized briefly the four types of his experiment:

(1) Dreams combining a number of *ideas*: the experimental persons are given a number of ideas, in accordance with which they are then to have dreams.

(2) Dreams of *stimuli and ideas:* not only ideas but also stimuli (actual as well as suggested) are given to the subjects.

(3) Dreams involving *time measurement:* the experimental person receives the order to raise her hand to her breast at the moment the dream starts, and to let her hand fall at the moment the dream ends.

(4) Thought-, symbol-, and censorship dreaming: the suggestion may be, for instance, about the "dream fulfillment of the strongest desire of which you now know"; or suggestions referring to symbols are given, etc.

It is typical of most of these dreams that the person of the hypnotist is drawn into them, that the respiration changes at the moment the dream is beginning, and that the motions made by the experimental person during the dream show a certain relationship to the content—even when nothing of this kind had been suggested in the hypnosis.

The speaker now relates a number of examples from his copious collection of such dreams. It becomes evident that dreamers can immediately weave into a dream, with all the elaborateness revealed by Freud's *The Interpretation of Dreams,* any suggestion they have received; the speaker can—on the basis of his exact knowledge of the living conditions and occupation of the persons used for his experiment at the time the experiments were carried out—trace the other elements of the dream back to day residues. An analysis in the Freudian sense was not undertaken. Whereas the dreamers dream all suggestions promptly and directly, nevertheless, in the case of suggestions drawn from the area of sexual ideas (for instance: "Dream about sexual intercourse with Mr. N," or "Dream about homosexual intercourse with Miss N"), the influence of the censorship becomes effective, insofar as the girl dreamer, who has not the slightest notion of the nature of symbolism, is able to find an often ingenious metaphorical disguise. For instance, in response to the first order: Mr. N. comes to visit the dreamer; he has a wine bottle hidden under his coat and asks her for a glass; the rug gets wet; then he wants to pour a second time, but she pulls the glass away.[4] Under the stimulus of the second suggestion, she dreams about Miss N. as a repulsively ugly person, who wants to seduce her; Miss N. carries a traveling bag upon which there is stuck a label inscribed with the words: For Ladies Only. The dreamer then receives a key from her; but before she enters the house, she is warned against the jealous husband (of her actually unmarried girl friend).

DISCUSSION

STEKEL is extremely grateful to the speaker for his interesting exposition, even though it merely confirms what is already known from our analyses—for instance, that the dreamer absorbs stimuli only in order to weave them into his dream, and that it does not make much difference what these stimuli consist of. The fact that the symbolism has been substantiated by way of experiments at the hands of a totally unprejudiced observer is of the greatest value.

The measurement of dream duration applies only to the dream that has been ordered by suggestion; in Stekel's opinion, people dream without interruption. He himself has made similar experiments, although without hypnosis; he directed his patients to form artificial dreams. If such experiments are continued, and the forms of suggestion well chosen, one will be able to bring to light quite a few findings that will be valuable for the exploration of dreams.

[4] This detail is told differently in the version in the *Zb.*: there, Mr. N., having poured wine, breaks the first glass, asks for a second one, and having started to pour wine into it, suddenly draws the bottle away.

PROF. FREUD interjects that those who do not want to become convinced will not be convinced by these experiments, either.

TAUSK, on the other hand, thinks that the two series of proofs will back each other up. The fact that the censorship remains so effective during the hypnosis and leads to symbolization sheds new light on the nature of hypnosis.

PROF. FREUD remarks, in this connection, that he has known that [fact], ever since he first tried to influence patients by hypnosis; they offer resistances and are lying while in hypnosis.

HITSCHMANN, too, thinks that Tausk underestimates the part played by consciousness in hypnosis. He believes that the experiments provide excellent support for the much disputed and attacked concept of symbolism.

FEDERN also finds the experiments most interesting and believes that it will be possible to approach a very large number of dream problems in this way, thus bringing them closer to a solution. These are ideal transference dreams. Just as children have some dreams that can be explained completely in terms of the day residues, so it may perhaps be that, in some hypnotized persons, childhood affectivity has been preserved so that they actually work with only the material that has been placed at their disposal. Besides, what a dream is like will also depend, as is assumed in reference to the genuine dream, upon the depth of sleep; this could perhaps be established experimentally. The directive to indicate the beginning and end of a dream may possibly modify the conditions of dreaming. The fact that the physiological state of a dreamer changes has been known since 1863, the year when certain observations were made on wounded men—for example, that in their dreams, cranial injuries appear to have been filled in.

DATTNER would focus more attention on the observation of affects in these dreams. The affect does not always, indeed, pertain to the manifest content, but usually to latent dream thoughts; it would be interesting to learn with what affect the experimental person woke up after the situation that had been set by suggestion had in one form or another made its way into the dream.

46

SACHS, by means of an example that is on occasion cited by Freud, points to the enormous role played in hypnosis by consciousness, affect, and will. Schrötter's symbolic dreams are of inestimable significance to us. It is true, though, that they seem to be closer to consciousness than are genuine dreams. In the homosexual dream, the dreamer's resistance was very nicely eluded.

PROF. FREUD would divide the paper into two parts. As far as the first part is concerned, which goes back to Swoboda's suggestion, he has to say that the attempt to construct the dream from the manifest fragments does not warrant the title of "synthesis." With the second part, that of the experiments, however, which were initiated by the speaker, a new branch of experimental psychology was born. If the speaker were to analyze those dreams, he would be able to see for himself that our analyses are right. The signal concerning measurement of time, as given by the experimental person refers, of course, to the *perception* of the dream; the dreamwork is certainly not measured thereby.

SILBERER would arrange these interesting examples in two major groups: (1) those in which the suggestions that were made influence the manifest dream content; and (2) those in which these suggestions influence what is *behind* the manifest dream. In the dream that took place upon the order to "Dream your present psychic state," there is ample functional symbolism. Then Silberer reads aloud some examples of hypnagogic experiments that were carried out by Dr. Schrötter upon his [Silberer's] suggestion.

SPIELREIN thinks it would be interesting to suggest the same words to different persons so as to learn how different people react to identical material. Further, one could analyze one of these dreams and then suggest the underlying wish to another person in order to see how the same wish is represented by various people. Some individuals will, for example, react in a positive way to the homosexual suggestion; others again will react in a negative way.

REITLER, too, would take exception to the term "synthesis." The substance of the experiment—giving the patients stimulus-words to which they then react—is reminiscent of Jung's "association experiments." These experiments are of the greatest significance for research in symbolism, not only because we can verify our interpretations of symbols (he proposes suggesting: staircase, flying, cravat), but also because we can learn of the employment of new symbols (rug as symbol of the vagina).

HITSCHMANN says: If the dreams turn out to be somewhat thin and unimaginative, one has to take into account the wish to dream only in terms of the elements suggested. Perhaps the reason why the dreams are so innocuous and veiled is that the hypnotist represents one parent.

TAUSK suggests that one might perhaps, after the dream has been produced, set the dreamer the task of reproducing, during the hypnosis, the infantile fragments underlying the dream.

FREUD doubts that such an experiment would prove successful.

ROSENTHAL does not at all agree with Hitschmann's opinion that the dreams are thin; the suggested ideas are utilized in line with complexes, *despite* the restrictions that are due to hypnosis.

SILBERER poses the question of whether, as Stekel believes, man actually dreams continuously. It is the arousal stimulus that puts the dreamer into the state in which he is enabled to perceive his dream activity. One might say that, even if there is continuous dream activity, perception of dreams takes place only when an arousal stimulus, or closeness to the waking state, makes it possible for the dreamer to become aware of his dream activity.

PROF. FREUD regards as unscientific the question of whether there is continuous dreaming. If Stekel, while dozing off during the daytime, keeps catching himself dreaming, that is no evidence of his dreaming without interruption also at night. For in order to be able to sleep by day, he has continuously to fend off the stimuli that intrude from the outside.

ROSENSTEIN would find it interesting if one were to give the suggestion to dream of no wish; he wonders whether in this case the desire to obey the hypnotist would be the only wish in the dream.

SCHRÖTTER, in his concluding remarks, expresses his gratitude for the suggestions received, which he is going to utilize. Stekel's objection that man dreams continuously, even if it were valid, would not mean anything as far as Schrötter's time-measuring experiment is concerned. Unfortunately, there is no method for determining the depth of sleep (Federn). Up to the present, he has paid little attention to the affects in dreams, but the latent contents of—for instance, the sexual dreams—clearly found expression in body movements.

As far as the question of proving symbolism is concerned, Schrötter has to cut down on that expectation, since the material at his disposal that refers to symbolic disguise is extremely meager. At the end, he defines precisely his basically different standpoint in the question of symbols: he cannot accept something that corresponds to a state of clear consciousness being characterized as a symbol. He reserves this term for phenomena of which the *entire meaning* lies in the symbol, and behind which there is a content that cannot be expressed verbally.

PROF. FREUD clears up this contrast by declaring it to be a mere dispute about words.

163

SCIENTIFIC MEETING on *February 21, 1912*

Present: Dattner, Federn, Freud, Friedjung, Hitschmann, Nepallek, Rank, Reik, Reitler, Rosenstein, Sachs, Sadger, Spielrein, Steiner, Stekel, Tausk.
Guests: Dr. Heller, Dr. Krauss, Dr. Scheu.[1]

PRESENTATION
The Parent Complex as Cultural Ferment[2]

SPEAKER: DR. THEODOR REIK

In several points, Reik shows the significance of the parent complex for one's cultural attitude. In the sexual jealousy toward the father he sees one of the roots of ambition; the father complex, which makes use of ambition, is, for instance, particularly marked in Schiller. This relationship often also gives rise to skepticism (Flaubert, Heine)—that is, if the child at an early age gets some

[1] This is probably Dr. Robert Scheu, a well-known Viennese author who was a friend of Federn.
[2] Reviewed in *Zb.* (1912), 2:547.

idea of the relativity of moral values. The speaker touches upon the connection between the father complex and religion, and points out the extent to which infantile sexual curiosity affects religious doubt, and how the latter, as well as atheism, is rooted in the father complex.

The speaker then passes over to a discussion of the influences that the mother has on the child's development, referring to Freud's investigations of object choice (love type). With this as his point of departure, he tries to find a way toward an understanding of the Don Juan problem: on the one hand, Don Juan cannot ever find enough women; on the other hand, he cannot ever find the one [he is seeking]. Doubt about women's faithfulness also has its roots in the infantile complex (Schnitzler); these infantile fantasies are of significance for the genesis of jealousy. The speaker would contrast with Freud's type another: the man who loves only the pure virgin, the mother-like aspect of her nature; the "long-suffering one"; one could speak directly of the precondition that there be a third who is not present. The preconditions for this "Gretchen-type" are rooted in childhood impressions. The child wishes to see his mother again as she seemed to him before he discovered the sexual relationship; in addition, his mother appears to him to be suffering. This glorification of the mother is true also of the "Madonna type" in which mother and pure virgin are combined.

Finally, the speaker deals with the relationship of the *parents* to their children. Parents too have to be resigned. The parental attitude shows itself, for instance, in the model they choose for their children's education. It becomes obvious that the psychoanalytic point of view needs to be introduced into the science of history. The struggle between the old and the new generation, the detachment from tribe and family, prove that the parent complex is one of the most valuable cultural ferments of mankind.

DISCUSSION

TAUSK would like to corroborate the speaker's statements by examples. The influence of the parent complex is demonstrated by the example of the obsessional neurosis of a 16-year-old boy. If religion is not observed at home, the influence of the school is not so significant; the teacher of religion cannot implant devotion to the god whom the father does not represent. Finally, the speaker relates some children's stories.

REITLER finds a contradiction in the thesis that when the father's authority suffers, then "God the father" springs into action. It is the other way round; if the father's authority suffers, then the child loses his faith in God. The desire to be redeemed by a woman is to be understood psychoanalytically as meaning that the child's wish is to be introduced into sexual life by his mother. The virginal mother serves an incest fantasy: the God impregnates a woman and is at the same time given birth by her.

SACHS relates a passage from Anatole France that shows his [France's] knowledge of the significance of the parent complex.

FEDERN, referring to the symbolism of the cross, remarks that the meaning of carrying a burden is not altogether clear. With regard to the "Madonna type," one will have to ask from what period of the person's life it derives; it is probably from the time when the mother appeared to the child to be asexual. Alfred de Musset has described both types in one poem. Those men who begin by loving the Madonna type will come to sexual knowledge only late in life, and will therefore be predestined for stronger sexual repression. Freud once construed as the precondition for Don Juan that he either lost his mother at an early age or did not know her at all and is therefore always searching for her. Federn can confirm the point, made in Reik's exposition, that mothers often react with melancholia when their children detach themselves from them. The father complex appears as a neurotic symptom in those working disturbances that result from a hostile attitude toward the father.

SPIELREIN relates the family romance of a girl who left her home in order to be able to study. Subsequently, in addition to self-reproaches, fear and hatred of her father set in; she projected her own desires onto her father. Besides, she was convinced that her parents could never be unfaithful to each other.

RANK, with reference to the Don Juan type, presents a case that shows clearly that one type of these "heterosexuals by compulsion" (Ferenczi)[3] is actually unconsciously anchored in homosexuality and that some details of their choice of a love object can be understood on this basis.

Luther is named as an example of the parent complex that is significant from the point of view of cultural history (pope = antichrist = devil; disbelief in the Virgin Mary).

The incest fantasy contained in the virginal Madonna type is no longer as clear in Christianity as it is in other mythological and cosmological systems.

As a counterpart to disturbance in working (Federn), Rank mentions that one also encounters excessive assiduity as a reaction to the father's actual or alleged laziness.

PROF. FREUD would like to begin by voicing some criticisms: the first concerns the sort of style that favors sentences turned into epigrams and strives to be too clever. His second objection is that the parent complex, which is about the most important piece of knowledge we have gained, must not be treated so lightly.

Turning to the content, Freud remarks that the mother type described is neither the only nor the most frequent one, but is merely a particularly striking one. The ideal of the virginal woman may perhaps arise only from the rejection of the usual motherly woman. This leads to the whole question of the origin of an ideal. Being both a reaction and sublimation, it must be connected with the most common experiences and go back to childhood impressions. The secret of love culminates in the demand to be loved in the same way as one has been loved as a child by one's mother. This applies mainly to men, for the authentic type "woman" does not love the man but has remained as a rule arrested at the stage of narcissism. Her child, too, she loves narcissistically, as a part of her own self. For the same reason, the overestimation of the sexual object that is characteristic of men does not exist in the case of

---

[3] S. Ferenczi, "Zur Nosologie der männlichen Homosexualität" [On the Nosology of Male Homosexuality], Z. (1914), 2: 131–142. Ferenczi presented this paper at the Third International Congress in 1911.

women.[4] With regard to the love types, one must not forget the complications that result from the fact that those persons who took care of the individual in his childhood merge with the mother. In reference to the detachment from the father, it should be noted that it ought to take place only when the son has grown strong enough. Sons have to suffer for a premature detachment, later on, when they themselves have become fathers: they are tyrannical fathers, and they earn the greatest ingratitude from their sons. The relationship of homosexuality to paranoia could recently be demonstrated experimentally in a patient who, well on the way to liberation from this homosexuality, attempted sexual intercourse and immediately afterwards had a paranoiac attack.

STEKEL, too, finds fault with treating such highly significant themes in a literary manner. It is true that the Don Juan is a homosexual: he is in love with himself, and each new conquest proves to him his irresistibility. Reik's Gretchen-type is the bipolar counterpart to the Freudian type.

Women who in their youth set themselves the ideal of the pure man, in analysis often show that their original ideal was the Don Juan.

When is that type (the virginal woman) formed? (Federn) When degrading his mother to a prostitute has become painful to the neurotic, he transforms the type into its opposite.

Even if children say they are nonbelievers, they are still not unreligious; they often become believers again at a later time. Even a religious education is no protection against the development of a religious feeling of guilt.

Father and God do not—as Hebbel's confession, presented by Sadger, shows—fall from their pedestal at the same time. God takes the father's place.

To study the father complex in poets—especially in Schiller and Shakespeare, who represent the type of the ungrateful son—would be a rewarding task.

The child often punishes not father and mother, but himself.

Woman loves man only because he admires her.

[4]See Freud, "On Narcissism" (S.E., 14: 69–102.)

54

Interesting as the case of the homosexual with the paranoiac attack is, it merely confirms Stekel in his conviction that homosexuality is not curable. If homosexuals go to women, they do it out of love for their physician.

DR. HELLER relates an observation concerning the origin of the notion that the mother is suffering (the result of overhearing parental intercourse), and its impact upon the entire outlook on life in later years.

DR. DATTNER cites an example that shows how difficult it is for the idea that the mother has sexual intercourse to assert itself. On the basis of his experiences, he can confirm Federn's remark that aversion to learning arises because of opposition to one's father. Finally, Dattner mentions his observation that those women who lay down the demand that the man be pure usually present a very markedly masculine type.

SCHEU misses the explanation of the type of man who has a hostile attitude toward his mother and love for his father (Hamlet, Orestes, Schopenhauer). He presents the life history of a boy who, having been raised as an atheist from the beginning, nevertheless acquired a father complex that was of great moment for his entire attitude.

TAUSK mentions an earlier work about the Ideal. He demonstrates, by way of an example, how God can be uprooted by the mother. He also poses the question of whether Don Juanism could not be brought about by any unconscious perversion.

ROSENSTEIN asks whether an analysis has yet been carried out on a patient who did not know his mother at all, and what form the complex took in such a case.

SPIELREIN maintains that man, too, loves at first narcissistically. Two types of women must be distinguished: the masculine women desire merely sexual objects.

FRIEDJUNG, in reference to the choice of a love object, remarks that the woman actually wants any man who comes to meet her half way; otherwise it could not be understood why it is that the same man can be successful with a great variety of women.

An example of a young woman whose precondition for loving consists in the man being suppressed, debased, and miserable—a condition that can be explained in terms of her identification with him.

164

Present: Dattner, Federn, Freud, Heller, Hitschmann, Rank, Reinhold, Reitler, Rosenstein, Sachs, Sadger, Spielrein, Steiner, Stekel, Tausk, Wagner.
Guest: Dr. Krauss.

SIXTH DISCUSSION ON MASTURBATION

Dr. Steiner, Dr. Federn

DR. STEINER begins by stressing that masturbation is neither a symptom of illness, nor a symptom of any sort, but merely an activity, one of the manifestations of sexual neurasthenia—which is what should actually be the topic of our discussion. In view of the difficulties that presented themselves when the attempt was made to establish a masturbatory type and the characterology resulting therefrom, it seems suitable to make the concept of masturbation as inclusive as possible so as also to comprise mutual masturbation, frustrated excitations, and nocturnal emissions.

[1] The original is erroneously dated February 21.

The question of whether masturbation is harmful must be answered in the negative, as far as the healthy individual is concerned: for him it is a physiological necessity. It is different in the
case of the sexual neurasthenic, whose sexual function has been
altered as the result of chemical conditions that depend on an
inner secretion, and in whose case the genital glands can be pre-
maturely stimulated. Such an individual will not tolerate sexual
intercourse either, and we are wrong in calling him a masturbator,
because he cannot tolerate masturbation, just as we could not call
a smoker someone who cannot tolerate smoking. It is not masturbation that produces sexual neurasthenia; masturbation intensifies
and worsens one that already exists. Ferenczi's correct observation
of a one-day neurasthenia is scientifically well founded.

Harmful effects of masturbation that are apparently not essentially dependent on the method employed are, in the case of the
sexual neurasthenic: (1) external-anatomical and (2) those that are
a result of the influence upon inner secretion and concern the entire organism (for instance, neurotic constipation); they can also
make themselves felt in the realm of the *sympathicus.* Therapy in
these cases will include treatment by probe and treatment of the
constipation, as well as drug therapy (spermin, etc.), whereas the
neurotic cases belong in the realm of psychoanalysis.

FEDERN emphasizes that it will not do to regard masturbation,
which is an equivalent of coition, as an etiological factor; he objects to the inexact use of the concept which leads to identifying
masturbation as "sexual activity without a partner."

That masturbation in infancy is ubiquitous, even in the case of
nonpredisposed children, has not been proven. The difference between merely temporary excitation and the experience of the sexual
act is one that can be expressed only in terms of quality and not
in terms of quantity. In normal development, what is called masturbation represents one consequence of the gradual maturing of
sexuality, and is innocuous; often, indeed, it even protects the
child from activity in perverse zones. Whether or not masturbation
is judged to be noxious will depend on the extent to which it is
capable of gratifying excitation for some length of time, as well as
on the type and degree of other possibilities of transforming the

58

sexual instinct. The longer the relaxation lasts, the more useful it is.

Masturbation increases the feeling of guilt because it implies acts of volition (as well as of concealment); many individuals, however, become deeply depressed, not as the result of feelings of guilt, but directly through masturbation. The noxious effect lies to a great extent in the reaction after the act. The main source of the feeling of guilt is found in the change that occurs in the psyche from before to after the act; what seemed so desirable before then becomes for some time worthless. Having turned asexual, the psyche rejects the sexual act that has taken place and promises itself never again to experience that. This rejection is a precondition of the feeling of guilt, which is intensified when the instinct suppression is not successful. Another consequence of the feeling of guilt is that the aggressive tendency of sexuality, ungratified as it is, turns against the subject.

FRIEDJUNG, who has been able to establish infant masturbation in a number of cases, replies to Federn's objection that, by the same token, these cases would first have to be proven to be pathological. One should not hold phimosis alone responsible for the states of excitation at the genitals of boys.

ROSENSTEIN singles out from the discussion four different views about masturbation and its relation to neurasthenia. Freud has asserted that neurasthenia results from excessive masturbation; Stekel denies the existence of an "actual-neurosis"; Steiner considers an innate behavior of the sexual glands to be the cause of neurasthenia; Federn, finally, thinks that masturbation per se produces certain disturbances, but—in agreement with Stekel's opinion —regards the feeling of guilt as the cause of these disturbances. Federn's distinction between a feeling of guilt that can easily be removed and one that is more deeply rooted is likely to clear up some misunderstandings and contradictions that have made their appearance in the discussion.

Nonsatisfying masturbation—which was also drawn in as an explanation—has to do with frustrated excitement, which belongs to a different realm.

SPIELREIN mentions a case which shows that the connection

between obstipation and masturbation is familiar also to physicians who are not involved with psychoanalysis. Federn's statements are quite plausible: that masturbation is tolerated without ill effect by some, but that on the other hand, it can generate neurasthenia, which in turn produces feelings of guilt; these again are capable of evoking pleasurable feelings and of intensifying masturbation.

HITSCHMANN regards as new Steiner's view of congenital disturbances of metabolism and congenital neurasthenia, even though it has not been denied that certain organ defects can be observed. In discussing the problem of the feeling of guilt, Federn failed to explain why masturbation remains unsatisfactory; can it be that a nonsatisfactory masturbation is one that is carried out with feelings of guilt?

In TAUSK'S judgment, some of Steiner's statements are not quite correct. The fact that it is possible to exert psychological influence in that case (of the sexual neurasthenic with neurotic constipation, etc.) shows that something must also have taken place in regard to inner secretion, so that to us the problem remains merely a psychological one. Federn's attempt to define the psychic contents of the feeling of guilt is of great value.

FEDERN cannot agree with Steiner's view that the problem of masturbation is settled with the assumption of congenital sexual neurasthenia.

PROF. FREUD remarks that Steiner was right in pointing out that a path must lead from the actual neuroses toward an understanding of the somatic processes of sexuality. Particularly significant in his discussion was the reference to constitutional changes in the sequence of the organic processes, or what he has termed "precociousness." There are two difficulties in accepting the rest of his exposition. One basic difficulty lies in his having settled from the start the question of why masturbation is harmful. The second objection would be that the sexual neurasthenic is not sharply distinguished from the normal individual. Besides, as Federn has correctly emphasized, seduction does play a role, inasmuch as it can provoke "congenital" neurasthenia.

Federn's argumentations were thoughtful but somewhat diffuse.

The feeling of guilt develops, as Rank also believes, similarly to the way in which anxiety develops: but it arises from social feelings and makes its appearance in those instances in which the child already senses that sexuality is a social obligation. Where the sexual instinct does not show any inclination toward an object, no feeling of guilt will appear. The social feelings are constituted of egotistical feelings, with an addition of erotic feelings (they also develop out of sadistic activity). What is involved here is a part of the libido that at an early age has been connected in this way with the ego instinct; at what point this becomes manifest in an individual depends upon his constitution.

STEINER did not at all have the intention of contesting the view that besides congenital neurasthenia seduction [too] can have a similar effect; insofar as it stimulates a premature inner secretion, it comes into account as an etiological factor.

STEKEL finds that the concept of masturbation has not been defined sharply enough. He can in no way agree with Steiner, just as he considers the assumption of a "one-day-neurasthenia" incorrect. The closer the neurotic comes to the type of hermaphrodite, the more easily will he be subjected to conflicts. Federn's statements, too, need to be criticized in some respects; it will not do to postulate a post- and an antesexual state of the psyche. The sense of guilt is social from the start; it refers to inhibitions that were created by higher agencies—e.g. by religion. The sense of guilt arises in those cases where children believe in God or fear him.

PROF. FREUD remarks, in reply to this, that he did not speak of religious feelings of guilt, because the sense of guilt has been proven historically to have existed at times when there was no question of religion. Stekel's objection, voiced last time, that equating masturbation and infantile sexuality is untenable because people do not fall sick from infantile sexuality but from their reaction to it, is itself untenable; it merely mirrors the psychoanalytic view that one of the two pathogenic factors is infantile sexuality, the other repression.

TAUSK thinks that with Freud's "social conscience" a later stage of development is being inserted as a primary one. If one considers the parents to be representatives of society, one can constitute the entire sense of guilt. Social conscience is a stage in the development of the child's relationship to father and mother; Tausk regards as a danger this replacement of a synthetic factor by analytical ones.

An extensive discussion ensues during the course of which PROF. FREUD once more defines exactly his view that the point in introducing the concept of social conscience is only to find a way of establishing the constitutionally varying point in time at which the sexual components unite with the egoistical ones.

165

Present: Dattner, Freud, Friedjung, Heller, Hitschmann, Rank, Reitler, Reinhold, Rosenstein, Sachs, Sadger, Silberer, Spielrein, Steiner, Tausk, Stekel, Winterstein.
Guests: Dr. Weiss, Pappenheim,[1] Krauss.

PRESENTATION

A Contribution to the Psychoanalysis of Traveling[2]

SPEAKER: DR. ALFRED FREIHERR VON WINTERSTEIN

The speaker discusses the various forms of the urge to travel, from the wish to travel, which at certain times makes its appearance spontaneously, to the pathological form of the fugue; on the basis of psychoanalytic findings, he attempts by way of a number of examples from the lives and works of poets to take up the spon-

[1] This was probably Dr. Max Pappenheim, who subsequently became Professor of Psychiatry at the University of Vienna and a member of the Vienna Psychoanalytic Society.

[2] "Zur Psychoanalyse des Reisens" was published in *Imago* (1912), 1: 484–506.

taneous drive to travel and trace it back to psychosexual roots. It may well be a question of the wish for libidinal gratification, as much as it is of a representation of the violent detachment of libido, or finally of death wishes clothed in sexual symbols (to depart = to die; mother's-womb fantasy).

Side by side with the psychosexual root, some role may be played by the inability to maintain lasting associations, which may be identical with the neurotic's need for introjection; besides, traveling, which is per se a form of motion, can also provide a pleasurable motor discharge. The sexualization of nature, too, contributes to the pleasure in traveling. Finally, as to the pathological drive to roam, which is, according to Heilbronner,[3] encountered predominantly in hysterical (not epileptic) individuals, it is often criminal desires and death wishes that are the propelling forces behind it. In all these cases, what is involved is the overwhelming of consciousness by the unconscious.

SACHS, referring to the points of contact between the presentation and his own exposition on the feeling for nature, remarks that traveling as an end in itself, in the contemporary sense, actually began with the epoch to which J.-J. Rousseau gave its character— an epoch that must be conceived of as a reaction against sexual excesses. Herein lies an additional confirmation of the erotic character of traveling.

In regard to the jealous father in *The Tempest* (Shakespeare) who torments his daughter's suitor, reference is made to the parallel with the Griselda-legend.[4]

STEKEL expresses his appreciation of the speaker's exposition, which coincides in part with his own essay, "Why They Travel." [5] Insufficient stress seemed to be laid on the fact that traveling usually represents a compromise between erotic tendencies and the tendency to liberate oneself from the shackles of neurosis.

[3] Heilbronner: "Über Fugue and Fugue ähnliche Zustande" [On Fugue and Fugue-like Conditions], *Jahrbuch f. Psychiatrie und Neurologie* (1903), Vol. 13.

[4] Rank: "Sinn der Griselda Fabel" [The Meaning of the Fable of Griselda], *Imago*, 1: 34–48.

[5] W. Stekel: *Was im Grund der Seele ruht.* Vienna: Paul Knepler, 1909. [*The Depths of the Soul; Psycho-Analytic Studies.* New York: Moffat, Yard, 1922.]

The interpretation of travels to America as mother's-womb fantasies does not seem to be sufficiently well founded.

REIK mentions the sect of the Paternians, who localized certain mental properties in certain areas of the body. For instance, they designated the abdominal region as the seat not only of sexual desire but also of the desire to travel.

SADGER has found the urge to travel a characteristic stigma of those who are severely encumbered by heredity. His own experiences confirm much of what was said in the presentation; yet there are some things that have to be criticized. An aversion to associations, for instance, is by no means identical with introjection; increased desire to travel in those who are severely encumbered by heredity does not invariably have to go back to increased libido; nor can one assume that longing for an erotic experience is generally the basis for that desire, even though that is true of a number of cases. The wish to flee from one's own tormenting ego is the chief motive for traveling.

RANK too points to the desire for "liberation" as being, psychologically, the more significant reason for traveling; it has to be regarded as a representation in reality of an unsuccessful inner detachment. This mechanism has its origin in the detachment from parents and family that takes place at puberty—which is the model for later behavior, as can be demonstrated especially in the neuroses of puberty, and in poets in connection with their poetic creations.

HITSCHMANN misses, in the presentation, the *fear* of traveling, as well as of kinesthesis in general, which is undoubtedly closely related to agoraphobia and to the psychological motivation for traveling. Also, the meaning of travel in dreams should have been given appropriate consideration. The custom of wedding trips can probably be understood only in historical terms; if it is true that the urge to travel springs from lack of satisfaction, one should rather expect a newly married couple to be capable of staying where they are. An explorer who was a breast fetishist confessed that it was the naked breasts of savages that particularly excited him.

TAUSK mentions two types of travelers that he has encountered in his analyses: in one case, it was flight from a decisive discussion with the father that was at the root; in the other, a passionate desire to triumph over the wretched conditions in the parental home.

The prototype of the traveler is the eternal Jew, who is in search of death.

The incest complex and detachment from the parental home are characteristic of the urge to travel; this is illuminated by the case of a young man who in his travels was unconsciously looking for his sister.

SPIELREIN knows from her experience of two roots of traveling: (1) the passionate desire for detachment; (2) strong desire to find something new, behind which incest is invariably hidden. The versatility of this passion is illustrated by an example.

ROSENSTEIN stresses that there can be no doubt about the motive of flight being a root of the urge to travel; but he also insists that the erotic motive leads to more problems, which are connected with the concept of instinct. The question is whether restlessness as a consequence of intensified libido is psychologically traceable to the instinct, or whether, as Swoboda and Schrötter believe, what is involved are transitions that are, as such, incapable of entering consciousness and therefore cannot be made conscious as can the repressed.

Reference is made to the urge to roam [*Wandertrieb*]; in animals this serves the purpose of providing numerous occasions for fertilization. According to Bölsche,[6] this stands in the way of the primal incestuous union, which had been recognized as harmful.

RANK points out that it has not by any means been proven that incestuous unions are biologically harmful; on the contrary, recent researchers (Marcus, etc.) have refuted that assumption.

PROF. FREUD, too, stresses that these problems have not yet been cleared up and that, in any case, knowledge of a harmfulness that has been claimed only by science could not have been the reason for avoiding incest. The speaker's unlikely interpretation of

---

[6] Wilhelm Bölsche (1861-?), German novelist, but known chiefly as author of popular works in natural science. An enthusiastic advocate of Darwin's theory of evolution.

the cloak as a symbol of the prepuce does find support in the phallic demons of antiquity, who are represented as wearing a hood.

Traveling in order to find a bride can be explained in terms of the earliest history of man, by way of the custom in accordance with which the father drove out his sons when they reached manhood; and these then won a bride in strange lands and, with her, a kingdom. The fairy tales in which a strange prince comes into the country and there marries the princess seem to repeat these primeval conditions.

To interpret traveling in the sense of tearing oneself away as a plastic representation of repression seems plausible. Attention must be called to the psychological significance of the notion of space. There are types—the obsessional neurotics, in particular, are such people—who have a much more solid relation with space than with time. In other persons, one sees clearly how they transfer their complexes onto other fields; they copy over their affects, for instance, onto localities—as do those who visit watering places. Transfer onto locomotion thus plays the chief role in agoraphobia, in which sexual restriction is represented by spatial confinement. Thus, there is a possibility of representing plastically the intensities of affects. Music, too, is perhaps nothing but a system of that sort onto which psychic processes are transposed. From a case of fugue it becomes evident that what is involved in flightlike hysterical states is a "tearing-oneself-away"—not infrequently in the sense of fleeing a crime.

WINTERSTEIN expresses his thanks for the suggestions received and endeavors to clear up some misunderstandings, as well as to round out some details.

166

SCIENTIFIC MEETING *on March 13, 1912*

Present: Dattner, Federn, Freud, Friedjung, Hitschmann, Nepallek, Rank, Reitler, Reinhold, Rosenstein, Sachs, Sadger, Spielrein, Steiner, Tausk, Reik.

Guests: Mrs. Sachs, Marcus, Krauss.

SEVENTH DISCUSSION ON MASTURBATION

SPEAKERS: DRS. SACHS AND ROSENSTEIN

DR. SACHS attempts by arranging things in order and by classification to solve the still unresolved problem of the variety of effects produced by masturbation, even though the cause remains the same. He distinguishes two characteristics in masturbation: (1) masturbation can produce a general predisposition to being harmed; (2) under certain conditions, masturbation can turn this latent predisposition into real harm.

Ad (1) Of the consequences of masturbation that are of a generally predisposing nature and have not yet been discussed, two are mentioned:

(a) In masturbation, the condensation of instincts that is characteristic of a number of psychic achievements, and makes possible the simultaneous satisfaction in sexual intercourse of many instincts, is missing. Some of these (sadism in particular) must seek, in the case of masturbation, extrasexual satisfaction (prison revolts).

(b) The relationship that must exist between gratification in fantasy and real gratification: in normal gratification, an object is offered to the libido, whereas in masturbation the course of regression is adopted, inasmuch as the object must first be imagined.

Ad (2) The specific etiologies for the appearance of, as well as the particular types of tangible harm vary, since activities of many kinds are subsumed under the term "masturbation." The phenomena can be classified from three points of view, so that each phenomenon is to be considered from each of these viewpoints:

(a) the kind of manipulation; in this regard, four factors are to be taken into account: in what area [of the body], in what way, quantity, and quality (intensity).

(b) the psychic content of masturbation, which will change in accordance with its being or not being autoerotic—that is, whether masturbation is carried out with or without fantasy and whether this fantasy is conscious or unconscious. Besides, the fact must be considered that certain instinctual drives cling to a form of gratification that is "comfortable" for them, even though the rest of the psychic system has already progressed further in its development. However, what represents progress at a certain age will become at a later age an obstacle to progress and can lead to harm. One has to conceive of special psychic and physiological conditions as existing for the psychic economy of each individual and each age; these conditions consist essentially in a proper distribution of libido. The most serious harm inflicted by masturbation lies in the fact that it prevents such a distribution.

(c) the masturbator's position with regard to his social milieu, already discussed by various speakers (especially by Rank). At this point, the only question raised is whether the alleged lesser harmfulness of masturbation in the case of girls should perhaps be attributed to the fact that with them no factor corresponding to the castration threat comes into question.

DISCUSSION

TAUSK finds the presentation, which was clear in its terminology and disposition, correct in every respect; most of what it said had already been said, but not as clearly or as well. The concept of "condensation of instincts" runs counter to the two established concepts of "confluence of instincts," and of the collaboration between the various components of the sexual instinct in its gratification. Over-determination of an instinct is known to us in the form of an instinct taking possession of an organ. The expression "condensation of instincts" could perhaps be used as a general term to express all these forms of the collaboration of instincts. Similarly, the fact that the masturbator has to substitute in his fantasy for what is not offered to him by an object is also known to us under a different name: he does not abreact either totally or adequately. Prison revolt can not be explained in such general terms; at its root lie specific forms of psychic conflicts. The speaker's conception of the principle of economy as being etiologically responsible for the harm that results from masturbation should be put almost the other way round. Normally, too, the object has first to be gained, and it is the dammed-up libido that is discharged in sexual intercourse. What is both new and correct is the view that regression is involved in masturbation. The statement about the distribution of libido is also true; it is only that various familiar things can be subsumed under it. In every neurosis what is involved is a disturbance of equilibrium because some elements have remained infantile. Masturbation fixates not only infantility, but also perversion; it is in general a way of fixating the infantile state.

STEINER is also of the opinion that the presentation offered nothing new *in merito,* and in particular that it failed to solve the problem of why masturbation is harmful in one person and harmless in another. The lesser harmfulness in the case of girls may perhaps be connected with the fact that fantasy is more fully developed in the female sex, and therefore lesser expenditures of energy are required.

FEDERN emphasizes that the increasing clarity of the individual presentations provides the best evidence of the fruitfulness of these

debates. He corrects Tausk's mistaken understanding of the "confluence of instincts"; this does not signify, in Adler's sense of the
term, the collaboration of a sexual instinct with an instinct of the
ego group (sadism), since in Adler's view sadism itself arises out of
a "confluence of instincts." What was said about the psychic economy is correct, but one must guard against disposing so casually of
the problem of pleasure and unpleasure. There are also feelings of
pleasure that are highly detrimental to the psychic economy. Also,
what Sachs has characterized as a "permanent result" is not necessarily always harmful; often the repression of harmful instinctual
drives succeeds better when the subject has masturbated. The essential
factor is the point at which the barrier of repression is broken
through.

SADGER thinks that on the basis of his experiences he can state
that girls masturbate just as much as boys do, and that, side by
side with complete harmlessness, one can also observe the most
severe forms of damage done to them by masturbation. He saw the
most serious damage in cases in which masturbation was practiced
relatively little. The castration threat does indeed have its analogues
in girls.

REINHOLD remarks, in reference to the term "condensation of
instincts," that it is true that a condensation does take place in
intercourse; it is not, however, a condensation of instincts, each of
which strives for its goal on its own, but rather a condensation in
the end-effect of pleasure. Nor does a regression to perception take
place; otherwise masturbation would not differ from the actual conditions. It is only a construct [without objective grounds] to say
that masturbation takes a reverse course; in both cases, the libido
precedes and the object follows.

As to pleasure, it is not the principle of economy that is the
determining factor, it is abreaction that is.

REITLER finds that Sachs actually holds the view that masturbation is harmful because the demands made on fantasy are too
great; but this cannot hold true of mutual masturbation, which often
has the same damaging effect. The most important factor has not
been taken into consideration—that is, the question of the period
at which the individual masturbates. It is altogether different whether

it is a sexually immature individual who is masturbating or a grown-up.

PROF. FREUD shares Reinhold's opinion that no condensation of instincts takes place in sexual intercourse, but rather that there is a condensation in the end result. The term "confluence of instincts" is preferable.

ROSENSTEIN singles out from the debate three important problems:

(1) the character changes caused by masturbation;
(2) the compulsion to masturbate (the fixation of the act);
(3) the question of the harmfulness of masturbation.

Ad (1): R. has no experience of these.

Ad (2): He makes several general statements that apply also to the neurotic. The compulsion to masturbate (when the opportunity presents itself or in addition to intercourse) rests on an inability of the organism to digest contrasting currents, an inability to perform a synthesis, which also underlies the neurotic's inhibition. Among the contrasting pairs that the neurotic individual is unable to combine in joint and unified action are: love and hate (Freud's explanation of obsessional neurosis); sadism and masochism—or, in more general terms: sexual instinct and ego-instinct, or, in quite general terms, instinct and repression. Freud has shown us, in place of "disposition," the play of forces; in the neurotic, however, ambivalence is perhaps more developed. This blocking of libido by inability to produce a synthesis makes necessary another compulsory discharge. Such damming-up of the libido may persist even though intercourse has been performed, since it is not able to influence the psychic processes.

Ad (3): The problem of the "actual neuroses" and the psychoneuroses in relation to masturbation has not been formulated correctly. Actual neurosis is an autointoxication; psychoneurosis has a psychic etiology. However, one can speak of a parallelism of the etiology in the two cases. The connection between these two etiologies can be established via the concept of inhibition, i.e., of resistance, which is the most important factor in neurosis. But inhibition is also the essential factor causing the damming-up of secretion. It is not anger ("bursting with venom and malice") that produces secretion, it is the inhibition of the affect. Instead of an innervation of the motor apparatus, an innervation of secretion takes place; in this lies the connection between the neuroses and intoxication. Masturbation carried out with inhibitions must have other consequences than masturbation without inhibitions. An important question is the one having to do with the nature and removability of these inhibitions. Are these inhibitions more pathogenic when they are conscious or when they are unconscious? There are inhibitions that disappear under the influence of mere discussion and instruction, and the harm resulting from these inhibitions vanishes simultaneously. It is more difficult to do away with the organic inhibitions of which Rank spoke. And finally, there are biological inhibitions (of a teleological nature).

FEDERN refers, with regard to the whole conception of inhibition, to Otto Gross; he does not, however, decide whether Gross is right in his view of the effect of inhibition. The concepts of dissociation and synthesis are rendered obsolete by psychoanalytic understanding. The interrelationship of glandular activity and psychic processes, which he himself dealt with in his report on masturbation, does exist and was correctly evaluated.

PROF. FREUD finds the exposition about a connection between psychic and toxic phenomena well worth noting. It does not seem superfluous to stress, as Rosenstein did, that the symptoms of the actual neurosis are to be regarded as symptoms of intoxication. On the other hand, he wanted erroneously to make use of the comparison with intoxication also for the psychoneuroses. If we once again introduce the concept of dissociation and synthesis, we renounce our psychology of the unconscious, which has traced these phenomena back to the active interplay of psychic forces. The opposites finally do combine—i.e., in the symptom that originally emerged out of their separation; those opposing forces do bind each other once again.

TAUSK remarks that it is not the fact that strivings are inhibited that is the most important factor in neurosis, but how this is utilized. Nor can ambivalence be considered the basis for the whole of neurosis, because the symptom proves to be determined by the

73

workings of *various* strivings, not only of contrasting ones. There is no synthesis between two opposing strivings from the same instinctual root; there is only an either/or, or else an alternation.

REINHOLD concurs with Tausk in the opinion that it is not the inhibition that produces the neurosis; however, neither is it the utilization of inhibition, which can also lead to sublimation. Repression must precede the inhibition.

FRIEDJUNG believes that the opposing opinions—namely, that the actual neuroses are caused by the influence exerted by psychic factors upon glandular secretion; or, as Stekel thinks, that the concomitant psychic phenomena remain the decisive factor—should be settled on the basis of the observation of a large number of idiots, for in their case these processes take their course without being influenced by the accompanying phenomena of civilization.

ROSENSTEIN remarks that, although he is familiar with Gross, he did not consider a reference to him to be important in the context of his presentation. Up to the present, it has not been disproved that inhibition is the ultimate cause of neurosis. "Sejunction" merely designates an *Anlage*.

SPIELREIN calls attention to the fact that Bleuler, in his conception of ambivalence, attributes the absence of a capacity for action to two forces working against each other. Normally, we perceive a complex only in the difference of the two antagonistic forces.

MARCUS counters that two opposing strivings directed onto an object, will not result in indifference toward that object, but the opposite.

PROF. FREUD remarks that nothing is gained by the assumption of a "sejunctive disposition." It is true that the inability to synthesize is in fact congenital, since it is expressed most clearly in the child. Only later do we feel it to be unbearable to tolerate, as the child does, two opposite kinds of behavior in relation to the same object. This can also be pursued in the history of religion, since often (for instance, among the Egyptians) all the figures of the Gods who succeed each other are retained alongside one another.

167

SCIENTIFIC MEETING *on March 20, 1912*

Present: Dattner, Federn, Freud, Friedjung, Hitschmann, Jekels, Rank, Reinhold, Reitler, Rosenstein, Sachs, Sadger, Spielrein, Steiner, Stekel, Tausk, Winterstein.
Guests: Dr. Marcus, Dr. Dorsay Hecht from Chicago.[1]

EIGHTH DISCUSSION ON MASTURBATION

SPEAKERS: DRS. DATTNER, SPIELREIN

Dr. DATTNER, following the course of development described in the *Three Contributions to the Theory of Sex,* traces the vicissitudes of masturbation from earliest childhood to the years of maturity. In so doing, he pays special attention to the influence exerted upon the kind and consequences of masturbatory activity by the individual's physical readiness and psychic development. In earliest childhood, sexual activity serves biological interests, and, unless it is practiced to excess or inhibited by powerful traumas of prohibition, it can do no harm. On the other hand, it is in the period of latency, during

---

[1] Dr. Hecht's identity could not be established.

which the first barriers against sexuality are erected, that the first psychological as well as physical indications of harm usually appear. The most significant consequences, however, develop out of masturbation during puberty. At that period, stimulation of any erotogenic zone may be harmful; genital masturbation, however, because of the loss of semen involved, will in general be more harmful than extra-genital masturbation; also, mental masturbation will have more serious consequences than manual masturbation: the ensuing disturbances will be all the more intense, the more the psyche is involved. Instinctive knowledge of the unsuitability of masturbation in terms of the perpetuation of the species will certainly also intensify the harmful consequences, just as the frequency of the act must exert some influence. The speaker establishes a connection between the persistence of masturbation, as well as the underlying lack of will power and the disturbance of inner secretion. On the whole, masturbation must be regarded as nothing worse than a necessary evil of the age of puberty; it is an inferior *Anlage* that is mainly to blame for harmful effects.

FEDERN concurs in general with these comments and wants to criticize only a few incorrect statements. The notion that the sexual organs are developing during latency seems to rest on a misleading wording; in general, it must be assumed that at times of more intensive genital development the period of latency is interrupted. Loss of secretion as the result of masturbation, as well as forceful discharge in ejaculation, cannot in any way be considered harmful factors. Also, in view of the fact that, during the course of our debate, various factors have been held accountable for the harmful effects of masturbation, it will not do simply to declare one or the other method to be more harmful.

Concerning the influence exerted by masturbation on secretion, MARCUS remarks that the generative and secretory functions of the genital glands are completely separated, to which

STEIN replies that nevertheless the parallelism is there.

TAUSK criticizes some formulations. For instance, it is not only in early childhood that sexual activity serves biological interests; it does so at all times. Disgust, shame, and morality cannot all be subsumed under the common term "sublimations"; they are of entirely different origin. Nor does it tally with actual observation to make the assertion that there is no masturbatory activity during the so-called latency period.

SACHS remarks in answer to this that, according to Freud's view, sexual activity does not come to a halt during latency, it merely remains stationary—that is, it does not undergo any further development. An important difference in terms of time is to be observed with regard to the complex relationship between the psychic effort connected with intercourse and that connected with masturbation. In the case of coition, the psychic effort is more intense before the act; in the case of masturbation, it is precisely at the peak of sexual tension that the fantasy must be maintained.

FEDERN cannot but maintain that during the latency period masturbation is stopped and sublimation takes place; in periods when the instinct is weaker, man attempts to sublimate it.

RANK, on the contrary, thinks that sublimation is more likely to occur when the instinct is strong.

HITSCHMANN finds that the concept of the latency period is often taken too literally; what is referred to is, as the term indicates, the fact that manifest masturbatory activity becomes temporarily latent. Tausk would like to see determined what is meant by the concept of "psychic masturbation": this means indulging in fantasies to the point of ejaculation—the sort of masturbation that is far more damaging to the safety valve and may easily lead to *ejaculatio praecox.*

A suggestion: in an appendix to the intended publication of these discussions, a collection of typical masturbation dreams or clinical material about dreams of prohibition should be presented.

PROF. FREUD comments that the concept of the latency period was intended at first to set up a sharply defined extreme type; this must now be modified wherever necessary, in accordance with careful individual observation. It may be that sexual interest and sexual activity do come to a halt completely during this period, but it is also possible that there are interruptions.

TAUSK believes that during this period, in which the erotic interest clearly turns toward an object, amnesia for masturbation is also more intense, as a result of the development of the sense of shame. On the other hand, the existence of an acute feeling of shame at this time indicates that there is something of which the individual has to be ashamed.

DATTNER clarifies some misunderstandings for Hitschmann, Tausk, Federn.

PROF. FREUD welcomes the attempt to fill the latency period with psychosexual content and stresses once again that this concept is merely a relative one, formulated by way of comparison with the period of sexual flowering at the age of three to four. The anatomical parallel to this would be interesting: it seems that the growth of the genitalia comes to a stop at a very early age; it could be that between the ages of three and four the thrust of growth sets in anew.

FRIEDJUNG relates that according to his observation it is true of the majority of cases that there is a comparative subsidence of sexuality during the period Freud has characterized as latency. Even though he has made no anatomical measurements, Friedjung has gained the impression that the genitalia grow rapidly up to the third or fourth year of life, and that a major thrust of growth does not occur again until the twelfth or thirteenth year.

STEKEL considers Dattner's statements to be wrong; in most cases, a period of latency does not exist. If children become asexual, it is not as the consequence of masturbation, but rather of their giving up masturbation. In some children, a seeming latency sets in because at the ages of three and four the child begins to be influenced by education.

HITSCHMANN makes the point that the significant sexual development during the third and fourth years of life is the best evidence against Adler's theses, for at that time there is no question either of a "masculine protest" or of doubt about one's sexual role.

DR. SPIELREIN thinks the delimitation of the concept of masturbation is still so very uncertain because of the variety of facts that have been learned by experience. In girls, masturbation can generally be observed less frequently because it often takes the form of retention of natural needs from which the child derives pleasure. The sense of guilt is regularly linked with religious ideas. Spielrein considers woman's application of the castration fantasy to man as an analogy to man's castration fantasy. A woman patient suffered from a continuous fear that her hand would fall off; another patient had strangulation fantasies. Mention is made also of the superstition that "one's mind is being sewed up."

The reporter further mentions that genital masturbation changes to other forms (hand-rubbing; tearing one's hair, etc.), and that psychic masturbation (heroes of novels) plays an important role (pictures: Leda, Jo). The fact that in the woman (who is generally more erotic), anything can serve as a means of stimulation is characterized as being a transition to fetishism. Special attention is called to a form of masturbation that occurs while listening to music. Finally, the speaker mentions that the desire to masturbate can be aroused by kleptomania. She cites a form of masturbation that is typical of women: it consists in pressing her child to her body, and leads over to girls' games (doll).

HITSCHMANN mentions the masturbation that follows states of anxiety and the masturbation that accompanies the reading of novels. It seems that there are two kinds of music: one that has a cathartic effect, and one that is exciting (playing the piano in dreams is a frequent symbol of masturbation). The relation of musicians to neurotics would deserve thorough study.

REIK believes that music offers the greatest opportunity for abreacting all complexes, while not making them conscious.

FRIEDJUNG, referring to the autoerotism of hair, remarks that it is an important starting point for stimulating oneself, without touching the genital itself.

It is true that there are two kinds of music, but not along the lines of Hitschmann's thinking. There is an autoerotic musical activity which exhausts itself in "fantasying" on the piano, and there is another that is meant for listeners, and aims at winning them over.

STEKEL finds it inadmissible to apply to hands the concept of castration fantasy; the fear of the hand falling off is a talion fantasy. A woman's fantasy of having damaged her genitals or her inner organs by masturbation and therefore of having become sterile, for instance, corresponds to the castration fantasy of the man. Women usually have bisexual (male) fantasies. The criminal fantasies of many men (that they have murdered someone) and of women (that they have murdered a newborn), which accompany masturbation, are counterparts to the fantasy of strangulation.

There do not exist two kinds of music; one and the same music is capable of generating totally different fantasies and of having various effects. It is correct to say that kleptomania is connected with masturbation, and it is interesting that in Spielrein's cases, something is taken away from the hated person. Frequently, homosexual inclinations also play a role in this: the woman wants to make up for the part of the man that she is lacking.

TAUSK thinks music represents a stage of the human spirit at which it still worked without ideas, and abreaction occurred only through the expression of affects. Music as a stimulus of associations is a different matter. As another equivalent of man's castration fantasy in women, mention is made of the fantasies of biting off (Zola: *Fécondité*). Passive castration plays a different role. The castration fantasy seems to be phylogenetically preformed; in a neurotic, it proved to be linked with the act of birth. An example is offered to illustrate the fact that kleptomania follows forbidden sexual acts.

RANK points out that, while the forbidden content of the kleptomaniac act may consist in various sexual activities, its mechanism is that of masturbation. As a female fantasy of punishment for masturbation—albeit for the most part imposed by men—we encounter in myths and fairy tales such things as sewing up (in displacement onto the mouth), securing with a padlock, and especially cutting off of the hands. In most instances, this latter punishment is inflicted upon the girl by her father, whose desire she has resisted. Narcissistic self-admiration in the mirror underlies the sexual excitement that may set in when a woman combs her hair (of course, the role played by the erotogenic capacity of hair must not by any means be disregarded). The woman's fantasy of cutting off the penis is based on complicated fantasies and not simply on castration performed on the man because of her own masturbation.

FEDERN surmises that Spielrein's patient, who suffered from strangulation fantasies with the image of dogs hanging on each other, suffered from vaginismus. (SPIELREIN remarks that the patient had suffered from cramps in the esophagus.) Birth fantasies are usually hidden behind the fear of suffocation. How cautious one has to be in interpreting disguised masturbation is demonstrated in the case of a little girl: her habit of pressing her doll to her chest was traceable to her previously having taken the doll between her legs, which in turn went back to masturbation with the doll, carried out on the toilet.

PROF. FREUD does not consider it useful to try in every way to find in the woman an analogue to the castration fantasy that has the same meaning for her as the castration fantasy has for the man. The woman has no need of this fantasy, since she has come into this world already castrated, as a woman. Later on, she may simply give her sanction to this fact by producing the fantasy that her penis has been cut off. With reference to the strangulation fantasy, the dream of an agoraphobic patient who strangled her husband in her dream; the actual theme of her dream is the vengeful castration of her husband, who does not satisfy her. The spasms in the esophagus and the fantasies of strangulation on the part of Spielrein's patient constitute a displacement upward of vaginal tendencies.

SPIELREIN is inclined to ascribe to all artistic activity the auto-erotic and heterosexual aspects mentioned before in relation to music. The creative act can be reduced to a re-differentiation of all auto-erotic elements, which are then adapted to the external world, by means of the heterosexual component.

STEKEL finds contained in the male castration fantasy the wish to be a woman. Not infrequently, castration fantasies have to do with characteristics of the female sex (breasts, thighs, reducing, etc.). If Freud derives the strangulation fantasies from rage, that is in accord with Stekel's own view about "criminal tendencies."

81

168

Present: Dattner, Federn, Freud, Graf, Heller, Hitschmann, Jekels, Rank, Reik, Reinhold, Reitler, Rosenstein, Sachs, Spielrein, Steiner, Stekel, Tausk, Wagner, (Karl) Weiss, Winterstein.
Guest: Dr. Robert Scheu

PRESENTATION

Sexuality and Ego

SPEAKER: DR. VICTOR TAUSK

The speaker proposes merely to unfold a problem and to offer some standpoints from which it can be approached. It is only if one is a psychoanalyst that one can become reconciled to the contrast that has been expressed, yet not sharply demarcated, in the concepts of the sexual instinct and the ego instinct. Sexuality indeed belongs to the ego; the "second ego," which could be contrasted with sexuality, should be conceived of as a censored breakthrough into consciousness of an unsuccessful repression. The problem can be approached only from a historical-psychological point of view; one must try to understand this concept of the ego by way of the vicissitudes of the instincts.

To begin with, it is only the instinct of self-preservation that can convey the idea of a contrast to the external world. Marking off the ego from the external world is, however, marking off the ego from the species. With that, the antithesis of species and individual has been drawn into the problem; what follows is the supposition of an order of precedence between these two groups of instincts. The sexual instinct serves primarily the preservation of the species and secondarily self-preservation. At this point, it should be particularly stressed that the two groups of instincts are served by the same organ, and that the simultaneity of these two sorts of activity must be left undisturbed.

By way of a comparison of the results of these two activities, one is led to the recognition that a contrast exists between the two groups of instincts. The resultant preservation of the species is independent of pleasure. The sexual instinct does not allow its primary tendency to be tricked with impunity by its secondary tendency (anxiety neurosis, etc.). If one considers the two groups of instincts with regard to their expression and without considering the consequences, one finds that the existence of the sexual instinct is rendered secure in the most diverse and most far-reaching ways (fantasy, dream, perversion, sublimation, etc.), and that it has at its disposal inexhaustible possibilities for gratification. As far as the instinct of self-preservation is concerned, we find in this respect a relatively poor milieu. What secures the sexual instinct most effectively is its significance as a source of pleasure for the individual (orgasm dissolves the ego).

There does exist, however, between ego instincts and sexual instincts, something that represents both; that is sadism, in which the battle between the two groups of instincts is carried out. Sadism has to be repressed in civilization; the lowest limit for it goes only so far as to permit the ego group to be still preserved; if more is repressed, disturbances appear in the form of symptoms. On the basis of the experience that these disturbances of repressed sadism often affect the organ that is most important for preservation—i.e., the intestinal tract—the speaker is inclined to regard manifestations of anal erotism as an organic substrate for sadism.

We can approach the problem of ego and sexuality only by showing in what way these instinctual activities confront each other and what the results of their battle reveal themselves to be. It then becomes clear that the ego can be used as an artificial concept in the Freudian sense, but also that it has to be used if we want to understand the neurosis.

DISCUSSION

REINHOLD argues against the speaker's basic conception on the grounds that the battle of the instincts cannot be comprehended psychologically at all, because "instinct" is not a psychological concept but a biological one. Yet, the instinct cannot actually be described in biological terms, either. To the discussant, the animal appears to represent the argument against the entire conception of a contrast between the two groups of instinct, the animal in whom there is ample room for both instinctual activities, one alongside the other. Human civilization forces the individual to renounce only a certain kind of pleasure—that is, a portion of sexuality; if we set aside the instincts, the problem that presents itself is: why does society offer resistance to this type of pleasurable activity?

ROSENSTEIN, in contrast to the previous speaker, concurs with the lecturer on the principle of his presentation, for it is only the theory of the instincts that gives psychology its foundations. Similarly, contrary to Reinhold's view, the battle of the instincts simply has to be included in civilization. Nietzsche postulates a hierarchy of the instincts for the individual who is to be considered a whole personality (as a result of the battle of the instincts, as it were). The fact that orgasm annihilates the ego feeling has been generalized by Klages, to the effect that any affect that exceeds a certain measure has a tendency to dissolve the individual.

Connection between repressed sadism and constipation would have to be proven by a larger body of empirical material.

SPIELREIN, too, turns against this view, which—for women in particular—does not hold true. The problem of why the individual defends himself against sexuality can be approached on the basis of the fact that the sexual instinct is bipolar: it contains one component that calls for the dissolution of the ego. In asserting that the ego is dissolved during the sexual act, Tausk is saying the same thing. Klages' opinion that every strong affect bears the tendency toward ego dissolution is advocated also by the present speaker, in a paper now in print. Every psychic reaction has a tendency toward dissolution of the ego into its phylogenetic past; the second factor is that of projection and adaptation to the present.

STEKEL feels the contrast between ego instinct and sexual instincts to be an artificial one. The sexual instinct is the most powerful of the ego instincts. Whatever belongs to instinctual life is unconscious, and it is a mistake to mark off as ego instincts those instincts that have been accepted by consciousness. A strong affect does not dissolve the ego; on the contrary, it awakens it; true, this is the unconscious ego, the same that comes forth during orgasm. It is incorrect to establish a connection between sadism and constipation; in analysis, quite different relationships can be demonstrated to exist.

Prevention of conception does not—as has already been mentioned by Rosenstein—in and of itself lead to anxiety neurosis.

PROF. FREUD stresses the philosophical naïveté of psychoanalytic conceptualization, which took its start purely from the practical experience that neurotic disturbances can be traced back to sexual components. What was left could then be brought together under the rubric of ego instincts. Psychoanalysis has to work at first with concepts that are philosophically vague; only afterward will it be possible to mark off their boundaries sharply.

Prof. Freud agrees most closely with Reinhold, who wants to allow "the instinct" only as a hypothetical concept, at the border between the psychic and the organic. In his conception, which ascribes the sexual instinct to the ego, Stekel is not in contradiction to the speaker, who did indeed stress how closely the two groups of instincts belong together. One could express this antithesis between the two groups of instincts in historical terms: everything that today is an internal conflict was once an external conflict. If today the ego defends itself against sexuality, this barrier was once upon a time transformed from an external into an internal one.

Wittels once developed the fantasy that men came to possess their excessive libido (annulment of periodicity, etc.) as a result of the overnourishment that occurred during the golden, paradisical epoch. Then, Ferenczi, in a conversation, referred to the supersession of this period by the glacial epoch, in which the scarcity of food made the libido a danger and its restriction a necessity. Ontogenetically, the individual repeats this destiny; in the present constitution and in the tendency toward repression, that destiny of the libido has been preserved. In the same way, the Americans have undertaken to explain national character in terms of the history of nations; perhaps the prehistory of animals would explain their character to us.

As far as Tausk's exposition is concerned, nothing conclusive can be said today about sadism as a point of convergence for the two groups of instincts. There does exist, however, a more important contact between the two groups: the stage of narcissism in which the entire libido has found its object in the ego itself. It is only from then on that the instincts clearly separate from each other.[1] Dr. Spielrein was right in stating that the problem of sadomasochism is identical with that of the instinct of destruction. Any connection between sadism and constipation must be contested; these things are not yet ready for judgment in either one direction or the other.

STEKEL would like to express some reservations with regard to Freud's ingenious hypothesis and to propose a simpler path to the explanation of repression: i.e., the principle of the increasing of pleasure, which by itself creates the barriers within that are no longer offered by the external world. Repression serves the purpose of effecting the increase in pleasure.

FREUD counters that interpolation of resistance for the purpose of increasing pleasure occurs only in the case of the sexual instinct.

STEKEL points out that it also occurs in the case of the drinker (teetotalism) and the eater.

FEDERN calls attention to the fact that long ago Rank had postulated the principle of increasing the libido by means of the inter-

---

[1] This is an intimation of an ego psychology. Freud's 1914 essay "On Narcissism" contains a clearer indication of the development of an ego psychology.

polation of resistances; by no means did Freud intend through his comment to invalidate that thesis. It seems plausible that during the glacial period the animals had a delayed sexual development.

In Tausk's presentation, nothing philosophical was to be met with. His error lay in the assertion that the sexual instinct primarily serves the preservation of the species; there is only one instinct in the human being that does serve the preservation of the species, and that is the woman's maternal instinct. Comparison of the activities and manifestations of the two instincts must necessarily prove inadequate because we in our culture no longer know or experience being overwhelmed by the intense hunger-instinct, whereas the overwhelming desire of the sexual instinct still makes itself felt in every human being. That is why man feels himself subjected to the sexual instinct, and why a conflict arises. From the standpoint of biology, Tausk is right. During the time when the cell was multiplying, while growing, no contrast existed between the development of the species and that of the ego. In the metazoan, one part is utilized for the creation of the individual, another part is preserved until maturity. The sexual organ was originally a part of the cell, and the individual himself is merely an organ of the sexual gonad.

ROSENSTEIN remarks, in reference to the difference in man's behavior as far as the instinct of eating and the sexual instinct are concerned, that according to Freud the need for alcohol is a substitute for sexual enjoyment, and that therefore it is precisely in that case that Stekel's view of the conflict might well be correct.

On the subject of methodology, the discussant comments that a sharp separation of concepts is not only a need and a requirement of any science; it is also of heuristic value.

REINHOLD reiterates that, in considering instincts from the standpoint of biology, we gain nothing for psychology. Perhaps it is more useful to follow up, not the instincts in their battle with each other, but rather certain forms of their activity; it may then turn out that the sexual instinct is fighting against the self.

SACHS would like to propose that in place of the inappropriate and awkward terms, sadism and masochism, we substitute the terms "active and passive erotism of aggression."

87

SPIELREIN mentions, in connection with the theory of repression, Jung's reference to "historical recall." The pleasure that, according to Stekel, is increased by abstention from eating, is encountered in eating-erotists, just as, in the process of acquiring food by conquest, sadism—pleasure in overpowering—is needed.

FREUD remarks that with the substitution of alcohol for sexual enjoyment, sexual gratification becomes a matter of the instinct of nutrition. The difference between the sexual instinct and the ego instincts can be formulated in the following way: whereas the other instincts from the very beginning have their object in the external world, the sexual instinct for a long time finds its object within the ego (autoerotism). With this is connected an attitude toward reality that remains at an earlier level (see formulations on the two principles of mental functioning).

A second essential characteristic of the sexual instinct is the latency period, which is particularly characteristic of the human being. In this period the sexual instinct, in the sense indicated by the hypothesis that has been presented, is defined in terms of its constitutional as well as its accidental qualities.

GRAF is astonished by the fact that one is speaking of a separate ego-instinct; this is, perhaps, not quite correct. One can speak merely of an ego-feeling whose developmental history follows, on the basis of Freud's theories, from the history of repression.

TAUSK comments, in his concluding remarks, that he intended merely to show how the term "ego instincts" can be confirmed by way of their counterpart. What presents itself psychologically is a representation of the biological. And if the nature of repression is explained by Freud in terms of the vicissitudes of the species, here too it is a question of the contrast between the representation of the species and the representation of the individual. The child wants to use everything for himself, and the species opposes this; hence the demands for renunciation and the corresponding reactions. With regard to the relation between constipation and repression, we have to refer to the fact that both groups of instincts can make use and take hold of the same organs, and that it is merely a question of the sequence in which this occurs (the rank order of the instincts).

Federn's remark that the individual is an organ of the sexual organ touches upon the problem in depth. The undivided individual simply has to work in accordance with two tendencies, and thereby the possibility is given of their being in contradiction and conflict with each other.

169

SCIENTIFIC MEETINGS *on April 3 & April 17, 1912*

REVIEWS AND CLINICAL COMMUNICATIONS

First Evening [April 3]

SILBERER: Spermatozoa Dreams (will appear in *Jahrbuch*) [1]

DR. REIK: Review of Rullmann, *Wit and Humor*; Baümer and Dröscher: *About the Child's Soul.*

DR. WEISS: Contributions to the Observation of Children

DR. SACHS: Jokes of Sexual Symbolism

PROF. FREUD: About One Particular Root of the Castration Complex: an Analysis of Numbers[2]

[1] *Jb.* (1912), 4:141–161.
[2] Freud's communication could not be identified.

Second Evening [April 17]

DR. HITSCHMANN: On the Symbolism in a Poem.
On Examination Dreams.
On Symbolic Representations in Painting.
A Contribution to the Clinical Picture of
Juvenile Obsessional Neurosis and to Child Psychology.[3]

ROSENSTEIN: A Criticism of Kronfeld's Comments about an
Alleged Contradiction between the Theory of Repression and that
of the Complexes.[4]

DR. van EMDEN: A Case of Unconscious Self-Punishment.

DR. FEDERN: The Inhibition-Dream (as an Expression of a Conflict of Will, in Freud's Sense).[5]

[3] Hitschmann's contributions could not be identified.

[4] Rosenstein published in *Jb.* IV/2 an essay entitled Eine Kritik [A Criticism]. It
refers to a paper by Arthur Kronfeld, which appeared in *Archiv für die Gesamte Psychologie,* Vol. XXII, as well as in book form as II/3 of the *Abhandlungen zur Psychologischen Pädagogik,* under the title *Über die Psychologischen Theorien Freuds
und verwandte Anschauungen* [On Freud's Psychological Theories and Kindred Views].

[5] "Zur Frage des Hemmungstraumes" [On the Question of the Inhibition Dream].
Z.(1920), 6: 73–75.

91

170

SCIENTIFIC MEETING *on April 24, 1912*

Present: Dattner, Federn, Freud, Hitschmann, Rank, Reinhold, Reik, Reitler, Rosenstein, Sachs, Sadger, Silberer, Steiner, Stekel, Tausk, Karl Weiss.
Guests: Dr. Hellmann, Loew, Spitzer, Marcus, Klebinder.

PRESENTATION

An Epilogue to the Discussions on Masturbation

SPEAKER: PROF. FREUD

PROF. FREUD begins by grouping the twelve contributions into general and specific presentations and giving a brief characterization of the individual efforts. On the whole, he finds a welcome agreement on the essential points, without serious contradictions; the various views have a place alongside one another.

Passing on to his own contribution, the speaker remarks that he is not trying to offer any solutions, but merely to define his own point of view precisely, with regard to the topics that were dealt with: the definition of the concept of masturbation, what it does biologically, and its harmfulness.

(1) A sharper distinction should have been made between masturbation in infancy and childhood masturbation, as well as between the latter and masturbation during puberty, which is either separated from childhood masturbation by the latency period or follows the former directly (Reitler's critique is referred to at this point).

(2) As far as the relationship is concerned between masturbation (emission) and neurasthenia, Stekel's objection must be met. The speaker adheres to his opinion that "actual neuroses" do exist— that is, neuroses in which a purely toxic component can be distinguished, a component that therapeutic means are unable to reduce. In reality, these disturbances, except where the individuals involved are still juveniles, will in most instances be blended with psychic disturbances. The essential factor in the relationship between neurasthenia and psychoneurosis is this: neurasthenic symptoms are not structured like psychoneurotic phenomena. The symptoms do not come about psychogenetically; rather, they underlie the psychogenic symptoms. What one could accept from Stekel as a new finding is the role of the psychic conflict; but the conflict generates the symptoms, not psychogenetically but toxically.

(3) *A priori*, one is forced to oppose the assertion that masturbation has to be harmless; on the contrary, there must be cases in which masturbation is harmful. Since the etiology of the neuroses is given by way of the conflict between infantile sexuality and the opposition of the ego (repression), masturbation, which is only an executive of infantile sexuality, cannot *a priori* be presented as harmless. The question of when masturbation is harmful and when it is not cannot be answered in general terms. Three factors can be singled out as contributing toward the overall result: the first factor contributing to pathogenicity is that of quantity; the second, concerted action with all sorts of other influences; the third, the constitutional factor, which can, however, be inferred only *ex post facto*.

Side by side with the harmfulness of masturbation, its usefulness must also be taken into account; much could be said about it, but only one point will be stressed. One part of the usefulness of masturbation lies in the harm it does, in that it effects the culturally necessary lowering of potency.

The harmful consequences can be distinguished as:

(1) Organic injuries (probably of a toxic nature), the causes for which are to be sought in physiological factors (inadequate gratification) as well as in toxic factors.

(2) The fact that masturbation becomes a psychological model insofar as no reaction to it develops; that is again of advantage.

(3) Masturbation, being an executive of infantile sexuality, allows fixation to take place and therewith brings about the disposition to neurosis. In this, most likely, lies the main harm inflicted by masturbation.

The following points were little dealt with, or not at all:

Unconscious masturbation (during sleep): cases in which the individual slips into unconsciousness in order to be able to masturbate. A hysterical attack will often bring masturbation into action once again, as will certain compulsive motions.

The masturbation of women should have been dealt with separately as well as more extensively.

The therapeutic return of masturbation—that is, the fact that persons who have fallen ill because they have given up masturbating show improvement by beginning to masturbate again.

The role of masturbation as an executive of fantasy. Fantasy, as an area between pleasure and reality, is a harmful compromise from which there is only one reasonable way out—that is, into art. Art offers the chance of acting in accordance with the pleasure principle and yet, at the same time, taking part in all the progress that one can otherwise make only in reality; without masturbation, this would not be possible.

There are some things the speakers have been in agreement on: the great significance of fantasy; the incurring of a sense of guilt; the impossibility of specifying under what conditions masturbation is harmful.

They were in disagreement, however, with regard to: the question of the ubiquity of children's masturbation; the negation of any harmfulness; the emphasis on the feeling of guilt. Where the sense of guilt comes from has not yet become clear. It was stressed that (1) the sense of guilt is nothing but an anxiety that is psychically bound; (2) repression in this instance proceeds from the social factor; and (3) whether or not the masturbatory act is gratifying is relevant.

The toxic mechanism is completely unknown to us at the present time, yet the significance of these processes deserves to be underlined by way of an analogy in the realm of anxiety. A person who suffers from chronic fears and worries loses weight and moves toward degeneration, whereas the neurotic anxiety arising from the libido is trophically harmless.

DISCUSSION

STEKEL says that he has observed in his cases how seemingly toxic symptoms come about psychogenetically, just as the conflict is purely psychogenic.

The view that masturbation is an executive of infantile sexuality does not *a priori* prove that it is harmful; in social life, too, we may hold only a bad law responsible for some harmfulness, and not the executive organs, which are not responsible for it. Whether or not someone falls ill depends on whether or not his attitude toward infantile sexuality is one of guilt. With regard to the influence of masturbation on potency, we have to take into consideration seeming impotence (with homosexuals, perverts, etc.) and relative impotence (with ladies).

TAUSK, referring to the point about the weakening of potency, raises the question of what consequences result from this for women, who do indeed suffer from that condition.

FEDERN states that he thought of masturbation as being useful only where criminal and sadistic characters are concerned.

Women certainly do suffer when potency is decreased. The difference between the effects of neurotic and normal anxiety may perhaps be explained by way of the fact that in the anxiety attack a sort of compensation of these toxins takes place.

REINHOLD, in connection with the question of the effect of anxiety, refers to melancholia and depression, which manifest themselves in somatic states. Stekel's proof of the psychogenic nature of neurasthenic headaches does not hold up, because all that was shown was that the headache is called forth by intense mental work (the work of repression), but not that it has a symbolic meaning, as for instance a stomach ache has ("That sits in my stomach"—Stekel).

ROSENSTEIN, with regard to the effect of anxiety, calls attention to the fact that, according to a remark made by Freud, edemas develop during the course of an agoraphobia.

FREUD: These edemas cannot be equated with a lasting disturbance; the patient simply receives the vasomotor and secretory stimulation in his legs, instead of in the genitals.

DR. WEISS stresses that it was not a question of neurasthenia in the cases Stekel cited as proof for the psychogenic origin of neurasthenic symptoms, because there was no actual neurosis (the patients no longer masturbate).

FREUD, too, cannot regard Stekel's cases as counterevidence. The picture of neurasthenia in these cases is explained by the fact that such persons, once they have acquired the mechanism, continue to react to the harm in the same way.[1]

[1] The debate about masturbation extended over a period of more than two years. It was fruitful: many concepts were clarified, many were not. The most important insight that can be gained from these discussions is that masturbation is a very complex problem, which can be subdivided into part problems, and that masturbation probably exercises an influence on normal intercourse, as well as on neurosis and the character. I should like to add the observation that masturbation, being an executive of the sexual instinct, is useful in that it offers sexual gratification.

Later discussions and articles on this topic did not succeed in adding anything of importance.

171

SCIENTIFIC MEETING on *May 1, 1912*

Present: Dattner, Emden, Federn, Friedjung, Freud, Heller, Hitschmann, Rank, Reik, Reitler, Rosenstein, Sachs, Sadger, Steiner, Stekel,
Tausk.

CRITICAL REVIEWS OF PAPERS PUBLISHED IN THE
ZENTRALBLATT

HITSCHMANN limits himself to a review of Freud's article *Über
Neurotische Erkrankungstypen* [Types of Onset of Neurosis].[1]

DR. WEISS on Stekel's essay "The Masks of Homosexuality":[2]
Criticism of this instructive work is leveled chiefly against its generalizations, which often neglect the multiple meaning of a symptom;
this the speaker tries to show in detail.

FEDERN would defend the author against this reproach, since
the meanings he has uncovered are surely correct. It is only that
Stekel does not distinguish between homosexual tendencies that go
back to certain organic dispositions, and those that are fixations

[1] *S.E.* (1912), 12: 229–238.
[2] *Zb.* (1912), 2: 367–372.

97

on certain objects; besides, some things are not masks for, but causes of homosexuality.

DATTNER stresses that homosexuality is the moving force that lies closest to the bottom in neurosis.

RANK would like to illustrate, by way of a case, the conception stressed by Stekel and criticized by Weiss—namely, that of jealousy having evolved from paranoiacally repressed homosexuality. At the same time, he would extend Freud's conception of the genesis of the paranoid delusion of jealousy (Schreber) to many cases of normal jealousy.

SADGER also emphasizes the significance of the homosexual tendency in neurosis, which he called attention to as early as in 1897, when he laid special stress on the bisexuality of every neurotic symptom.

PROF. FREUD comments that Stekel's work presents copious factual material even though it is derelict in its theoretical points of view. A stricter definition of the concept of homosexuality would have been of great advantage to the work; the distinction is insufficiently sharp between the behavior of the subject and the object that he requires. Besides, homosexual longing should not be described as a component of an instinct. Homosexuality cannot be represented as the general root of Don Juanism; it is for the most part a question of a substitution, by way of the series, for a lost love-ideal. Homosexuality plays a supreme role in the genesis of normal jealousy as well: this is the repressed homosexuality that engenders a feeling of disgust with the genitals of the same sex, which have come into contact with the genitals of the beloved person. One must, however, distinguish between the really deeply repressed homosexuality that engenders this disgust and the homosexuality that is still active and merely latent.

To Sadger, one has to reply that it is not at all true that every symptom, in addition to its other roots, also has to have homosexual roots. As a rule, if this is the case it will occur only with fully developed symptoms.

FEDERN, in reference to the genesis of jealousy, points to the pimp, who represents a complete contrast to the jealous person and has no feeling of disgust with the stranger's genitals either.

REIK points to the fact that jealousy also arises as a result of projection onto the partner of one's own feelings of insecurity in the face of seductions.

ROSENSTEIN calls attention, in this context, to a work by Juliusburger.[3]

FEDERN on Abraham's article: "The Manic-depressive States" (*Zb.* 2:6). To begin with, Federn singles out for approval the statement that the love life of these persons continually takes an ungratifying course; further, that the manic and the depressive phases are both governed by the same complexes. However, when Abraham, comparing these states with that found in obsessional neurosis, draws upon the sadistic instincts as the pathogenic ones, the objection must be made that his case gives no indication thereof. It shows only what Adler has called a "whipped-up aggressive drive"; this anamnesis can be found in all neurotics and in all poorly endowed individuals, but it is no proof of the presence of a stronger sadistic component. That depression arises out of the conflict between love and hate is not true; there are cases without any sadistic disposition. Similarly, the assertion that ill-humor is based on repressed libido appears to be disproven by the fact that during the depression the ill-humor has completely disappeared. One of the most frequent causes of this is the lack of success of the libido. Also, the formula proposed by Abraham, by analogy with Freud's formula for paranoia, does not seem to be correct.

PROF. FREUD is inclined to blame the deficiencies in that [Abraham's] work on the deficiencies in our present-day knowledge. Three different principles have been utilized, only one of which seems to be significant: (1) the not particularly convincing similarity between these patients and the obsessional neurotics; (2) barely related to this, the very engaging connection that has been made with the affect of mourning; (3) the conception of mania as being an attempt at repression, a conception that is of great value for our

---

[3] It has not been possible to establish the identity of the work referred to.

understanding. Mania is an attempt at defense by means of a change of mood. In these cyclothymias, the repression is replaced by a toxic mechanism of mood (Otto Gross).[4]

---

[4] Otto Gross: *Das Freudsche Idiogenitätsmoment und seine Bedeutung im manisch-depressiven Irresein Kraepelins* [*The Freudian Theory of the Origin of Concepts and Its Meaning in Kraepelin's Manic-Depressive Psychosis*]. Leipzig: Vogel, 1907.

172

SCIENTIFIC MEETING on *May 8, 1912*

Present: Brecher, Dattner, Emden, Federn, Freud, Friedjung, Heller, Hitschmann, Rank, Reitler, Rosenstein, Sachs, Sadger, Steiner, Stekel, Tausk, (Karl) Weiss.

Guests: Kelsen, Schwarzwald,[1] Rosenberg,[2] Dr. Heller.

PRESENTATION

On Schopenhauer

SPEAKER: DR. HITSCHMANN

The essay, which is to appear in print,[3] is not intended to offer a philosophical evaluation of Schopenhauer, but rather a psychography—that is, a psychological genesis of the basic ideas of Schopenhauer's conception, which he himself declares to be the outcome of intuitive production. The feasibility is discussed of applying the

[1] Probably the husband of Eugenie Schwarzwald, who was a well-known pedagogue; she directed a coeducational school that was extremely progressive for her time.

[2] A pediatrician, personal friend of Freud. Dr. Anny Katan is his daughter.

[3] It appeared in *Imago* (1913), 2:101–174, under the title "Schopenhauer, Versuch einer Psychoanalyse des Philosophen" [Schopenhauer, an Attempted Psychoanalysis of the Philosopher].

psychoanalytic point of view to the philosophically productive genius. After a concise biographical sketch concerned with internal events and characterological peculiarities, the doctrine as such is traced in three sections back to its psychological instinctual roots: the theory of will and the negation of will; the morality of compassion; and pessimism. Finally, the similarity of psychotic clinical pictures to individual traits is touched upon and, in view of his emphasis on the significance of instinctual life (will, sexual instinct) and his knowledge of repression and the unconscious, Schopenhauer is considered to be a precursor of psychoanalysis.

Schopenhauer proves to be an excellent example of the individual root of a philosophical system—the connection that exists between the philosopher's personality and personal fate on the one hand, and his *Weltanschauung* (philosophy of life) on the other. He further shows the significance of the instinctual disposition, of infantile experiences, and the vicissitudes of the libido, in pointing the direction for the development of the personality and of the philosophy of life. In addition, we see at work the mechanisms of repression, of reaction formation (ethics), and of sublimation as they bring about the evolvement of spirituality from his human frailties.

(There is no discussion of the paper.) *

* [Footnote to original Minutes]
Following this meeting, up to the end of the working year 1911–1912, three more meetings were held. Of these, however, no minutes have been preserved, nor does the *Zentralblatt* contain reports about them. There is no entry about the meeting on May 15. On May 22, Freud spoke about "The Taboo." Those present were: Brecher, Emden, Federn, Freud, Friedjung, Heller, Hitschmann, Rank, Reitler, Reik, Reinhold, Rosenstein, Sachs, Sadger, Steiner, Stekel, Tausk, Winterstein, Karl Weiss.
Guests: Mrs. Sachs, Kelsen, Hellmann, Krauss, Klebinder.
For May 29th, there is entered: *Reviews and case reports.* Present were: Emden, Federn, Freud, Friedjung, Hitschmann, Rank, Reik, Reinhold, Reitler, Rosenstein, Sachs, Sadger, Steiner, Tausk, Wagner, Winterstein, Karl Weiss. Guests: Krauss, Mrs. Sachs.
The next entry is also dated May 29—obviously an error. There is no list of those present. Reik spoke on "Cynicism." The paper was published in *Imago 2:* 573–588, under the title "Psychoanalytische Bemerkungen über den zynischen Witz" [Psychoanalytic Comments on Cynical Jokes].

173

REGULAR GENERAL MEETING

Accounts given by the officers of the Society.

Re-election of the Executive Committee by acclamation.

On a motion by Sachs, Dr. Stekel is co-opted by the committee as the editor of the *Zentralblatt.*[1]

On a motion by Prof. Freud, a Review Board is established to which are assigned Federn, Hitschmann, Reitler, and Tausk. Their task is to review the *Jahrbuch* regularly.

---

[1] On November 6, Stekel resigned his membership in the Society.

174

SCIENTIFIC MEETING *on October 16, 1912*

Present: Dattner, Federn, Freud, Friedjung, Heller, Hitschmann, Nepallek, Rank, Reik, Reitler, Rosenstein, Sachs, Sadger, Silberer, Steiner, Stekel, Tausk, (K.) Weiss, Wagner, Winterstein. Marcus is invited (as a member).

PRESENTATION

The Methodology of the Theory of Instincts

SPEAKER: DR. SACHS

(The paper is to appear in the *Jahrbuch*) [1]

DISCUSSION

PROF. FREUD finds fault with the view that the instincts have acquired their ambivalence with the choice of an object. Not all

---

[1] The paper was never published in the *Jahrbuch*, nor could we find it published anywhere else.

psychic actions are ambivalent [2] by nature; among the sexual components are some that are characteristically ambivalent—for instance, the sadistic drive and scoptophilia.

FEDERN thinks that one has to distinguish whether a specific object or an object in general is chosen. Besides, it is a question of whether the instincts only *become* object loving or are so from the start.

WINTERSTEIN endeavors to clear up some misunderstandings that Sachs is supposed to have been guilty of, in reference to Jung's paper about the libido.[3] The question of whether it is pleasure or unpleasure that is primary can be said to be beside the point. Pleasure in excreting and disgust is not an ambivalent pair, but rather, respectively, instinct and reaction formation. One cannot understand why the instincts should obtain their ambivalence only with object choice (to which Rosenstein, as the first speaker, has already drawn attention).

FRIEDJUNG voices some doubt about the theory of the ambivalent instincts. One should perhaps try to answer the question of how it is that the instincts develop in the direction of ambivalence by referring to a secondary formation of ambivalence.

PROF. FREUD calls attention to the fact that a variety of things are concealed within the concept of ambivalence: (1) the transformation of activity into passivity (sadism); (2) the actual ambivalence—that is, the transformation into the material opposite, of which the sole example seems to be the transformation of love into hate.[4]

---

[2] It was Bleuler who coined the word "ambivalence." If one wishes to learn what Bleuler meant by this concept, one should read his *Affectivity, Suggestibility, Paranoia*. Utica, N.Y.: State Hospital Press, 1912. Freud himself points out that the concept has several meanings and aspects.

[3] "Wandlungen und Symbole der Libido. Beiträge zur Entwicklungsgeschichte des Denkens" [Changes and Symbols of the Libido. Contributions to the Developmental History of Thought]. *Jb.* (1911). 3: 120–227; (1912), 4: 162–464.

Jung maintained that all psychic energy is sexual. He forgot that in addition to sexual energy there also exists ego energy. Freud has dealt with these questions in more detail in his paper "On Narcissism" (*S.E.*, 14: 69–102).

[4] The theory of instincts changed considerably after "Beyond the Pleasure Principle."

ROSENSTEIN criticizes the fundamental position taken by the speaker, who did not succeed in working without psychological prejudice, since he did not start from established truths. The question here is one of causality and not of finality. Even in animals the instincts are changed. The love of a companion, to which the speaker referred so much, is a late cultural product which cannot be regarded as a criterion of sexuality as such. The drive to eat cannot be sublimated for a simple reason: because otherwise the creature would die from hunger. (To this teleological conception Sachs raises the objection that at first man certainly does not eat in order to preserve his life, but because his instinct drives him to eat; this is evidenced, for instance, in the individual who is determined to commit suicide and yet does not abstain from food.)

In deriving ambivalence from object love, no distinction has been made between the idea (of a countercurrent) and the existence of the instinct itself. The reaction formation differs from ambivalence in that with the latter the two instincts co-exist, whereas with the former one instinct is replaced by the other.

TAUSK can subscribe to many of the remarks made by the previous speaker. From a "methodology," however, one was entitled to expect more. Besides, Sachs has left out the entire mechanism of forming ideas; this is indispensable, for instance, with the concept of the surplus amount of pleasure, which can indeed become active only as an idea. The speaker attempted to pursue the thesis that everything occurring in the psyche takes place in order to obtain more pleasure and has thereby made himself guilty of several incorrect conceptions. Tausk tries to demonstrate this in detail.

FEDERN objects to the derivation of ambivalence from object choice; but he is of the opinion that culturally it is of great significance that the other instincts have dead objects, whereas sexuality has living ones.

SACHS endeavors to refute individual objections and to clear up misunderstandings, especially those that concern the relationship of ambivalence to object choice and the teleological conception.

175

SCIENTIFIC MEETING on *October 23, 1912*

Present: Dattner, Federn, Freud, Friedjung, Heller, Hitschmann, Jekels, Marcus, Nepallek, Rank, Reik, Reitler, Rosenstein, Sachs, Sadger, Silberer, Stekel, Weiss, Winterstein, Wagner, Tausk.
Guests: Kirsch (M.D.), Blum (Student), Klebinder, Krauss.

REVIEWS AND COMMUNICATIONS

HELLER: Lou Andreas-Salomé as a Writer

DATTNER: A Supplement to Marcinowski's Number Analysis[1]

ROSENSTEIN: Critical Comments on Juliusburger's "Alcoholism" [2]

RANK: Psychoanalytic Items from Multatuli's Writings[3]

TAUSK: Analysis of an Instance of Forgetting

[1] What is referred to seems to be Marcinowski's essay, "Drei Romane in Zahlen" [Three Novels in Numbers]. *Zb.* (1912), 2:619–638.
[2] Probably Otto Juliusburger, "Beitrag zur Psychologie der sogenannten Dipsomanie" [Contribution to the Psychology of the so-called Dipsomania]. *Zb.* (1912), 2:551–557.
[3] Rank published two articles on this: "Multatuli über die Wissbegeirde" [Multatuli on Inquisitiveness], *Imago* (1913), 2:534–536; and "Multatuli über Hysterie" [Multatuli on the Subject of Hysteria], *Z.* (1913), 1:607–609.

176

Present: Dattner, Federn, Freud, Friedjung, Hitschmann, Holz-
knecht, Jekels, Marcus, Nepallek, Rank, Reik, Reitler, Rosenstein,
Sachs, Sadger, Silberer, Tausk, Wagner, Karl Weiss, Winterstein.
Guests: Lou Andreas-Salomé,[1] Bass,[2] Blum,[3] Kelsen, Krauss.

PRESENTATION

Communication about a Case, Combined with
Some Polemical Observations

SPEAKER: PROFESSOR FREUD

The patient in question is a woman who is 23 years old and married; as a girl, she was completely well, but following her marriage

---

[1] This is the first time that this famous woman is mentioned in the Minutes as a
guest; in later entries, she is called only by her given name, Lou. Born in St. Petersburg
in 1861, she died in 1937 in Göttingen. During recent years, her writings have been
republished, some of them in English; this, together with her friendship with Freud, has
been responsible for her having also become known in America.
[2] Bass had left the Society in 1909–1910; such a separation did not by any means
always imply a break with psychoanalysis.
[3] Blum is one of the many names that cannot be identified today.

she began to suffer from states of angry excitation, which were linked with confusion and finally with amnesia. (At the height of this condition, suicidal impulses.) After she had given birth, these attacks were replaced by lassitude and depressions.

She had always had a good relationship with her father, with her mother a very bad one; the relations to her brother presented nothing out of the ordinary. As to childhood material, the only thing that came to light was that, between the ages of six and seven years, she used to be on the lookout, together with her brother, for what the parents were going to do at night; further, that a nursemaid in her parental home had had an affair with a physician and had given birth to a child.

After four months of treatment, she brought a dream that explained the essentials of her childhood history and of her neurosis—provided one did not try to interpret it merely symbolically, but drew upon the patient's associations.

It turns out that there was a seduction by her brother, and also that in her childhood she had wanted to be a boy, and now wants to be a man. This would seem, therefore, to be a case of masculine protest, but to us it presents itself differently. For girls, too, the castration complex plays a role, in that they are already castrated, as it were, when they are born. In the girl, therefore, penis envy develops, instead of fear for the penis (as in the boy), and it is typical that these emotions are invariably tied in with sexual activities.

What speaks particularly against Adler's conception of the universality of the masculine protest is the fact that there are cases in which no trace of this penis envy can be found. For instance, another patient, who has four sisters, falls ill when she learns that she is unable to have a child: she wanted a child by her father. This is a case of (purely feminine) envy, referring to the bearing of children and directed against the mother.

The relations of these emotions to the Oedipus complex seem to be that these conditions probably exist everywhere, but become pathogenic only when they flow into the core complex. In the boy, then, the hostility against the father takes as its pretext the castration threat (no matter whether it is actually uttered or merely fantasied).

In the girl, the hatred for the mother obtains its justification from penis envy: the mother is to blame for the fact that the child came into the world as a girl. Adler's conception is valid, even on his own grounds, only for the woman. As the result of the castration complex, there develops in the man almost regularly the wish to be a woman.

Further, it is a question of what use the child makes of the castration complex. The boy becomes timid and recalcitrant; the girl feels herself to be treated unjustly and flies into a rage. Adler's instinctual drives thus derive from the castration complex, which lies in a deeper stratum. The theory of inferiority also refers to the penis: the girl feels that her clitoris is inferior; the boy, that his penis is too small as compared with that of the adults.

Out of this may develop a general feeling of inferiority. As a way of preserving itself against this, the child has its narcissistic self-overestimation, which prevents it from sensing that what is infantile is inferior. The feeling of inferiority in the neurotic comes about later; it is a complex conclusion, drawn from general perceptions. Neurotic doubting does not stem from any primary doubt, but is the reaction to the perception of one's ambivalence, just as the feeling of inferiority is the reaction to the feeling of one's inner inhibitions.

As to the neuroses of women who complain about their husbands, there are two strata that can be distinguished: the relationship to the mother and the relationship to the husband. If these women have chosen the husband in accordance with the model of father, brother, or even their own person, then, when they have fallen out with the husband, they displace upon him the feelings that originally referred to the mother.

DISCUSSION

FEDERN thinks the appendix symptom in the dream should rather be interpreted as a symptom of pregnancy. No doubt, in the Adlerian symptoms it is the libido directed to the penis that appears to be sublimated. As to penis envy in girls, Federn is inclined to trace it back, not to an inherited castration complex, but to identification.

Adler himself traces inferiority, for the most part, back to the inferiority of the sexual organs; inferiority does not, however, have to refer to a small penis. It may be that the feeling of inferiority develops earlier in those children who are not protected by adequate narcissism. As for the feminine attitude in man, Adler explains it quite consistently within the framework of his system by way of the individual's realizing that he cannot reach his goal with the help of his masculine attitude.

TAUSK: Adler has conceived of inferiority as if it were the psychic representation of a somatic condition; on the other hand, he bases the masculine protest on something psychic (a reaction). With regard to a higher state of civilization, his general observations are commonplace.

In the discussant's experience the existence of the castration complex is betrayed by (1) anesthesia of the penis during coition and (2) exhibitionism. One patient, for instance, has to perform intercourse so as to be able to observe his own coition. Polyuria has proven to be the wish to see that one still possesses a penis.

DATTNER remarks, with reference to dream symbolism, that on principle it must be possible—and indeed he has already succeeded in so doing—to obtain associations to the symbols and in that way to verify them. It is interesting that at first it is the constitutive characteristics of a symbol that are stated, whereas the accidental ones are left out.

ROSENSTEIN poses the question of how it is that penis envy arises. It does not represent any sexual envy for the individual, but goes back in the last analysis to the ego instinct. Rosenstein could not confirm that the feeling of inferiority was, as Adler maintained, identified with femininity.

WEISS thinks that perhaps penis envy might be explained in the following way: the idea that the brother is more like the father is antecendent to it.

FREUD emphasizes that the relations of the castration complex to neurosis and character formation are still to be investigated. The girl wants the penis when she sees another human being with a powerful organ, the possession of which appears to be valuable to him. Sexual envy has its sequel in later years when the girl envies her mother for her full form. Sexual envy is a narcissistic phenomenon; under these circumstances, there is no distinction between ego- and sexual instincts.[4]

---

[4] One is so to say relieved to hear, after quite a few rather sterile discussions, these simple and clear words. As if with a spotlight, they illuminate Adler's error and show, in an unambiguous manner, the vicissitudes of the castration complex in the man, and of penis envy in the woman. Besides, we here learn something that, I believe, is not to be found anywhere else: that neurotic doubting is, among other things, the perception of one's own ambivalence; and that the feeling of inferiority is, among other things, a reaction to the perception of one's inhibitions.

177

SCIENTIFIC MEETING *on November 6, 1912*

Present: Dattner, Federn, Freud, Hitschmann, Jekels, Marcus, Nepallek, Rank, Reik, Reinhold, Reitler, Rosenstein, Sachs, Sadger, Steiner, Tausk, K. Weiss, Winterstein.
Guests: P. S. Krauss, Lou Andreas-Salomé.

PRESENTATION

On the Sadomasochistic Complex

SPEAKER: DR. J. SADGER

(The paper is to appear in the *Jahrbuch*)

DISCUSSION

(First Evening)

HITSCHMANN can confirm, on the basis of his experience, the hereditary character of masochism. If, however, this attitude had its source in infancy, one cannot understand how it is that a female partner could require a male sadistic object. For then, sadomasochistic women would have to show homosexual traits, which is not indeed universally the case. In addition, it would still have to be determined specifically under what conditions sadomasochism comes about in the child.

PROF. FREUD remarks that the fundamental facts presented by the speaker have not taught us anything new; as to the idea that the organic substance of sadomasochism necessarily has to be the surface of the skin, to that we can only agree.[1] It is to be doubted, on the other hand, that masochism can be primary, as the speaker seems to assume.[2] As for the paper as a whole, one finds it lacking in organization and structure.

SACHS criticizes the fact that the concept of skin- and muscle erotism, which is indeed nothing but an auxiliary and transitory concept, is presented as something absolute. Moreover, he found missing an evaluation of the psychic aspect of sadomasochism.

WINTERSTEIN raises the same objection to the concepts of skin- and muscle erotism, as well as to the neglect of the psychic factors; in addition, he criticizes some less significant things.

ROSENSTEIN emphasizes the absence of the psychoanalytic point of view from the paper, as well as the fact that manifest and suppressed sadism were not distinguished. Sadism is probably to be traced back to the suppression of other instincts, and it is in this way that it, too, is reachable by therapeutic influence. One misses, besides, incontrovertible evidence that the period of infancy exercises an influence upon the development of the later man.

RANK, too, thinks the impression is created that the speaker regards masochism as a primary phenomenon; this runs counter to our entire conception of instinct life.

TAUSK finds that the relation that has been established in the main thesis (he wants to cause the partner pain because pain gives him pleasure) is questionable. The pleasure of an abreaction is confused with the pleasure that is found in pain as such. Cruelty, which

[1] Psychic masochism will be discussed later.

[2] It is interesting that in the year 1912 Freud was not yet willing to hear of primary masochism. In "Beyond the Pleasure Principle" (1920), primary masochism comes fully into its own.

114

was drawn in as an explanation, actually has nothing to do with sexuality.

FREUD, referring to Winterstein's remark that children who are brought up strictly become sadistic, states that he has also seen the opposite—with particular clarity in two brothers: the one who had been badly treated became masochistic, while the other, who had been treated well, became sadistic. Rosenstein is correct in that the starting point for the treatment of sadism is to help suppressed developmental components toward their development.

FEDERN approves of almost every detail, but not, however, of the whole. As far as the *first thesis* is concerned (that sadomasochism goes back to a constitutionally intensified skin-, mucous membrane- and muscle-erotism), it is correct that skin-erotism and sadism coincide; mucous membrane-erotism corresponds to the erotogenic zones; under muscle erotism, one cannot conceive of anything at all. It is a question whether skin erotism is primary or secondary; it could be a matter of tenderness or of cruelty.

With regard to the *second thesis* (that sadomasochism goes back to very earliest childhood, and is acquired with the infant's bodily care), it has to be noted that infant care, which occurs in equal measure to every person, cannot be presented as an etiology. It is true, however, that the determination of most of the symptoms of sadomasochism does go back to childhood.

In reference to the *third thesis* (that it is by no means a question of submission, etc., but invariably a question of pleasurable childhood experiences), we have to state that submission does often play a significant role, and should not be simply ruled out.

REINHOLD finds missing any evidence that all masochists show intensified skin erotism and vice versa; consequently, the connection appears merely constructed, but not evident. Furthermore, sensations that belong together anatomically cannot be regarded as belonging together physiologically as well. Moreover, no bridge has been built to the psychic forms, and the actual problem of why pain provides pleasure has not been touched upon.

DATTNER voices the objection that the patient's assertion—that he felt relieved after the uncovering of the infantile etiology—cannot be decisive for the value of this insight. He would also definitely speak against the opinion that was set forth about the formation of the hymen.[3]

WEISS thinks that a reinforcement of individual erotogenic zones, such as is necessary for a specific etiology, could set in during the stage of narcissism. The child's sadomasochistic activity can be explained on the basis of his bisexual *Anlage.*

[3] The objection refers to Sadger's thesis that the hymen came into being because the anthropoid monkey female wanted to force the male to inflict pain upon her, thus increasing sexual pleasure. Sadger then presents a number of examples in order to show that' in the human female sex is linked with pain.

178

SCIENTIFIC MEETING *on November 13, 1912*

Present: Federn, Freud, Friedjung, Hitschmann, Jekels, Nepallek, Rank, Reinhold, Reitler, Rosenstein, Sachs, Sadger, Steiner, Tausk, K. Weiss.

Second Evening of
Discussion of Sadger's Paper

HITSCHMANN presents an example of verbal sadism.

REINHOLD repeats his objections concerning skin-, etc. erotism and finds any psychoanalytic working-up missing in the patients' resolutions, as they were presented.

REITLER shares the preceding speaker's opinion that the clinical material has not been suitably worked up, and that no proof has been furnished of a skin-, etc. erotism in these cases (especially, none of a urethral erotism). That sadomasochism is connected with the surface of the skin is a matter of course; it is doubtful, however, whether there does exist a muscle erotism. In the assumption of a specific instinct of cruelty in the child, an error has been committed similar to that committed by Stekel with his "criminality"; often it

117

is merely a question of instincts of mastery. To recognize urethral erotism to that extent would mean to get rid of the sexual instinct altogether; in cases of this kind (such as, for instance, Rousseau), it is simply that the children involved are sexually precocious. One thing that was right to the point was the patient's observation that the instruments of torture symbolize the penis.

TAUSK finds that what was demonstrated was only that the erotogenic zones are *utilized* sadomasochistically, not however *where sadism comes from;* nor was it stated why urethral- and muscle erotism should have a particular share in that, or under what specific conditions a person with a sensitive skin becomes a sadomasochist. What has been shown is only that all the experiences from childhood that were mentioned are later made use of in a certain sense; the question is, *why?*

FEDERN stresses that the speaker did not touch upon the problem of sadomasochism. Two observations are correct: that blood-sadism goes back to the specific pleasure women often take in menstruating; the tracing back of fettering symptoms to the infant's swaddling. Finally, the discussant remarks that he regards publication of the paper in its present form as inadvisable and harmful.

SACHS mentions that Rousseau did not know his own mother and grew up in an intimate relationship with his father. It is correct that he suffered from urethral difficulties, but from this one cannot infer urethral erotism. That these complaints were of a nervous nature may perhaps be suspected on the basis of the fact that, upon being offered an audience with the king, Rousseau, in view of his *incontinentia urinae,* declined it. In one respect, the speaker has been misunderstood: he did not intend to set forth the mechanism of the connection between sadism and skin erotism, but merely to call attention to the fact that in all cases of sadism there can be found an increased excitability of the skin.[1]

ROSENSTEIN is essentially in agreement with many of the preceding speakers. The high pulse mentioned by Federn is not essential so far as sadism is concerned, but would indicate that rage is

[1] On the margin of the original is a penciled note: "Sad—abgelenkter erotog. Masochismus?" [Sadism—deflected erotogenic masochism?]

a significant factor. The most valid objection to the derivation of certain symptoms from infant care is the statement made by Prof. Freud that in England, the classical country of flagellomania, children are not swaddled. The self-analyses presented prove to be successes of suggestion.

HITSCHMANN mentions that recent research has explained Rousseau's suffering in anatomical terms.

PROF. FREUD presents, to begin with, an example of verbal masochism. It is the case of a lady from the higher circles of the art of living, who has a strange love life. She demands of the man a certain scene, upon whose success the peculiarity of her love life is dependent. He must, after an altercation, throw her down, denude her, pull her legs apart, and inspect her genitals—and in so doing obscenely revile her. At the end, he has to masturbate her. During this procedure, she imagines that spectators are present, and it is from this that she chiefly derives her pleasure. Once she imagined her father among the spectators, but she became so terrified that for a while she gave up these scenes. The vilifying derives from a peculiar characteristic of her father who is at present—since he is old and incapable of working, as well as suffering from vertigo— being quite well-supported by his daughter. It is easy to turn the sequence around, so that masturbation comes first, then the examination, and finally the vilification. The core proves to be the fact that the little girl, before her third year, had been forcibly examined by a physician, probably while the parents were present as spectators. In her fantasy, she now puts her father in the physician's place. The examination was undertaken at that time because of bedwetting. For the pathogenesis of her neurosis—which set in when she was in danger of losing the income from which she had supported her father—it is the father who is of significance; in her symptoms, she emulates his attacks of vertigo. In this identification, her tender feelings find expression, as well as the repressed wish to be freed from any obligation by her father's death.

As to the paper itself, it is to be noted that the predominantly clinical material placed great demands upon the listeners and that the work lacks organization and structure.

SADGER tries, in his concluding remarks, to take issue with some of the discussants, and in particular objects to the reference to England, insofar as he had not in any way established any connection between flagellomania and the fettering of infants. Nor did he assert that masochism is primary, but rather that the active as well as the passive forms are rooted in skin erotism. In order for a person to become a sadist, the component of cruelty, which stems from the ego instincts, must be added on.

179

SCIENTIFIC MEETING *on November 20, 1912*

Present: Dattner, Federn, Freud, Ferenczi, Friedjung, Heller, Hitschmann, Jekels, Marcus, Nepallek, Rank, Reitler, Rosenstein, Sachs, Sadger, Silberer, Tausk, K. Weiss, Winterstein.

REVIEWS AND CLINICAL COMMUNICATIONS

PROF. FREUD: *Fate of Two Women*

The case history of the former Queen Carlotta of Mexico,[1] who is at present dying, contains problems that are of interest to us. She suffered from a delusion of poisoning, which broke through before her husband was murdered. She had her first attack during her interview with Napoleon III. She felt secure only with the Pope. She seems to have had the same feeling of security in an orphanage near Rome, for there she pulled a bone from a pot of hot soup and began to gnaw it.

It cannot have been her fate alone that caused her to fall ill, for we see that Eugenie of France,[2] who suffered a fate that was surely just as hard—she had to flee after her husband's downfall, and later

---

[1] Carlotta of Mexico, 1840–1927, wife of Emperor Maximilian, became mentally ill in September 1866.

[2] Eugenie, 1826–1920, wife of Napoleon III.

121

endured her son's being slain in Africa—nevertheless stayed well.

If, then, we attempt to guess at the secret motives behind the symptoms in the first case, the delusion of poisoning would correspond to the wish to get a child, or rather to the defense against this wish. Now we learn from a reliable source that her husband was absolutely impotent and never attempted to have sexual intercourse with her. That is why, like Lady Macbeth, she projected all her energy into ambitious plans, and it was to be her destiny to fail in precisely this. The fact that she feels secure with the Pope and in the nursery, where there is no danger of temptation, is then comprehensible.

RANK mentions, in this connection, the delusion of a paranoiac woman who believed herself to have been poisoned by her husband. She had two half-grown children, but for years she had been living without having sexual intercourse with her neurasthenically impotent husband, to whom, upon the advice of a female relative, she had from the beginning given herself only with the greatest reserve. Her delusion turns out to be the justified accusation that it was against her will that her husband had impregnated her. Her jealousy toward the female household help, whom her husband had to call in because of her illness, points to homosexual roots, as does her anaesthesia during coition.

FERENCZI remarks that the ambition put forward in place of a child may perhaps also play a role in the feminist movement.

*   *   *   *   *   *   *

HITSCHMANN: *Goethe—a Father Symbol*
Three dreams of different persons, which have an Oedipus-like tinge in which Goethe proves to be a symbol of the father.

WEISS thinks it would be interesting to obtain some information about the fathers' personalities: they are most likely insignificant people.

SADGER mentions that Napoleon is frequently made use of for the same significance. In women, too, Goethe-worship betrays a bit of a father complex.

SACHS is inclined to believe that the dreamer has come to know the insufficiency of his father and has thereupon substituted for it the most sublime thing he knows. It is a correlate to the myth of the hero, in which, upon the attainment of a certain cultural level on the part of the individual there appears an ideal substitute for the symbol of the emperor.

FERENCZI thinks that from the personalities of the fathers (Weiss) we would learn nothing about the choice of a symbol, since it may be based on the attitude of overestimation as well as on the negative attitude.

* * * * * * *

REITLER: *A Contribution to the Sexual Symbolism of the Eye*

The matter in question is an obscene wooden figure which under appropriate pressure shows an erect penis. What is striking is that the figure has on its forehead a third (Cyclopic) eye. The man who made the figure, a simple peasant in the Salzkammergut, says, upon being asked about it, that the eye signifies that an obscenity is hidden behind it. By the way, persons who can no longer procreate are called "blind" (half-breeds are called *blender*).

MARCUS calls attention to "oculation," and

FERENCZI to the formation of eye symbolism on the basis of the mobility of the eyeball, which

PROF. FREUD corroborates, referring to the fact that in the child the formation of symbols generally occurs via the impression of movement. In this context belongs also the history of a man who represents his castration in a singular manner. Deterred from masturbating at an early age by means of the threat of castration, he later has the masochistic fantasy of being seduced by a man; he resists persistently, giving in only when he is threatened with being blinded.

* * * * * * *

ROSENSTEIN: *On Periodicity in Dreams*

By means of several examples, the tracing back of striking dream elements to the "periods" of Fliess-Swoboda (or their multiple) is demonstrated; the speaker does not, however, fail to point to the fact that in many instances the precipitating causes for the appearance of the elements in question can be shown to have been present on the preceding day. Yet this is not always sufficient; residues often remain, gaps that the speaker believes he can fill in, in terms of periodicity. No contradiction between the theory of periodicity and Freud's interpretation of dreams can be found therein; it is a matter merely of a new kind of overdetermination.

DATTNER can, on the basis of his own experience, support Rosenstein's view.

PROF. FREUD too finds no basic difficulty in acknowledging this influence in that form. With Swoboda, however, it never became quite clear whether it was a matter of manifest elements or of latent ones. His own experience has taught Prof. Freud that in cases in which the period is valid, the actual precipitating cause from the preceding day can also be demonstrated regularly, but that, on the other hand, very often the influence of the period cannot be ascertained. For a decision in this question, one also has, of course, to draw in these negative cases.

In the first case presented, it was the actual "period" of the woman that was also involved; obviously, this has to be kept out of these experiments; since then the period would coincide with the periodicity of sexual life.

FERENCZI points to the basic precondition of all experiments of this kind—namely, the dreamer's total ignorance of the theory of periodicity.

* * * * * * *

FEDERN: *Repression in a Visual Person*

In the case of a man who was being instructed rather than treated during the course of his analysis, the recollection of important repressed childhood experiences emerged by way of the *visual scenery* of these experiences (the apartment of his childhood), which comes into consciousness bit by bit; moving parts are recalled sooner than immobile ones, shining ones sooner than dull ones. The part of the room in which the gravest experiences took place is the very last to be recalled.

HITSCHMANN calls attention to the fact that dreams often take place in the locality of pathogenic traumas.

DATTNER has, in hypnosis, found the opposite of Federn's observation: what is cathected with affect is the first thing to come to light.

TAUSK points to the general validity of this experience: the first bit that comes to the patient's mind in connection with a topic is the closest one—from which, it is true, he immediately tries to get away once again.

* * * * * * *

TAUSK: *A Dream Interpretation,* in which the person's entire destiny is brought together in a single word and unfolds in his associations.

180

SCIENTIFIC MEETING *on November 27, 1912*

Present: Dattner, Federn, Ferenczi, Freud, Friedjung, Heller,
Hitschmann, Jekels, Marcus, Nepallek, Rank, Reitler, Rosenstein,
Sachs, Sadger, Silberer, Tausk, K. Weiss, Winterstein.
Guests: Lou, Blum.

PRESENTATION

Two Contributions to the Psychoanalysis of the Inhibition of Artistic Productivity

SPEAKER: DR. VICTOR TAUSK

By way of two analyses of inhibitions in the artistic production of
professional artists, the speaker pointed out that the setting-in of the
inhibition coincides with that moment at which the artist suffers an
intensification of an instinct or of an instinct component so strong
that the libido can no longer be shifted and the instinct inexorably
demands its original specific type of gratification.

This extraordinary intensification of instinct occurs on occasions
that at the same time prove the instincts involved to have been

subjected to infantile fixation on certain persons and conditions. These occasions admit of the conclusion that it is precisely the inability to detach the infantile fixation, at a time when the fixated instinct is undergoing an abnormal increase in intensity, that constitutes the nature of the inhibition of [artistic] production.

From the specific character of the instinct, or instinctual component whose sublimation had become impossible on certain occasions, for the reason mentioned above, the speaker inferred certain conditions for artistic production and concluded that the contents of the work of art can be traced back to infantile prototypes of the objects of instinct gratification.

(Self-report)

181

SCIENTIFIC MEETING *on December 4, 1912*

Present: Dattner, Federn, Freud, Friedjung, Hitschmann, Jekels, Marcus, Nepallek, Rank, Rosenstein, Sachs, Sadger, Silberer, Steiner, Tausk, Winterstein.
Guests: Dr. phil. Emil Lorenz.

REVIEWS AND COMMUNICATIONS ABOUT CASES

PROF. FREUD adds to his "Case Report with Polemic Observations" [1] that in the case of this patient one may speak of a castration complex *sensu strictorii.* At the age of seven she was caught by her mother on the toilet with her brother; she was threatened and came to believe that the punishment of castration had already been carried out on her.

FEDERN remarks that in his comment he had merely wanted to suggest the use of the term "penis complex" in place of "castration complex."

ROSENSTEIN asks whether the patient's wish to become a man goes back to that [experience] and whether this sort of connection is assumed to be a general one.

[1] See This Volume, Minutes 176.

RANK tells about a four-year-old boy who, upon seeing the genitals of his little sister for the first time, gives expression to his aversion. In this one sees how the lower estimation of the woman starts with the genital.

FEDERN observes that some children who have not experienced any castration threat think of the lack of a penis quite simply and without any cruelty.

FRIEDJUNG reports on a three-and-a-half-year-old boy, who notices the difference of sex when he sees his sister being diapered; he asks where she has her "wiwi"; he is shown the remnants of the umbilical cord, and for the time being he is satisfied. But later on he asks again, and he then becomes very proud of his own genitals; perhaps we may see in this one of the roots of exhibitionism.

TAUSK draws attention to the type of woman who takes revenge on the man for the fact that she is a woman; this results in a castration that the woman carries out on the man.[2]

HITSCHMANN reports the case of a hysterical girl with a despondency that can be traced back through the superficial motivations to an early childhood scene in which she saw a little boy nude.

Further, the case of an obsessional neurotic with *delire de toucher* and protective devices, who takes revenge upon himself for the successes of his erotic rivals. This goes back to childhood when his governess told him that his membrum was still too small and she could not do with him what she did with his brother. Genital defects do, by the way, play a role, according to Adler, in the feeling of inferiority.

PROF. FREUD believes that there is no such thing as an affect-free conception of the lack of a penis, as suggested by Federn. These children do not yet believe in castration and are calming themselves.

ROSENSTEIN raises the question of why it is only the lack of the penis that should come to be of account in the genesis of this feeling of inferiority, and not all the other social advantages that fall to the boy's share as well.

[2] See Freud: "The Taboo of Virginity" (1918), *S.E.*, 11: 191–208.

FEDERN reports on a little girl who at first felt very comfortable in her feminine role and in whom penis envy genuinely came into being. The child who is quite capable of renunciation in every other respect does not yield in this one, and she declares that she can still become a boy. Inferiority, in Adler's sense has, to be sure, a certain significance; but it is not something primary.[3]

FRIEDJUNG, in support of this view, points out that the genital simply does acquire a special significance in the child's eyes, such as he does not see in any other part of the body.

PROF. FREUD, replying to Rosenstein's question, comments that the social factor simply does not exist, as far as the child is concerned; these factors come to be added later on, and Adler overlooks the psychic stratification; besides, with him the etiology of the neuroses is thrown together with the etiology of all sorts of other things. The envy that results from social disadvantage has no bearing on the formation of a neurosis. Above all, [the sense of] inferiority is absolutely not found in the child. The child simply expresses a need; he wishes to have something he does not have. Moreover, inferiority does not by any means create the disposition for neurosis.

* * * * * * *

SACHS: *A Dream of Bismarck* (appears in print) [4]

HITSCHMANN finds that the symbolism interpreted as masturbation would also fit a defloration fantasy.

PROF. FREUD, too, thinks two points would fit in with that: (1) that he absolutely cannot make any progress; (2) that he tells his wife his dream in the morning. It means: just as I have intended to conquer you, so I shall also conquer the country.

* * * * * * *

RANK: *On the Inhibition of Artistic Production*

History of a sculptor whose creative activity is sustained mainly

---

[3] It is obvious that part of this sentence is missing.
[4] Z. (1913), 1: 80–83.

by sadistic impulses and changes in keeping with their vicissitudes. In life and in love he is masochistic; in art he gives full play to his sadism.

TAUSK finds this case parallels not only what he had spoken about, but also what he had not said about that case. The John-the-Baptist-motif is important for a certain kind of people, those who did not get on in life. He is the son, the prophet who never sets himself free. The desire for prison is to be understood as a safeguard against temptation.

The adoration of the breasts can be explained as a displacement onto this permitted genital; sympathy for the breasts is sympathy for the mother who is being raped. The sympathy for the mother's genitals is displaced upward; as early as in the fourth to fifth year, tenderness and worship of the breasts are combined with it.

Masochism that has been satisfied forms a protection for creativity, for in this way going after the other sex is rejected.

* * * * * * *

HITSCHMANN: *Cases of Social Anxiety* (with women's vomiting)

SACHS thinks that in the fantasies of these patients the disgusting (the excremental) must play a major role; the vomiting may also be connected with infantile birth-theories.

The dream of coition with a man does not have to be a homosexual one; it could be a skillful disguise of the desire for a woman with a penis.

FEDERN considers this anxiety with vomiting very interesting, but one cannot infer anything typical from a single case. Whether the vomiting is the result of anxiety cannot be determined at first. Anxiety can also make its appearance along with lack of appetite. Feelings of disgust toward urine and feces seem to play a great role in childhood.

The essential elements in the patient, who for years had undressed, smelled, and licked his sister, seems to have been suppression of sexual release.

PROF. FREUD emphasizes, to begin with, that vomiting of that sort may have a great number of meanings; combined in it are all the sexual instincts the patient did not discharge. One has to be familiar with many cases in order to be able to single out the most important motive. The cases show, above all, some rejection of sexuality. If one transforms the effect into a tendency, then one comes upon repressed instincts. At this point, the general question arises of why it is precisely on this apparatus that these phenomena come to the fore. It is here a matter of an erotogenic zone that is constitutionally hypertrophic, that could never be fully sublimated and gratified, and that is ready for regression so as to give expression to the repressed. Thus, all suppressed instincts express themselves in the vomiting.

What the repressing force is can be guessed from the preconditions for this single case: to begin with, homosexuality can be pointed out. The model event in this case is the *cunnilingus* with the sister. The influence of the father causes him to repress it, and he gets the vomiting as an expression of the disgust he feels for it. Whenever he meets up with any sexual demand, he promises not to do it again. What sustains the symptom is the fear of his father.

Boys' vomiting before school regularly has psychic components and is homosexual by nature; in addition to what is purely somatic reflex, there is invariably superimposed a layer of psychic determination. The vomiting of children disappears, by the way, and its reappearance in the adult shows that it is intensively bound psychically.

The fully developed form is the feminine attitude. The patient not only promises his father not to do it again, but adopts the feminine role vis-à-vis the father: he shows that he is himself, a woman, for the vomiting also has the meaning of a female birth-fantasy.

* * * * * * *

HITSCHMANN: *Dreams of Homosexuals,* from which the infantile conception of the easily shifted genital becomes evident (it can be exchanged, lent out, joined on externally). It is not the entire individual that is male or female, but only the genital.[5]

---

[5] "Totem and Taboo" had just been published. Robertson Smith's hypothesis of the totem meal had inspired Freud to enlarge upon further aspects, implying the murder of the primeval father, the longing for him, and the attempt to revive him.

Freud's disciples were, of course, acquainted with the concepts Freud expounded in "Totem and Taboo." Yet in their discussion, they behaved as if they knew nothing of them. With infinite patience, Freud explained his ideas over and over again.

182

Present: Dattner, Federn, Freud, Hitschmann, Jekels, Marcus, Nepallek, Rank, Reinhold, Reitler, Rosenstein, Sachs, Steiner, Tausk, Winterstein.
Guests: Krauss, Lou.

PRESENTATION

Psychoanalytic Observations on the History of Philosophy

SPEAKER: DR. WINTERSTEIN

The speaker characterizes his task as a rather negative one, since he intends to examine the following:

Which elements of a philosophical system are of heterogeneous origin; what role the unconscious plays in philosophical production; to what extent the validity of a philosophical position is affected by psychoanalysis; and, finally, which philosophy of life is the only one that, from the standpoint of psychoanalysis, can come under discussion.

133

The speaker takes as his point of departure the sexual investigation of the young child, from which, according to Freud's presentation (*Leonardo*), three possibilities emerge: (1) neurotic inhibition; (2) the neurotic brooder; and (3) the researcher. The two latter types are both found among the philosophers; they show traits that bear a particularly striking resemblance to the obsessional neurotic and to the system-formations of some mental patients.

The speaker now sets out to demonstrate, by way of several philosophical systems, the mingling of wish material with cognitive material. Two things make their appearance here as dogma: the concept of a supernatural world and the introduction of God; these the speaker now traces historically. In their psychoanalytic reduction, the speaker points to the mechanism of projection, of which he distinguishes two kinds, corresponding to two different degrees of intensity of repression: (1) the personifying projection (functional), and (2) the paranoid projection of affect.

Then two kinds of cosmic system are discussed: that derived from emanation, and that established by creation. In the former, the projection of endopsychically perceived libidinal processes leads to object cathexis and regression, in which the stage of narcissism (identification with the father image) is of special significance. At this point, the mystics are also touched on. In the latter kind of system by contrast with the myth of "world-parents," and in pathological overvaluation of the father-libido and estrangement from the mother-libido, the world is created by God alone. (Art, in contrast to religion and philosophy, seems to be more under the mother's influence.) The typical doctrines of these systems (belief in pre-existence, the wandering of the soul and the return of the same) as well as the systems themselves, are traced back by the speaker in the last analysis to libidinal processes.

Then the various types of world concepts are examined, with the aim of finding out which prove to be least influenced by unconscious motives. It turns out that the idealistic systems contain less knowledge and more wish material, whereas in the formation of other philosophies in which the drive to investigate has a part, there exists, along with a libido that is sublimated to the craving for knowledge, libido that works merely as a motor of thinking.

Plato's system is now discussed and an attempt is made to demonstrate, by way of this example, the relations that exist between philosophy and psychosexual constitution.

Finally, the two types (the type of infantile curiosity, which has been sublimated into a craving for knowledge, and the type of the obsessional neurotic and the paranoiac) are characterized with regard to their specific mode of system formation, and it is emphasized that in reality they are not sharply set off from one another. Finally, the speaker stresses that the only conception of the world that can legitimately arise on the basis of Freud's teachings is the realist-dualist one. According to Freud, too, there are two realities: the external world, and the unconscious, as psychic reality.

DISCUSSION

TAUSK stresses the particular significance of the factor of narcissism and distinguishes within it three parts: homosexuality, sadism, and anality. It seems that it is from the latter that there actually emanates the power of the fixation in narcissism (a part of one's own body). The deepest part of narcissism is, according to Jekels, identification with the father's penis.

HITSCHMANN is on the whole in accord with the exposition, for which he offered proof some time ago in his paper on Schopenhauer. He regrets that no attention was paid to those philosophers in whom optimism or pessimism has some significance; further, that the fact that philosophers remain single was not mentioned.

SACHS attempts to sum up in three points the typical relationship between psychoanalysis and philosophy: (1) psychoanalytic theses may be discovered in a philosophical system, as intuitive findings; (2) this may occur indirectly, by virtue of the libido having been worked over along the lines of neurotic or psychotic mechanisms (which was what the speaker mainly showed); (3) mental activity may stem from sublimated libido. From this follows the question of what is the primary characteristic of the libido of the philosopher, and what transformations it has to undergo in order to re-emerge precisely as philosophy.

ROSENSTEIN is skeptical with regard to the exposition, which was, in part, no more than suppositions. For instance, it is still a question whether death is a problem of the libido. In contrast with the libido, the will to power seems to have been greatly underestimated by the speaker.

PROF. FREUD would like to join in the praise, even if with some reservations. Not only are the libidinal processes important, but the ego-processes as well. The question is why only the vicissitudes of the libido can be projected onto the external world, and not the other processes as well. That the father is of the greatest significance for religion, he had quite some time ago formulated in the following way: law is what the father does; religion, what the son has [*Totem and Taboo*]. The homosexual origin of this, the greatest sector of civilization, is rather evident since, indeed, our social feelings are also of a homosexual nature (it is woman who renders the man asocial). The speaker has brought forward the proof of a possibility in which Freud has expressed his belief: that one can discuss the relationships of the libido to the psychology of religion and to the evolution of civilization without having, as Jung thinks, to modify the concept. There are secondary interactions that take place mutually between libidinal disturbances and the ego.

Regarding the speaker's objections to the psychological formulations about the relationship between consciousness and unconscious (in the last section of *The Interpretation of Dreams*), it has to be admitted that these are still far from final formulation, as well as far from the end of their usefulness. The designation of consciousness as a sense organ is meant to be only an analogy. What we call "qualities" find no analogy in the actual psyche; they are created only by way of the organ of consciousness, out of the purely quantitative processes of the psyche.

If the present speaker had to choose among the views of the philosophers, he could characterize himself as a dualist. No monism succeeds in doing away with the distinction between ideas and the objects they represent.

The speaker's conception that the symbols of the libido were originally objects of the libido can be verified by the course of development. Primitive people personify all objects; it is only when the difference between the animate and the inanimate becomes prominent that things are no longer made objects of the libido, but they are still retained in the form of symbols.[1]

---

[1] Winterstein's paper was published in *Imago* (1913), 2: 175–237.

183

SCIENTIFIC MEETING *on December 18, 1912*

Present: Brecher, Dattner, Federn, Freud, Friedjung, Hitschmann, Jekels, Nepallek, Rank, Reitler, Rosenstein, Sachs, Sadger, Silberer, Tausk, Winterstein.
Guests: Lou, Prof. Montague.

CASE REPORTS AND REVIEWS

1. DR. L. JEKELS: *A Case of Slip of the Tongue* (being published) [1]

2. DR. SADGER: *Slandering by Children* (being published) [2]

[1] "Ein Fall von Versprechen" [A Case of Slip of the Tongue]. *Z.* (1912), 1: 258–260 Briefly summarized, the content is as follows: a lady of Jekels' acquaintance asks him for an explanation of a slip of the tongue that occurred to her: when her daughter reproached her for taking so long cutting her nails, she replied that of course it took long, since she had twelve nails to cut; to her daughter's exclamation of astonishment, she replied with impatience, "Of course I have twelve fingers to take care of." The lady's associations disclosed an intense wish for the death of an old uncle from whom she was expecting a formidable inheritance; they also led Jekels to assume an equally strong wish for the death of her two mentally abnormal daughters.

[2] "Kinder und Jugendliche als Verleumder" [Children and Juveniles as Slanderers]. Zeitschrift für Psa. Päd. (1929), 3: 21–29.
With the help of some clinical examples, as well as of examples from literature

3. DR. SADGER: *Brief Contributions to Anal- and Urethral Erotism* (being published) [3]

4. DR. HITSCHMANN: *A Case of Blushing*

5. DR. RANK: *Review of Sanitzin: "Resolution of a Mystery of the Soul of a People (Volksseele)"* [4]

6. DR. RANK: *Contributions to Symbolism in Poetry* (both are being published) [5]

7. DR. TAUSK: *Observation of One Form of Obsessional Neurotic Fantasies*

DISCUSSION

Ad (1):

ROSENSTEIN refers to rage against the daughter as one factor bringing about the parapraxis.

SACHS points out that according to Artemidorus [6] "cutting nails" equals "interest-taking."

PROF. FREUD remarks that the slip may have to do with a turning back of the death wish from the relatives to the subject's

---

(Rousseau's confessions; Gottfried Keller's *Der Grüne Heinrich*), Sadger expounds his theory about the roots of slandering by children and adolescents. They are, according to him: (1) in terms of the organic condition, a certain degree of sadomasochistic disposition; (2) in terms of psychic determinants, (a) an excessively intense fantasy life, which causes the individual to take his wishes for reality and (b) love for the victim of the calumny, whom the child falsely accuses of having done to him what the child would like to suffer at his hands, what he dreams of.

[3] Sadger's contributions were not published under these titles, but he did publish a number of articles on these subjects.

[4] Could not be identified.

[5] This was published under the title: "Um Städte werben" [Symbolism in Poetry. "Conquest" of Cities] in Rank's *Psychoanalytische Beiträge zur Mythenforschung* [Psychoanalytic Contributions to Research on Myths]. Leipzig, Vienna: *Internationaler Psychoanalytischer Verlag*, 1919, pp. 164–176. Numerous examples from folksongs and legends, as well as from other literature, are cited to show the symbolic representation of cities as women—sometimes virgins, sometimes harlots—as well as the other way round.

[6] Artemidorus Daldianus, Roman soothsayer of about 180 A.D., who left an interpretation of dreams.

own person; it would then imply, "She does not allow herself to be pressed by her daughter into dying."

TAUSK stresses the difference that lies in whether such a condensation takes place with or without damage to the word.

SILBERER thinks the 12 fingers mean: We are two too many.

Ad (2):
HITSCHMANN finds the explanation inadequate.

FEDERN finds missing the problem of the white lie, consideration of the concepts of the pleasure and reality principles, the factor of spite, and further appropriate conclusions concerning the lack of compassion and of the sense of truth in children. The sadistic *Anlage* of these children would not have to be abnormal.

Ad (4):
PROF. FREUD has not declared that ambition plays a specific role in erythrophobia (on the other hand, it does in agoraphobia). It appears in persons who have a special disposition for blushing, and after puberty this is fixated most often as anxiety. It is then divided into shame and rage—a contrasting pair which expresses itself in blushing. It is regularly a feeling of shame because of sexual impressions.

FEDERN raises the question of whether the special *Anlage* for the feeling of shame is the precondition for blushing, or the other way around. Shame, by the way, calls forth blushing on the cheeks, rage on the forehead.

Ad (5):
PROF. FREUD considers too narrow the author's interpretation that the lawful parricide is rooted in *jus primae noctis,* exercised by the father on the son's wife (more about this in his forthcoming work on totemism).

Ad (7):
HITSCHMANN remarks that it is in only one definite type that all ideas arising spontaneously have the meaning of self-reproaches (Tausk). (TAUSK: the obsessional type.)

184

.

Present: Dattner, Federn, Freud, Friedjung, Hitschmann, Jekels, Rank, Reitler, Rosenstein, Sachs, Sadger, Silberer, Steiner, Tausk, (K.) Weiss, Winterstein.
Guests: Eder[1]

PRESENTATION

An Example of Libido Displacement During the Course of Treatment[2]

SPEAKER: DR. PAUL FEDERN

Displacement of libido during treatment counterbalances the incorrect displacement of libido that occurred in the genesis of the illness.

The case in question is one of *asthma bronchiale,* which goes

---

[1] M.D. Eder, one of the first British psychoanalysts, came to Vienna for an analysis of short duration (see Jones, *Life and Works of Sigmund Freud,* II, p. 98. New York: Basic Books, 1955).

[2] An abstract of Federn's paper was published in Z. (1913), 1: 303–306.

back to when the patient was seven-and-a-half years old; it made
its appearance after a severe pertussis (at six-and-a-half years old).
The patient had not been subject to any harmful influences in
childhood.

His sexual interest during childhood was guided by the sense of
smell, and this predisposition of his olfactory sphere has considerable bearing on the localization of his neurosis as asthma. His
characteristic of being a sensitive man and subject to moods
(*sentire* = to sense) is also closely connected with it. Besides, as
a child he had copro- and urolagnial interests, as well as interests
in the genital—in particular in that of his mother, to whom he
was attached in love and tenderness. In his seventh year, he was
enlightened by his mother about birth; in his ninth year, he learned
the essentials about sexual life. Then he wanted, quite consciously
and without any defense, to have a child with his mother. Altogether, the patient was from the start fully aware of his perversions and his incestuous attitude, and thus he had apparently
repressed nothing. Indeed, he practiced all perversions—cunnilingus,
in particular—and had many dreams of incest. In his tenth year,
a sister was born.

After his pertussis, which has no etiological connection with the
asthma, he was even more pampered; a year later, upon being
separated from his mother when he went on a trip with his grandparents he had his first attack of asthma. During the course of his
analysis, he had intimations of asthma; characteristic of this was a
certain "asthma-mood." To the "asthma-attitude" belonged a wish
that was not fulfilled, and then a fear that someone might be an
onlooker (mother), and the feeling: "Someone ought to help me."
All this points to a child's feelings of unhappiness.

Then the conditions (specific) are discussed for the attacks
of asthma, which are determined predominantly by the sphere of
smell (olfactory impressions that are connected with moods and
people), but also by intimations of certain illnesses (tuberculosis,
carcinoma, etc.), or by sleeping with other persons, etc. All these
conditions can be traced back to certain childhood impressions.
Even the atmospheric and cosmological conditions proved to be
symbols of experiences and thoughts that had a libidinal emphasis.

The same is true of the railway trip that had preceded the very first attack and which offers so many opportunities for rationalization. A certain kind of laughing and running, which shows characteristics that go far back into childhood, also provokes asthma. Among the general roots are things that can be characterized as "feeling of inferiority," "suppressed masculine protest," and the like. The patient has typical asthma-dreams, which correspond to the already mentioned causes of his suffering.

How does it come about that someone who practices all the perversions and is aware of his incestuous attitude nevertheless falls ill with a neurosis? The individual attack arises as a result of the fact that the patient reacts to an unfulfilled wish that reaches back into childhood, not in accordance with the reality principle but in accordance with the pleasure-unpleasure principle. That is how he succumbs to a child's mood of unpleasure, which is a kind of powerlessness and desperation. He wants to free himself of this unpleasure, and what now takes place is what Freud calls "after-expulsion." In consciousness it is desperation or consolation, as the case may be, that emerges; in the unconscious, what appears in response to the old wish is the reaction that came forth in childhood.

The asthma in childhood came about in the following way: the child had intense wishes for his mother. Then he was taken along on a trip by his grandparents; feeling lonely at night, he longed for his mother and got his first attack. The asthma is a cry (for his mother) to the point of loss of breath; it is the helpless cry of a child. The asthma is tantamount to fulfillment of the wish to return to the mother. The cunnilingus, too, can probably be explained as the wish to go back into the mother (birth in reverse). Cunnilingus takes its organ from the mouth, its object from the sphere of smell, and its goal from the penis (that is, to enter the vagina). Before the child knew anything about the genitals, he was tied to the mother via the oral and olfactory spheres. Under these circumstances, all that penis sexuality was able to accomplish at first was to re-enforce that oral and olfactory sexuality. This is a case of displacement upward, not in order to repress the crudely sexual, but rather as a result of attraction on the part of those erotogenic zones that are inordinately predominant. That is why, with the breakdown, a symptom was formed that was tied in with oral erotism.

In order to be able to love, man has to allow the pleasure principle to govern penis sexuality. The patient had his pleasure principle totally fixated; this explains why he was overcome by the mood of misfortune with all its consequences. It was for this reason, too, that he could have his sexuality free, but could not love. The asthma is a consequence of the failure of his application of the pleasure principle.

In what way, then, is the libido displaced by means of treatment, or what does treatment change in man?

1. The treatment has brought to consciousness the factors calling forth the attacks.

2. Where the patient has incorrectly and to his own detriment allowed the pleasure reaction to set in, the treatment has taught him to work in accordance with the reality principle.

3. It has made conscious the unconscious processes that lead to the asthma attacks. This renders it possible to undo the displacement of the libido (so as to make it go back to the genital zone from the oral zone). And with this reverse displacement of the libido, the patient was enabled to change the object to which he was attached by way of the displacement: he became detached from the mother.

DISCUSSION

SADGER finds some splendid statements and good observations in the paper, as well as some things that are unclear. The main topic was not dealt with fully enough. The case itself shows some peculiarities: for instance, the particular relationship to the railroad, which he himself has not found in any of his cases and, further, the connection with the sense of smell and with oral erotism.

It would be interesting to investigate which cases can be cured by way of the nose, and which cases are not at all helped by this treatment. Erotogenicity of the throat (tickling sensation) is a more frequent finding, as is erotogenicity of the breast. The absence of repression is also striking. This sort of asthma cannot be termed hysterical. Pertussis and asthma are, as the speaker also mentioned, seldom found together.

TAUSK remarks, in reply to the question of whether the man had or had not engaged in repression, that he had actually repressed everything having to do with his mother; he had not, in point of fact, done any of the things he really wanted to do. What is important are the *individual* affects and their vicissitudes; it is not the libido as a whole that is repressed.

PROF. FREUD stresses that the speaker had entered into the theory of hysteria somewhat more deeply than it actually exists today, and this is the explanation for all the merits and all the shortcomings of the presentation.

With regard to hysteria, some things can be guessed about the organic conditions of sexuality. When the hysterical symptom has been constituted, one sees that the individual has replaced his genital by another, a secondary genital (which had, as a rule, an erotogenic meaning in childhood). The disposition to hysteria has not yet been studied; it is probably to be sought in that stage at which subordination to the primacy of the genital zone should occur. In hysteria, it is not a question of a regressive formation of sexuality; the instincts have arranged themselves anew, in terms of a different primacy. Essentially, this is determined by the perverse *Anlagen.* In that case, Federn's example would gain particular significance: it would explain what is puzzling about repression. Repression in hysteria becomes reduced to organic repression—that is, organic fixation; all the rest in hysteria is after-expulsion. It is only these apparent exceptions, however, that constitute the confirmation of the thesis.

Tausk's objection has not eliminated the difficulty. In every hysteria, we are used to the phenomenon of oscillation between conscious and unconscious. What is essential is the fact that the patient is capable of oscillating. Obviously, man first has to have gone through a constitutional repression, from which the oscillation then emanates.[3]

[3] "Constitutional repression" obviously means withdrawal of genital libido, with concomitant fixation.

Strictly speaking, Federn's case should not be classed with hysteria. Cases like this have particular predisposing conditions. These organ neuroses tack themselves onto hysteria, to be sure, but they have to be separated from it. Erotogenic stresses on organs overwhelm the psychic mechanism, forcing the neurosis to manifest itself in organic ways. These neuroses differ from the usual hysteria in that they do not represent repression but, rather, infantilism.

FEDERN, in his concluding remarks, mentions among other things that the primacy of the oral zone had become possible to that extent because there had been no interval between strong infantile oral erotism and genital erotism. The desire, as well as some of the reaction to it, also enter into the symptom.

PROF. FREUD suggests calling these cases "fixation hysteria."

185

SCIENTIFIC MEETING *on January 15, 1913*

Present: Dattner, Federn, Ferenczi, Freud, Friedjung, Heller, Hitschmann, Jekels, Marcus, Rank, Reik, Reitler, Rosenstein, Sachs, Sadger, Silberer, Steiner, Tausk, Karl Weiss, Winterstein.

Guests: Frau Lou, Mrs. Weiss, Mrs. Jones (Frau Prof. Jones), Dr. Gustav Scheu,[1] Dr. Hellmann, Dr. Lorenz, Dr. Krauss, Dr. Eder.

PRESENTATION

Animism, Magic and Omnipotence of Thoughts[2]

SPEAKER: PROF. FREUD

DISCUSSION

SACHS calls attention to a place in Spitteler that corresponds with one point made in the exposition.

---

[1] Gustav Scheu, a brother of Robert Scheu, was a prominent lawyer in Vienna, a friend of Federn and Friedjung.

[2] Part III of "Totem and Taboo" (1913); *S.E.*, 13: 75–99.

SADGER would like the following facts to be taken into consideration (they are contradictory to the conception of narcissism that we just heard): (1) small children already show object love; and (2) woman's narcissism, too, speaks against its evolving under the primacy of the genital zone.

ROSENSTEIN, in view of various objections that occur to him, would like to have delineated exactly at what period narcissism appears.

PROF. FREUD replies—without thereby going more closely into the important question of narcissism—that the narcissistic organization of man sets in early—that is, before the stage of object love. Furthermore, it is a development that takes a chronic course.

FEDERN remarks that the statements about narcissism are not contradictory. The exposition we heard today has shown that those views of the world (*Weltanschauungen*) that arise not out of intellectual problems but automatically are the beginnings of what Jones has called "rationalization." The import of a name may have to do with "being discovered," and with the fact that speech is a specific act of will.

FERENCZI points to certain analogous conclusions at which he has arrived in his essay on the ontogenetic development of the sense of reality (in Number 2 of the *Internationale Zeitschrift*). It becomes evident that the omnipotence of thoughts plays an important role in the child and changes its form gradually.

TAUSK notes that another problem follows from the assumption of narcissism. In the artist, regression goes as far back as narcissism; from this standpoint, what the artist says is: "I am my desires." The child does not make this judgment of identification initially; he does so only at the stage of narcissism. It is at this stage that sublimation begins. A portion of the libido is withdrawn from the ego, and is transferred to objects that are of account as objects of mastery. It is not, however, the object that is loved, but the relationship to it—that is, the functioning of the libido.

As a counterpart to the taboo of women during the absence of their husbands, there exists a (neurotic) yearning: to become a father, which in the last analysis means being by means of the pregnancy assured of the woman's faithfulness. The wish not to be obliged to perform sexual intercourse may also be hidden behind the longing for a child.

FRIEDJUNG thinks that the objections raised to the concept of narcissism arise from the fact that things have to be taken as occurring not one *beside* the other or one *after* the other, but one *above or under* the other.

Investigations have shown that the neuroses are not, as was previously assumed, a product of civilization; on the contrary, in a primitive state, what we call neurosis is the usual condition.

149

186

SCIENTIFIC MEETING on *January 22, 1913*

Present: Federn, Freud, Friedjung, Hitschmann, Jekels, Rank, Reitler, Sachs, Sadger, Steiner, Tausk, Karl Weiss, Winterstein. Guests: Lou, Fr. Okmann, Mr. Peter Breithut, Mrs. Sachs, Krauss.

PRESENTATION

The Story of the Miner of Falun[1]

SPEAKER: DR. EMIL LORENZ

The speaker begins by first offering some historical and literary information about the incident that forms the basis of his paper, as well as about how the story was handed down and the poetic elaboration

---

[1] Dr. Emil Franz Lorenz (Klagenfurt, Carynthia) published this paper in *Imago* (1914), 3: 250–301. It deals with the following story: In December 1719, the body of a man was found in a copper mine near Falun, Sweden. The face and body showed no disfiguration or changes by death, although a wound was discovered that had apparently been inflicted by the falling rocks that had killed the man. Investigations led to the conclusion that the body was that of a certain Mathias Israelson who in 1670 had entered the mine alone and had never come back. The identification was made by several old people, among them a woman who had been betrothed to Mathias.

of what had happened before it, by Arnim,[2] E. T. A. Hoffmann,[3] Richard Wagner[4] and Hugo Von Hofmannsthal.[5] Then, with special reference to the versions by Hoffmann, and Hofmannsthal, he offers an analysis of the hero's delusions and dreams that reveals his infantile fixation on the mother, with its neurotic representation in a mother's-womb fantasy (the inside of a mountain).

DISCUSSION

SADGER finds no contradiction in the contents of the presentation, but he would like to caution the speaker against criticism by historians of literature.

The story also embodies the fantasy in which the father himself invited the son to go to bed with his mother.

The red stone probably represents, as it does in Hebbel's *Ruby*,[6] a symbol of the vagina. Hofmannsthal is not convincing in the role of witness because he is familiar with symbolism and translates it directly.

SACHS mentions that the interpretation of Novalis' fairy tale (*Hyacinth and Rosebud*) was already given by Immermann[7] about 90 years ago.

Oscillating between the earthly bride and the mysterious one is characteristic of the romantics (Fouqué's[8] *Undine*; Hoffmann's *The Golden Pot*; similarly, the Lanval-motif[9]). It has not been clearly stated that the mortal beloved is an image of the mother, just as is

---

[2] Ludwig Achim von Arnim, 1781–1831, German romantic poet dealt with the event in a poem, "The Miner's Eternal Youth" (*"Des Bergmanns ewige Jugend"*), 1810.

[3] E. T. A. Hoffmann: "The Mines of Falun" (Die Bergwerke zu Falun), part of his "Serapionsbrüder," 1810.

[4] Richard Wagner outlined the text for an opera "The Mines of Falun" (*Die Bergwerke zu Falun*), but he never completed it. The outline was published in 1905.

[5] Hugo von Hofmannsthal wrote a drama "The Mine of Falun" (*Das Bergwerk von Falun*) in 1899, of which, at the time of Lorenz's paper, only the first act had been published.

[6] *The Ruby (Der Rubin)*, a comedy, 1850.

[7] Karl Leberecht Immermann, 1796–1840, German dramatist and novelist.

[8] Friedrich Heinrich Karl de la Motte-Fouqué, 1777–1843, German romanticist, whose most famous fairy-tale, *Undine*, appeared in 1811.

[9] Marie de France, 12th century: "Le Lai de Lanval," an Arthurian legend (see This Volume, Minutes 139).

the supernatural or subterranean one. Particularly obvious is the mother's-womb fantasy; in general, one can declare oneself in full agreement with the contents of the paper, whereas one has to sharply criticize its form, in which the diffusiveness and repetitiveness were quite detrimental.

FEDERN would like to see the symbol of the inside of the mountain separated from that of the mountain as such.

What the speaker has characterized as "paranoiac" are simple hallucinations. One of Federn's patients had, like Dr. Lorenz's hero, only two sets of fantasies: fantasies of the sea and fantasies of heights. The symbolic meaning of the red gem seems rather to indicate blood. The fantasies do not, as the speaker thought, have to have direct models in the poet's life.

RANK comments that the speaker has mentioned only the hero's longing for the mother, whereas one can see just as clearly the desire to become detached from the mother (sea and the mountain's inside flowing together into one in the great dream). A similar symbolism of mines can be found in Ludwig Brinkmann's[10] novel *The Awakening of Maria Carmen.*

PROF. FREUD is of the opinion that investigations such as this should be carried out in a different way: above all, in dealing with topics as simple as this, one should not make use of the whole heavy panoply of psychoanalysis.

The question arises of how it has come about that an incident that even though interesting is yet not "the stuff of poetry," has become poetic material. This event is apparently stimulating in two directions: it includes an erotic motif as well as a social one. The point is the contrast between erotism and professional activity. Since nothing came of their union, the first thought that comes to mind is: could that be an accident? Did he not extricate himself by these means? That is how the matter becomes poetically interesting.

The protagonist's fantasies can be summed up in the term "Mother

---

[10] *Aus meiner Bergwerkszeit* [*From the Times when I Worked in the Mines*]. It also has the subtitle *Die Erweckung der Maria Carmen.*

Earth" (Dieterich[11]). He is tied to the subterranean, to the dead mother. The word "mother" was at one time something that was pictured materially, and it may be from that point that one can explain historically the identity of birth and death. Interment, which is a very late product of civilization, appears to be a preparation for rebirth (out of mother earth).

The interpretation of the red stone as vagina seems forced; one could with more justification decide in favor of blood. Even more likely in this context, in which the protagonist brings the stone to his bride as a wedding gift, is its interpretation as a child. It is quite possible, however, that this element derives from an alien context and, in this layer, does not entirely admit of a satisfactory inter-- pretation.

REITLER adds that in his experience the stone has the meaning of testicle, and the red stone that of the *glans*.

[11] Albert Dieterich: *Mutter Erde. Ein Versuch über Volksreligion* [*Mother Earth. A Study on Folk Religion*]. Leipzig, 1905.

187

SCIENTIFIC MEETING *on January 29, 1913*

Present: Dattner, Federn, Freud, Friedjung, Hitschmann, Jekels, Nepallek, Rank, Reitler, Rosenstein, Sachs, Sadger, Steiner, Tausk, Karl Weiss.
Guests: Lou, Lorenz.

BRIEF COMMUNICATIONS

ROSENSTEIN: *Supplement to Dattner's number analysis.*[1]

ROSENSTEIN proves that the hour at which the patient gave birth —which, according to Dattner, was delayed by way of psychic influences—tallies with the birth formula put forward by Fliess; it was therefore determined in accordance with organic laws.

DATTNER calls attention to the fact that the patient consciously counted on the fact that she wanted to give birth to a "Sunday-child." Psychic influence is therefore more probable than cosmic influence.

[1] See This Volume, Minutes 175.

ROSENSTEIN concedes that the hour of birth may have been determined psychically, but maintains, nevertheless, that the day was determined cosmically.

FREUD points to the fact that Fliess's original theory was fatalistic and connected with the question of death. Later, he did take into account the objection that men die under varied circumstances, and made a distinction between those who live out their life to its natural end, and those whose life is brought to an end by external circumstances.

The mathematical conception and the psychological one prove to be incompatible. The analyst is only too familiar with the influence that medical activity exerts on symptomatic expressions—something Fliess was not willing to admit.

FEDERN does not see the contradiction that has just been mentioned. Tabular comparisons he made from this point of view reveal that in some cases the periodic influence comes clearly to the fore as soon as during the course of treatment the psychogenic repetition of symptoms subsides. The periodic course also plays an important role in neurotic disturbances—a role that is, however, nullified or covered up by psychogenic repetition.

HITSCHMANN, too, is of the opinion that the influence exerted by psychic factors is no evidence against periodicity. This view finds support in the female "period," which can indeed also be influenced by psychic factors.

SACHS also finds that the contradiction is not so sharp, provided that the doctrine of periodicity is couched in sufficiently modest terms. Certainly the two kinds of influence exist, but they are entirely disparate.

FREUD calls attention to the fact that by means of hypnosis there can be a shift in the menstrual period. He would like to formulate his opposition to Fliess in the following way: laws of nature simply cannot express themselves in a pure form because they come into conflict with other laws, whereas it is in a pure form that Fliess's laws are supposed to assert themselves.

Besides, according to Fliess, birth takes the place of the tenth

155

period; just as the normal periods can be shifted, so this particular period too should be able to be put off. More than that, Dattner did not assert.

There is another observation of Fliess, however, that deserves to be verified: namely, that men die at the hour at which they were born.[2]

* * * * * * *

HITSCHMANN reports on striking similarities among neurotics.

PROF. FREUD describes the representation, in the dreams of two patients, of an infantile theory of sexuality.

A room that is later divided by a partition represents a progression of understanding, from the original cloacal theory to the correct perception of two localities.

RANK shows a drawing and reports two dreams.

SADGER speaks about the necessity of distinguishing erotism of the nates from anal erotism.

STEINER has no objection to raise on principle, but thinks he ought to point out that actually it is only a matter of shading that distinguishes acts of tenderness from acts of violence.

TAUSK stresses that it was a fundamental error, which led to the introduction of this new erotism. The speaker represented the nates as being the *object* of erotic excitations; the sexual object cannot, however, ever constitute an erotism.

FEDERN thinks that the speaker did not speak of sensations on the nates. The sensations of flagellants result from the excitation of the contiguous genitals. He considers the classification of erotism according to various bodily zones superfluous.

* * * * * * *

TAUSK: Dream mechanisms and dream symbols.

Change of scenery means a reminiscence of an event that contains an essential element belonging to the most important part of the dream.

[2] On this point, Freud does not seem to disagree altogether with Fliess.

FREUD points out that this coincides with his own conception of change of scenery as being the insertion of a subordinate clause.

TAUSK: The rat and the mouse in dreams invariably turn out to be penis symbols. In those instances in which the rats appear to be female, they show relations to the castration complex (biting off). Cats are as a rule female symbols.

SACHS objects that the mouse is not at all invariably male. ("Little mouse" as a term of endearment for a woman.)

FREUD too believes that the mouse is not a penis symbol, but always a female symbol. Symbolism does not attach great importance to the sexual difference. If the male or the female principle is represented by a symbol of the opposite sex, this is no proof whatsoever of the utilization of the symbol in a specific sexual sense. It is dream representation—that is, the dream wants thereby to express something quite specific.

RANK points to the fact that the cat, too, is not always, even though predominantly, female. In the typical symbolization of sexual intercourse as cat-and-mouse-play, the man in a sadistic conception is represented as a cat.

188

Present: Federn, Freud, Friedjung, Hitschmann, Jekels, Rank, Reik, Reinhold, Sachs, Sadger, Tausk, Winterstein.
Heller co-opted into Executive Committee.

PRESENTATION

Sexuality and Erotism in Childhood [1]

SPEAKER: DR. SADGER

If one adheres to the etymological derivation, the use of the two terms is quite plain: sexuality is what is crudely sensual, linked with the activity of the genitals; erotism is the psychic aspect of the sexual instinct. These boundaries have, however, gradually become blurred in usage.

The speaker then criticizes Moll's dissection of the sexual in-

[1] Sadger's paper "Sexualität und Erotik im Kindesalter" was published in *Moderne Medizin*, VI/23 (1915). It appeared in English as "The Sexual Life of the Child," in *J. Sexol. Psa.* (1923), 1: 337–348; 486–499; 579–590.

stinct,[2] as well as his objections against infantile sexuality, and brings forth all the indubitable evidence we have in that regard. He mentions the observations made by Kassowitz[3] and Friedjung on early erection and masturbation with all the manifestations of sexual orgasm. It is more difficult to demonstrate the child's extragenital sexuality; however, Lindner's[4] and Bleuler's[5] observations (thumb sucking, anality) speak clearly of these.

The speaker then deals specifically with muscle erotism which, he says, has met with resistance even in psychoanalytic circles. He cites as an example the erections that occur when children are scuffling (already referred to in the theory of sexuality), as well as the observations made by gynecologists on orgasm produced in anaesthetic women by muscle contractions. Otto Adler[6] flatly states that orgasm in coition is produced by the contraction of muscles.

One is justified in speaking of sexuality (in children) when phenomena occur that are well known from sexual orgasm or when there are inclinations that reassert themselves over and over again despite all obstacles and threats.

Dancing (Havelock Ellis), as well as sports, has a sexual effect because of muscle erotism.

Sexuality in a narrower sense is what is linked up with the genitals; but then one must also include the extragenital and psychic aspects, which are better termed erotism.

DISCUSSION

HITSCHMANN finds almost everything that has been said correct, insofar as it has to do with observations. What may be objec-

---

[2] A. Moll: *Das Sexualleben des Kindes* [*The Sexual Life of Children*], Berlin, 1909.

[3] Max Kassowitz, Professor of Pediatrics at the University of Vienna.

[4] S. Lindner: "Das Saugen an den Fingern, Lippen etc. bei den Kindern (Ludeln)" [The sucking of fingers, lips, etc. in children]. *Jahrbuch für Kinderheilkune* 1879; *Zeitschrifte für Psa. Päd.* (1934), 8:117–138.

[5] E. Bleuler: "Sexuelle Abnormalitäten der Kinder" [Sexual Abnormalities in Children]. *Jahrbuch der Schweizer Gesellschaft für Schulgesundheitspflege* (1908), 9:623.

[6] Otto Adler, sexologist, 1864–?: *Die mangelhafte Geschlechtsempfindung des Weibes. Anaesthesia sexualis. Anaphrodisia* [*Insufficient Sexual Feeling in Women*]. Berlin: Kornfeld, 1924.

tionable is only the speaker's incorrect use of the term erotism and its assignment to individual areas of the body and the skin. With many of the things adduced, it is not merely a question of muscle contraction, but also of the relation to the other object (scuffling). Sports do not absolutely have to be sexualized motion; they may be asexual repression as well.

KRAUSS, in confirmation of the existence of infantile sexuality, refers to pictures in antiquity, in which coition among children is a preferred subject of representation. Besides, the ancients represented Amor with an erect membrum. Among Negroes and in the South, children have sexual intercourse at a very early age.

SACHS is inclined to draw a parallel between Moll's drives of contrectation and detumescence on the one hand, and the concepts of sexual object and sexual aim on the other, rather than between those drives and sexuality and erotism.

FRIEDJUNG finds the proofs superfluous, inasmuch as we are convinced in any case of the existence of infantile sexuality. It should be pointed out, however, with regard to muscle erotism, that any organ activity is accompanied by pleasure.

PROF. FREUD is of the opinion that the speaker has chosen a rather petty point of departure, since Moll is not to be taken seriously.

There is a second reproach, however, that is more serious. Up to now we have been using the term erotism in a narrower sense (as erotogenicity): erotism was what arose out of the stimuli provided by an organ. Sadger's examples have nothing to do with the muscles as a source of erotism. The muscles are executive organs; they are the paths by which sexual excitation is discharged. This distinction is of greater importance than that between erotism and sexuality, in which it is after all only a question of the use of terms.

Orgasm brings about a muscle contraction; but the notion that the contraction of muscles itself produces orgasm is nonsense. Intensive muscle activity is, to be sure, also a source of erotogenicity, but proofs of this would have to be offered that are quite different from those presented by the speaker. This becomes quite clear if one takes the neurotic as one's point of departure. In patients who are

160

suffering from walking disturbances (abasias), muscle activity is an exquisitely sexual act. Moreover, it is probable that the processes in any organism exercise an influence on sexual production; that is what makes heredity possible.

In general, our most reliable proof of infantile sexuality, if we do not wish to refer to the sexuality of children among primitive peoples, is the neurosis. What is now sexual in a neurosis goes back to infantile activity. It is true, to be sure, that it then remains a matter of one's conception how far one wishes to acknowledge the existence of sexuality in childhood. One is, of course, going to take the extreme cases as the basis for one's judgment. The question is, however, whether it is orgasm that is the specific characteristic of sexual pleasure, or whether we may identify sexual pleasure with pleasure in general.[7] In addition, in any view on infantile sexuality, one has to take into account the fact that after puberty people do sexualize more intensely much that was previously only weakly sexual.

FEDERN criticizes the nomenclature; however, in support of some of the statements made, he points to the fact that, in all of animal life, scuffling and playing is found as preparatory action of a sexual nature. He sees one proof of the erotogenicity of the oral zone in the fact that nursing women often speak of a feeling of highly sexual enjoyment; this makes it likely that the child has similar pleasurable sensations. It is noteworthy, too, that children who have given up genital masturbation thereupon hit on various substitute gratifications (nose-picking, etc.).

[7] Later on, Freud seems to have equated sexual pleasure with pleasure as such.

189

SCIENTIFIC MEETING on *February 12, 1913*

Present: Dattner, Federn, Freud, Friedjung, Hitschmann, Jekels, Rank, Reinhold, Reitler, Rosenstein, Sachs, Sadger, Tausk, K. Weiss, Winterstein.

REVIEWS AND CLINICAL COMMUNICATIONS

1. TAUSK: Review of essays by Ferenczi and Putnam on Philosophy and Psychoanalysis.[1]

2. RANK: Review of *Zentralblatt* 4/5.

3. SACHS: The star as a genital symbol.

4. HITSCHMANN: Paranoia and anal erotism.[2]

5. HITSCHMANN: Parapraxes.[3]

---

[1] S. Ferenczi: "Philosophie und Psychoanalyse." *Imago* (1912), 1: 519–526. J. Putnam: "The Role of Philosophical Views and Training in the Further Development of the Psychoanalytic Movement." *Imago* (1912), 1: 101–118.

[2] *"Paranoia, Homosexualität und Analerotik"* [Paranoia, Homosexuality and Anal Erotism]. *Z.* (1913), 1: 251–254.

[3] "Ein wiederholter Fall von Verschreibung bei der Rezeptierung" [A Case of a Repeated Slip of the Pen While Writing Prescriptions]. Published under the title "Two Cases of Forgetting of Names" in the *Psychoanalytic Quarterly* (1913), 1: 266–267.

190

SCIENTIFIC MEETING *on February 19, 1913*

Present: Dattner, Federn, Freud, Friedjung, Hitschmann, Jekels, Rank, Reitler, Reinhold, Rosenstein, Sachs, Sadger, Tausk, K. Weiss, Winterstein.
Guests: Lou, Krauss.

PRESENTATION

On the Psychogenesis of Refrain and Rhyme

SPEAKER: DR. KARL WEISS

The speaker attempts to explain refrain and rhyme in terms of the unconscious—that is, to explain the psychic conditions of their formation and use. As the point of departure, he selects the factors that are typical of both—namely, consonance and rhythm. Consonance has its infantile prototype in the language of children, and rhythm in sucking. The pleasure obtained from recognition which has its origin in saving on psychic energy, is the motive force of consonance; rhythm, however, is a self-sustained source of pleasure. It obtains

163

the capacity for affording pleasure in that it represents the pleasure derived from an elementary instinctual gratification.

Then the speaker discusses the relation of refrain to affects and distinguishes two types of refrain: the nonsensical unarticulated one and the one that appears in choral song. One function of the refrain is the changing of an affect; the form overcomes the resistance we feel toward the expression of this particular affect. In other instances, the refrain tones down the affect and checks its discharge; this is shown by way of examples.

On the basis of the analysis of a child's rhyme, rhyme is explained as being the result of a compromise between two tendencies that are in conflict with regard to the censor. Rhyme and rhythm are autoerotic (the lyricist speaks only about himself). At the end, the speaker touches upon the question of why antiquity did without rhyme, and says that the sexual repression of Christianity is partly responsible for the emergence of rhyme.

DISCUSSION

DR. KRAUSS calls emphatic attention to Bücher's paper, which the speaker has also quoted. The examples of refrain ought not to have been taken from modern poets, who quite intentionally calculate its effect on the well-educated reader, but rather from the poetry of primitive people, in which alliteration and other forms are generally used.

DR. REIK finds that the etiology of rhyme has been oversimplified. Rhyme has not only an inhibiting, but often also a releasing effect.

TAUSK, speaking in opposition to Krauss, remarks that as far as the genesis of rhyme is concerned, it is immaterial at what [historical] position it is located. What the speaker wanted to show was the relations of refrain and rhyme to affect.

Dancing is obviously an inhibited sexual activity. Rhyme is a compromise, insofar as it gives expression to what the instinct desires, but not in its direct form. The examples (Heine) cited by Reik are secondary [worked-over] achievements.

164

SACHS refers the speaker to Weiss's article (*Imago*).[1] Sachs himself has expounded in this circle the view that rhythm goes back to sucking—a view that called forth general disagreement. Genetically, the formation of rhyme probably has nothing directly to do with Christianity. The similarity of rhyme to certain types of jokes should have been spelled out more clearly.

FEDERN rejects any connection of rhythm, which is a universal phenomenon, with sucking. Another misconception consists in bringing together refrain and repetition. The central idea of the exposition is correct, just as one has to agree with the speaker's view regarding the late emergence of rhyme—an assumption corroborated by the fact that dancing was tabooed by Christianity.

Besides, in searching for and finding a rhyme, a bit of sexuality is functionally expressed.

SACHS does not find any valid contradiction in Federn's objection, since the pleasurable transformation of the biological rhythm does indeed occur during sucking at the breast.

HITSCHMANN would like to see the topic dealt with *ab ovo*, more than it has been. Too little was said about the primitive; there were too few genetic viewpoints, and not enough use was made of what is known. Music was likewise not sufficiently drawn into the discourse, and the stanza has remained unexplained.

FRIEDJUNG too would claim sucking to be the ontogenetic source of rhythm.

REINHOLD would distinguish two things with regard to rhythm: the temporal sequence of facts and what is psychically represented as rhythm. Psychologically, rhythm means the organization of what occurs in sequence. Any physiological derivation of rhythm is therefore bound to fail. There is simply the psychological question of why these physiological processes are organized in accordance with a certain law.

---

[1] "Von Reim und Refrain. Ein Beitrag zur Psychogenese dichterischer Ausdrucksmittel," *Imago* (1913) *2*; 552–572. [Rhyme and Refrain. A contribution to the Psychogenesis of Poetic Expression." *Psychoanalytic Review*, 5: 101–104.]

The psychological factor is explained as being a result of the need to organize the entire variety of processes. That means a saving of labor, from the sensory standpoint and from the motor standpoint as well, for work that is divided into sections is easier. In poetry, one encounters the same need to accentuate certain elements (rhythm) and to mark them off (stanza).

FREUD finds it gratifying that once again a psychoanalyst is occupying himself with aesthetic problems, of which there are quite a few still awaiting elucidation from our point of view. It is true, though, that here the task is an especially difficult one because, with regard to these problems, one has to do everything and all strata have to be linked up. Freud would like to suggest to the speaker that in case he submits the paper for publication, he reverse its arrangement and start from the analysis of a sample rhyme. Freud would recommend for this purpose a less complicated example be chosen than the one by the little girl that was presented here.

191

SCIENTIFIC MEETING *on February 26, 1913*

Present: Dattner, Federn, Freud, Friedjung, Heller, Hitschmann, Jekels, Marcus, Rank, Reinhold, Reitler, Rosenstein, Sachs, Sadger, Tausk, K. Weiss.
Guests: Lou, Krauss, Landau, Lorenz.

PRESENTATION

Disturbances in Work and Professional Activity Resulting from Neurosis.[1]

SPEAKER: DR. FEDERN

The relations between work and neurosis are reciprocal. Not everything, however, that makes its appearance in the neurotic as a disturbance of working has to be a consequence of his neurosis. On the other hand, there are cases in which it is only the capability for work that is disturbed, without any other neurotic symptoms taking shape. In these instances, there is a displacement of libido disturbance

---

[1] The title of Federn's paper as given in the attendance book is "Disturbance in Learning and Working" (*Gesellschaft und Neurose* I).

onto that area. The disturbance in working usually goes back to childhood; in addition to infantilism, ambivalence (subjectively felt as doubting) and hereditary inferiority come into account as predisposing factors.

The speaker then endeavors to show how the normal capability for work develops, and to indicate at what points weaknesses and disorders may appear, causing the neurotic's development to take a wrong turn. The first step toward normal capability for work—that is, learning how to work— demands of the child two accomplishments: (1) the correction of activities that were heretofore incorrect; (2) renouncing the carrying out of other impulses that do not pertain to work. A number of pleasure-premiums make it possible for the child to do so: (1) the drive to activate his organs; (2) libidinal stimuli that, coming from the component instincts, are linked with the activation of the organs; (3) the pleasure taken in the intellectual activity that steers performances in accordance with their purpose; (4) later on, the pleasurable idea of the success to be achieved.

Those first steps are counteracted by corresponding sources of unpleasure: (1) giving up the playful activity the child is accustomed to; (2) libidinal resistances directed against giving up beloved persons or objects; (3) atavistic resistance to going over to a higher level; (4) notions of lack of success and of vexation in and after work.

By way of identification and transference onto the person who is teaching the child, a considerable reinforcement is made to the libidinal sources. The sublimation of these libidinal desires must also succeed, however, if the work is not to be disturbed. The activities and successes that lie in the work itself have to comprise the libidinal reward. The work becomes, for a portion of the libido, itself the object. To this is added the supreme organ pleasure— namely, joy in the activity of the organ of thinking and willing.

Neurotic working-disturbances should be grouped according to: (1) whether they set in with a specific work-activity; or (2) to what type of neurotic illness they belong. There are disturbances of working that show a *marked tendency,* in which it is an unconscious counterwill that is hampering the individual; there are disturbances of the *will,* which does not function, and disturbances (due to a *complex*) of the functions necessary for working. We characterize those cases in which the relationship to an employer or co-worker plays a role as disturbances due to *transference.*

It is more difficult to understand professional disturbances. Where a component instinct is in operation, with strong libido, the disturbance takes hold of the sublimated form [of that instinct].

The form the working disturbance takes depends on the type of the neurosis. A working disturbance is connected either with the secondary function of the neurosis or with the primary conflicts. Decidedly neurotic working disturbances include the following: (1) the attitude toward certain individuals (transference; masochism); (2) the kind of attitude adopted in general toward one's goal in life (a missing or misdirected sexual goal); (3) neurotic conception of money; (4) masochistic attitude.

Truly neurotic disturbances in the form of symptoms are: hysterical absences (phobias); minor anxiety attacks which add up; compulsive obsessions; hypochondriacal disorders; paranoid attitudes (with a homosexual foundation). The most important symptom is the occupational neurosis, which is to be classified with the fixation hysteria.

DISCUSSION

WEISS objects to a classification of working disturbances into tendentious, associative, and transference disturbances. Any work disturbance is, as a symptom, tendentious. Moreover, the restoration of the capacity for working is not merely a secondary gain of analysis.

FRIEDJUNG is of the opinion that in many instances in our milieu one cannot speak of a choice of profession.

HITSCHMANN finds in the presentation a complete description of the working disturbance; the details, however, were scattered about. The connection with society (influence of the family, etc.) was barely touched on. An apparent working disturbance of young people should be mentioned—a disturbance that is nothing but preparation for the profession of artist. Working disturbances are characteristic of artists (inhibitions in creating); they may, perhaps, be altogether unable to produce without taking a pause.

169

Loafers and perverts should have been mentioned, as well as those aristocrats who start to work when they become neurotic (just as women do—studying, etc.).

ROSENSTEIN thinks that, as far as the statements made in the presentation are concerned, too little evidence was furnished. A challenge has to be made to the assertion that in our civilization work is a sublimation of component instincts (nor does there exist any choice of profession [Friedjung]. Finally, the phrase "unconscious pleasure" is to be objected to; the feeling of pleasure exists only in consciousness.

MARCUS characterizes learning how to work as giving up the pleasure principle in favor of the reality principle. This in itself enables work to become an important point of attack for illness.

TAUSK considers the theoretical aspects in the presentation unintelligible. Giving the reason for the appearance of a working disturbance is merely the lesser portion of the task. What should have been set forth in addition is what the working disturbance means in terms of society. The social function comes to a halt if an organ or its function is taken hold of by sexuality; from that point onward, the individual is antisocial. The relation of the working disturbance to society can be discussed only if one takes into consideration broad work-tendencies—if, for instance, one follows up the effect of such a disturbance in an organizer. Family or vagabondage, etc. has to be taken as a unit, and we have to consider the protection of society vis-à-vis those disturbed people.[2]

SACHS finds that too little importance has been attached to the anal complex: spite and stubbornness coupled with the money complex play an important role. Exaggerated pedantry, too, may often degenerate into a working disturbance. At the head of our considerations should be placed the tendency of the working disturbance.

FREUD thinks that what is involved in this undertaking is an elementary presentation, which should grow out of the material and should avoid sinking into general psychology, as well as, wherever possible, into the use of any sort of technical language.

[2] This is not altogether clear.

170

The problem of the specific topic under consideration today is the following: one's love life is indeed, to begin with, a private affair; how is it that it is able to produce disturbances of performance that involve society? It is advisable to consider this effect separately in men and women. (In women this relation is more obvious; in men, it is of a more complicated nature.) One would have to distinguish between childhood disturbances in learning to work and disturbances of an already acquired capacity for work, which are the result of neurosis.

A general classification of the etiology, from the viewpoint that the neuroses are disorders of the sexual function (type: impotence), would have to consider: (A) direct and (B) indirect effects of a person's love life on his ability to get things done.

Indirect effects would be:

1. certain dispositions, such as inferiority or hypererotism which make excessive demands on the organs;

2. energic points of view, such as the expenditure of energy that is required by suppression;

3. the fact that sexual life serves as a prototype;

4. the narcissistic standpoint of self-assessment, from which inferiority evolves as something secondary—as a result of neurosis and not as its cause.

Direct disturbances of social life brought on by the symptoms, from the viewpoint that whatever is the result of a neurosis has been its intent:

1. disturbance by way of homosexual inhibition (a main point);

2. sublimation and transference onto work (this also serves the ego as a way of diverting the libido);

3. working disturbances resulting from the removal of the sublimation;

4. the secondary tendencies of the individual, just like the narcissistic tendencies, have to be taken into account.

Furthermore, the father complex is an important viewpoint.

Working disturbances in women and children are then compared with those of men.

192

SCIENTIFIC MEETING *on March 5, 1913*

Present: Federn, Freud, Friedjung, Hitschmann, Marcus, Rank, Reik, Sachs, Sadger, Silberer, Steiner, Tausk, (K.) Weiss, Winterstein.
Guests: Krauss, Lou, Stoecker.

PRESENTATION

Psychoanalytic Remarks on Schnitzler's Poetic Works[1]

SPEAKER: DR. THEODOR REIK

The speaker makes use of the principle that has proven itself in the interpretation of dreams and neuroses: starting from small, unnoticed, seemingly arbitrary details—namely, the episodes of the poetic work—he singles out as a typical motif in Schnitzler's work the dying of the male protagonist (predecessor), who thereby makes room for another. What is operative here is the *omnipotence of*

---

[1] Arthur Schnitzler, 1862–1931, famous Austrian writer, author of numerous plays, novels and short stories, was also a physician.

thoughts,[2] or the principle of the power of wishing, which has a close connection with artistic creation. The poetic work is indeed the expression of a wish and realizes narcissistically a power that is denied in real life—the power of ruling over men. If Stekel maintains that the inability to love is characteristic of the poet, that is true, but only with the qualification that there are many different causes that are decisive for this (homosexuality, incestuous love, etc.). One of these roots is the narcissistic component.

Where the figures created by the poet gain power over him (as Schnitzler has shown in one of his novels), poetic creation and neurosis come close to each other in the vacillation between reality and fantasy, between waking life and dreaming. In these cases, poetic production is no longer sufficient as a way out of the conflict between egotistic and sexual desires, on the one hand, and social life, on the other. Fatalism, which is a leading motif in Schnitzler's poetic work, does offer a way out of these conflicts. If one wanted to draw conclusions from the poetic work about the type of neurosis the poet escaped by way of that creation, one would in Schnitzler's case have to say that it was the obsessional neurosis.

DISCUSSION

WINTERSTEIN, on the basis of his personal knowledge of the poet, considers the concise exposition to be to the point. Much that we now improperly call narcissism is identical with egotism.

The poet does not necessarily have to have escaped a neurosis by means of his work; he may also be a neurotic.

SACHS, who concurs in general with the previous speaker, even with regard to his praise, notes (as did the latter) the confusion of narcissism with egotism, the generalizing of individual observations, and the fact that things were represented as being certain that are still in doubt.

The artist's essential characteristic is that he feels the need to cast his fantasies into a form in which they have an effect on others: his fellowmen are of the greatest importance to him; so there have to

---

[2] *Die Allmacht der Gedanken* [The omnipotence of thought in Arthur Schnitzler] appeared in *Imago* 1913), 2: 319–335.

be other factors that are significant in the artist, in addition to narcissism. The relationship between neurosis and artistry is extremely fluctuating.

The motif of dying so that somebody else may live has been correctly placed at the center of Schnitzler's poetic work (*Call of Life*). In the aging Schnitzler, one can observe the change to the standpoint of the father, which is significant for myth formation.

TAUSK finds that the principles of narcissism and the omnipotence of thought were established correctly. Yet narcissism has not been explored in sufficient depth; what was not taken into consideration, in particular, is the poet's actual relationship to love, which as a rule looks quite different from the way it does in the work of the poet. Forbidden desires seek to gain actual power, and sublimation breaks down at a certain point; the conflict cannot be worked through because one part of it is linked up with the unconscious ambivalence.

MARCUS quotes Schnitzler's aphorism to the effect that the poet is a person who does not want to take any risks, a criminal without the courage to commit a crime.

SADGER considers narcissism an essential aspect of the poetic personality. One evidence thereof is the fact that the married life of artists is almost invariably unhappy. It may be that women's anaesthesia also has to do with their strong narcissism. The fear of death (the novel *Dying*) one can depict in this way only if one has experienced it oneself.

FEDERN is familiar with the history of the origin of *Dying*, and knows that the story renders a bit of something that was witnessed in reality. This demonstrates how dangerous it is to draw conclusions with regard to his personality from the poet's works. The obsessional-neurotic traits in Schnitzler were correctly pointed out. These, as well as dramatic talents, have a close relationship with sadism. Furthermore, the dramatist and the obsessional neurotic have this in common: their uncertainty in thinking, as well as their being able to regard as real what is only possible. One would, however, have to separate the purely egotistical motives from sadism, just as one had to separate them from narcissism.

RANK thinks it was correct to single out the death theme as Schnitzler's central problem, but finds that the underlying fear of death has not been sufficiently elucidated from the viewpoint of psychoanalysis. It is true, though, that for this purpose investigations of pathological material would be necessary. Sentimentality, which is quite conspicuous in Schnitzler, seems to be an offshoot of the fear of death.

The fact, mentioned by Federn, that it was in his medical practice that Schnitzler came upon the material for *Dying*, does not in the least speak against the subjective psychic motivation for the selection of the subject and the working out of the death-motif.

PROF. FREUD stresses that the principle of considering the bagatelle, as applied by the speaker, is particularly valid for art criticism. As to the principle of the omnipotence of thought, it would be tempting to establish in other fields how far it is still active among us. With regard to narcissism, it is to be observed that it has nothing to do with introversion, as Jung believes. Introversion has to do with the relation between fantasy and the external world; narcissism has to remain for us an irreducible phenomenon, the basis of the libido theory.

The thesis that poets are strongly narcissistic cannot be positively proven; but it finds corroboration in the fact that artists have selected precisely the field that is the only one in which, even today, narcissistic intents can be realized. On the other hand, the artist does not, of necessity, have to have remained egotistic.

Tausk was right in pointing out that it is by means of her narcissistic attitude that the normal woman gains the normal progression of love.

193

Present: Federn, Freud, Friedjung, Hitschmann, Jekels, Reik, Reitler, Reinhold, Rosenstein, Sachs, Tausk, K. Weiss.
Lou as guest.

PRESENTATION

The Father Problem

SPEAKER: DR. TAUSK

The speaker takes for granted familiarity with the fact that the father complex is both vehicle and content of the neurosis, and sets himself the task of considering the factors in the life of the individual that are decisive for the formation of a neurosis and of examining their role as factors in the formation of society and in social life. In this endeavor, one has of necessity artificially to isolate the father-problem.

It is not in all civilizations that the father counts as a power factor. To begin with, the speaker discusses the institution of the matriarchate, which Bachofen[1] inferred from judicial, religious,

---

[1] Johann Jakob Bachofen, 1815–1887, Swiss historian and professor of Roman law at Basle. *Das Mutterrecht* [*The Matriarchate*] appeared in 1861.

mythological sources as well as from certain forms of worship, symbols, and customs.

The institution of the patriarchate is directly contrary to this, as is demonstrated in the example of the Roman patriarchate. Here, in contrast to the father's plenitude of power, is found the barrier against incest with his own daughter, while at the same time, he is able to dispose of his children's life and liberty. With respect to the ego instincts and sadism, instinctual activity is prohibited without regard to the object; here it is the object that is forbidden.

The father, who formerly had the right to all the women of the house, must at one time have renounced his daughter of his own free will. From the standpoint of biology, the view seems to have prevailed that incest is destructive to the species. But even where this was not the case, with the separating off of smaller packs and the discontinuance of rut [animal sexual periodicity], the prohibition of incest became necessary. From this resulted the dominion over the women and the cutting off of the son from these women. It may also be true that the first incest barrier was a prohibition of sodomy.

Society rests on the existence of the father, and it is for this reason that patricide was prohibited, while the killing of the son for the protection of paternal rights was permitted. Later on, killing the son was cut down to castration (there is a residue of this in circumcision). After the father renounced incest with his daughter, he continued to retain the right to choose her husband and thus, despite his renunciation, a sort of power to dispose of her genitals. The father then vouches to the son-in-law for the daughter's virginity—that is, he guarantees that *he* has not used her; that is how the ideal of virginity evolves out of the prohibition of incest.

Up to this point, it has been shown how the formation of society was conditioned by the father; it remains to show the lot of the individual in the patriarchal family. The son has an ambivalent attitude of love and hate for his father. This hate has two roots: rebellion against restrictions (after displacement, this hate remains conscious and permitted); its motive power is the love for the mother, which results in the son's object choice. The second root stems from ambivalent homosexuality: it leads to overcoming of the father. It is homosexual love that brings about the introduction of God, as a result of which the hated father is no longer a person while, on the other hand, identification with the father can take place.

Through displacement onto another object of the love for the father, friendship arises, and later on society develops. Ambivalence as such also has certain cultural effects (investigation, skepticism, work, etc.).

Finally, the father complex in neurosis is discussed briefly and it is pointed out how, on the one hand, the unconscious hate for the father impedes sublimation while, on the other hand, the homosexual fixation disturbs the neurotic's love-life. In this discussion, the speaker touches upon the problem of the first-born, of succession, and of the disposition of Jews toward neurosis.

It is the father who created culture. Society rests on the father complex, which extends as far as homosexuality: the father complex is the form in which homosexuality is able to spell itself out and to which it has to adapt itself. A great man is someone who has overcome the father. Narcissism is connected with the father complex, inasmuch as the liberation of the son proceeds from successful identification with the father.[2]

DISCUSSION

DR. SACHS, to begin with, raises the formal objection that the set topic: "Society and Neurosis"[3] has not been dealt with.

As to the contents, it is to be noted that the matriarchate is still quite hypothetical and hardly adequate to serve as the basis for investigation. Besides, psychoanalysis provides arguments against it, in that the material Bachofen drew upon does not have to consist of historical *reliquae,* but may just as well represent wishes. By the same token, it is risky to draw in the conditions in ancient Rome.

A voluntary renunciation of incest seems most unlikely. Also, the question of whether incest is detrimental to the race has not yet been decided unequivocally.

[2] See Freud, "Totem and Taboo" (*S.E.,* 13: 1–161), as well as Rank, *The Myth of the Birth of the Hero.* New York: Nervous and Mental Disease Publishing Co., 1914.

[3] Tausk's paper was given as one of a series of sessions on Society and Neurosis.

FEDERN remarks that the exposition is to be taken only as an introduction to a later elaboration of the topic.

The damaging effect of incest upon the race has been proven. (Animal breeding does not come into consideration here, because that is concerned only with the breeding of certain characteristics, and not with the breeding, in general, of higher beings.) The necessity for a defense against incest has not been elucidated by the speaker. Incest itself can come into question only when the patriarchal family has already been introduced. It is improbable that the prohibition of incest was introduced through the roundabout way of totemism; the other way round is more likely. A strong father-complex alone is not sufficient to explain the disposition of Jews toward neurosis, because among the peasants, too, the father complex is usually pronounced, and yet it is only comparatively rarely that they fall ill with a neurosis.

RANK, too, finds that the topic has not been presented with sufficient sharpness. One should rather have started from the other end—that is, with the neurosis, then moved on to the individual's father complex with its social and asocial consequences (assassin, etc.), and finally cast a glance at the history of culture. Tausk, however, has presented only cultural history; he has disposed of the neurosis in passing, instead of establishing a relationship between them, as the topic calls for.

The father's voluntary renunciation of the daughter is altogether unlikely; from the myths, one could rather conclude that the daughter ran away from the father.

The destructive effect of incest on the race is by no means proven.

ROSENSTEIN finds it quite correct to draw upon biological motives for the incest barrier. As to the requirement of virginity, it is a question—as it is with any superstition—of whether it can be interpreted solely by way of motives that were valid only for our ancestors.

WEISS is inclined to find a reason for the father's renouncing the daughter in the fact that the expelled sons of other fathers lay claim to the stranger's daughters.

HITSCHMANN thinks Tausk has made himself guilty of throwing the topic into confusion. His paper has little to do with neurosis and father complex.

FRIEDJUNG calls attention to the fact that the requirement of virginity as a social institution is limited to only a small portion of the population. Perhaps this aspect could be approached from the viewpoint of the mother problem.

SACHS believes he can back up Weiss' supposition by way of a reference to the institution of the carrying away of women by force. The weak old father was slain by his sons—which may have been one motive for the renunciation.

FREUD, too, finds that the speaker did not present what was called for—namely, to show how the neurosis rests on the father complex, and in what way the neurosis thus formed then acts on society.

There are two gaps in the exposition: nothing has been said about the relation of the matriarchate to the family, or about the origin of the incest prohibition—about which one cannot indeed say anything. The biological explanation is untenable. But even if we were to grant its validity, we would still have to show how the biological tendency has asserted itself in psychology. In glaring contrast to the assumption of a degenerative effect of incest is the fact that among highly civilized peoples it was at one time a holy privilege and the law. Furthermore, it can be stated with certainty that prohibitions of incest are older than marriage. The problem of virginity in connection with the patriarchate would deserve an independent treatment. As to the relation of totemism to incest and to the father, Freud himself is going to speak on that within a short time.[4]

[4] Freud obviously refers to *Totem and Taboo;* it was probably because he expected to talk about this topic very soon that he took so little part in this discussion.

194

Present: Dattner, Federn, Freud, Friedjung, Hitschmann, Jekels, Rank, Reik, Reinhold, Rosenstein, Sachs, Sadger, Steiner, Tausk, (K.) Weiss, Winterstein.
Krauss, Lou as guests.

PRESENTATION

Clinical Communications and Reports

(1) PROF. FREUD: A dream representation which, in hypocritical clothing, reveals part of the dreamer's infantile sexual behavior (penis envy).

(2) DR. FRIEDJUNG: *Observations on the Source of the Infantile Feeling of Shame (Masturbation).* (This is going to be published.)[1]

FEDERN remarks that only the feeling of guilt has been disclosed.

REINHOLD finds that nothing has been offered toward an explanation of the feeling of shame, since in the cases cited it is not

[1] "Über verschiedene Quellen kindlicher Schamhaftigkeit" [On Different Sources of Infantile Bashfulness]. *Z.* (1913), 1: 362–364.

really a matter of shame. One would have to inquire further: why was the child ashamed on account of his masturbation?

TAUSK, like Federn, sees in the feeling of shame a reaction formation, behind which one finds, in analysis, the opposite: exhibitionism and, even earlier, defecation.

RANK confirms the fact that in many individuals the complex of defecation is intensely charged with shame; he cannot, however, find in Reinhold's objections any argument against Friedjung's statements.

ROSENSTEIN stresses the connection of the feeling of shame with fear.

FEDERN sees in the feeling of shame a reaction to sexuality on the part of the eye. With regard to defecation, it is to be noted that in such cases it is anal erotics who are involved, and that people are generally bashful where they are sexual.

PROF. FREUD remarks that the children whom Friedjung mentioned appear to be truly bashful.

(3) RANK: *On the Psychology of the Assassin* (Examples to show that the assassin experiences the family romance as real).[2]

FEDERN remarks that in children such as these it is only the hostile component of the father complex that achieves development.

FREUD mentions that in equating acting with thinking these people are carrying out the paranoid fantasy of vengeance.

(4) DR. REIK: *Gleanings from Psychoanalytic Literature.*

(5) DR. SACHS: *A Contribution to the History of Religion.* (The evidence utilized by Reinach,[3] to show that Barabbas and Jesus are one person).

(6) DR. WEISS: *Experimental Dreams.*

---

[2] "Der 'Familienroman' in der Psychologie des Attentäters" [The "Family Romance" in the Psychology of the Assassin]. *Z.* (1913), 1: 565–569.

[3] Salomon Reinach, 1858–1932, French archeologist and prolific writer.

195

Present: Federn, Freud, Friedjung, Hitschmann, Rank, Reik, Reitler, Sachs, Sadger, Silberer, Steiner, Tausk, Wagner.
Guests: Mrs. Jones, Krauss, Lou, Mrs. Sachs.

PRESENTATION

Swift

SPEAKER: DR. SACHS [1]

DISCUSSION

KRAUSS would caution against drawing conclusions of this sort from a poet's works, with regard to his character. For instance, at that time the English took pleasure in scatological writings—an inclination that Swift took into account. A more careful study of the literature of that time (especially of travel accounts) would be needed in order to establish what Swift added on his own.

[1] Apparently Sachs did not have this paper published.

HITSCHMANN considers it obvious to characterize Swift as impotent. In the fantasies of individuals who have small genitals is often found the element of the gigantic. He mentions a patient who wanted to be dressed only by male persons; he found it humiliating to be helped by women.

PROF. FREUD comments that the speaker has assumed that Swift had infantile genitalia, in which case impotence is self-evident. The stress on the number eleven in the Gulliver fantasies, for instance, might signify the limit of the time up to which the poet had felt happy. It is only genital inferiority that plays any role.

FEDERN emphasizes that any abnormality of pubertal development generates a feeling of inferiority. The child's narcissistic feeling of superiority indeed contradicts Adler's "feeling of inferiority." If there is a genital inferiority, narcissism is disturbed. It is a question whether the cruel impulses that every child shows are, in Swift's case, to be characterized as sadism. To be sure, it is one of the roots of the satirist, just as the small genitalium is another one. Swift's bashfulness vis-à-vis women, as well as in relation to his works, goes back to his being ashamed to show his genital. Persons who have infantile genitalia also retain infantilisms in other respects.

JEKELS sees a parallel between hate for children and the disavowal of authorship, in that both are to be traced back to the rejection of fatherhood.

PROF. FREUD comments that a special relation of the Adlerian "feeling of inferiority" to *neurosis* does not exist. To be sure, it plays a part in the formation of character, but Adler had blurred the boundary between the theory of neurosis and general psychology. The psychological feeling of inferiority comes into consideration only as a contradiction to narcissism.

196

Present: Federn, Freud, Hitschmann, Jekels, Reik, Reitler, Sachs, Sadger, Steiner, Tausk, Winterstein.
Krauss, Lorenz, Lou as guests.

PRESENTATION

An Autoerotic

SPEAKER: DR. J. SADGER [1]

DISCUSSION

PROF. FREUD comments that the patient, a case of perversion (infantilism), is not suited for analytic treatment; for, above all, narcissism forms the limits of accessibility to influence, and, further, what patients such as this one generally want is merely to prove to themselves their own incurability. In that case, one ought to reconcile them to their perversion. If, however, one does analyze

---

[1] "The Psychoanalysis of an Autoerotic" appeared in *Jb.* (1913), 5: 467; 528.

patients of this type, the psychoanalytic technique is to be strictly applied; under no conditions must one allow the patients to form theories about their illness. True, some associative relations were quite correctly interpreted by the patient, but he does not know the actual dynamic problem—for instance, that of fetishism (how it is that the libido comes to be transferred from persons onto objects) —nor has that been touched upon by the speaker. In any case, a special kind of repression (splitting of the complex) lies at the root of fetishism. The patient finds contained in the fetish everything he wishes; to him it is a collective object for his libido.

Just as this case does not lend itself to therapeutic treatment, so it is not suited for scientific use. It is a case of psychic infantilism, from which we cannot learn anything for our understanding. The case would be interesting in view of his inferior genital; but unfortunately he has in addition been neglected by his mother, so that we cannot establish the roots of his masochism. For the treatment by the mother also has a bearing on whether it is sadism or masochism that evolves.

FEDERN stresses that it is difficult, by way of associative connections, to discover the ultimate roots in perverts, because new components are continually being added on. In the present case, it is the patient's training in particular that interferes.

Whether the infantilism has remained fixated because of internal developmental inhibitions or for external reasons is hard to determine; only a successful treatment could do so.

Objections have to be raised to some of the associative interpretations.

The discussant can confirm that masochists do have peculiar genital sensations.

PROF. FREUD adds a remark on the therapy of perverts—namely, that it is not the true field of psychoanalytic work. It is only unhappy perverts who can be considered for analysis; the task of analysis can be performed in the undoing of the perversion. In the majority of cases, however, analysis has reconciled the individuals to their perversions: it is not the task of analysis to make people normal, but to make them harmonious and to solve their conflict.

197

Present: Dattner, Federn, Freud, Hitschmann, Jekels, Rank, Reik, Rosenstein, Sadger, Steiner, Tausk, K. Weiss, Winterstein.

PRESENTATION

Neurosis and Celibacy

SPEAKER: DR. ED. HITSCHMANN

The lecturer first speaks about married life in general as being under present cultural conditions man's natural form of loving, and he points to its advantages and its limitations. The marriages of neurotics and artists demonstrate that marriage can by no means serve as a cure. Whether there are, on the other hand, neuroses that are produced by marriage cannot be answered in general terms.

The speaker then considers celibacy as a cause of neurosis; he gives their due to the objective obstacles to marriage (inversion, perversion, being crippled, lack of money, etc.), and depicts the harmful consequences of celibacy, with special emphasis on prostitution.

The main theme dealt with is neurosis as a cause of celibacy, the roots of which consist of unconscious inhibitions which can be uncovered by way of analysis. Incapacity for marriage lies on the one hand in incestuous object fixation, on the other hand in the masturbation of puberty, the replacement of which by normal sexual life has become more difficult. The consequences of these conditions include absolute as well as relative impotence, marrying a relative and the choice of older objects. The type of man's object choice described by Freud is drawn in and evaluated as to its significance for adultery, as is the tendency toward the debasement of love life.[1]

Among those impotent in married life are superior as well as inferior types; the type of the bachelor, of the "mother's darling," is mentioned, and the rationalizations are spelled out by which celibacy is justified in such cases.

DISCUSSION

TAUSK finds that neither the material nor the points of view have been treated exhaustively in the presentation. The problem of marriage and celibacy is the problem of love, which begins at a time when there is no question of marriage. Love resists any attempts to fit it into a framework, and it is from there that inhibitions start. Marriage and the need for love, as a problem, can only be set in contrast to each other.

JEKELS refers, in this connection, to the polygamous instinct.

ROSENSTEIN finds the wish not to be together to have been insufficiently motivated; egoism and the lack of empathy also play a role here. The question should have been asked why people do get married. Marriage is fixation to an object.

WINTERSTEIN thinks one should have differentiated between whether the celibate merely does not lead a normal sex life or lives ascetically.

DATTNER believes a biological element is also involved—that is, a certain sensation of inferiority in the organ.

There is one type who wants children, and another who cannot understand that at all. For superior people, their works are their children.

---

[1] "A Special Type of Object-Choice Made by Men" (Contributions to the Psychology of Love) (1910), *S.E.*, 11:164–175.

REIK finds missing from the enumeration of obstacles to matrimony obsessional jealousy, which may extend to the past or to the future. Marriage is a compromise between polygamous strivings and monogamous ones. The neurotic attitude is rooted in narcissism.

FEDERN remarks that marriage is incorrectly looked upon as a cure for neurosis; if neurotics get married, they do so out of their neurosis. Besides, most neurotics are *drawn into* marriage (masochistic motives). The tendency toward marriage or the aversion against it goes back to a great extent to the model of the parental marriage. Another motive for marriage is a purely erotic one. People whose erotism is strong get married easily.

RANK can confirm this last fact and—in contrast to the emphasis on the polygamous instinct and the instinct of love in general—points out that for many persons, marriage is the only possible form of love life because their rejection of sexuality—the normal part of which we call fidelity—prevents them from practicing polygamy or aggression.

PROF. FREUD stresses that one part of the obstacles to marriage is connected with the general retardation of love life.[2] The sort of marriage the parents have does exert the greatest influence on one's decision whether or not to get married. Small children have, almost without exception, a wish to get married.

The man who has a neurotic attitude is actually the right husband; not, however, the neurotic. Matrimony is a difficult cultural task and one has to be healthy to fulfill it.

HITSCHMANN in his concluding words mentions that more is expected from married life than mere love gratification; in the discussion, a certain undervaluation of marriage has become apparent. The idea that people cannot always be together, occurs for the most part only to the neurotic (Grillparzer); the *fear* of being together, however, is definitely neurotic.

The incapacity for getting married has nothing at all to do with sexual gratification (Winterstein).

---

[2] "On the Universal Tendency to Debasement in the Sphere of Love" (Contributions to the Psychology of Love) (1912), *S.E.*, 11: 178–190.

198

SCIENTIFIC MEETING *on April 23, 1913*

Present: Freud, Hitschmann, Jekels, Rank, Sadger, Tausk, K. Weiss, Winterstein.

PRESENTATION

Autoerotism and Narcissism

SPEAKER: DR. J. SADGER

On the basis of detailed clinical material, the speaker points out that, in the coming into being of narcissism, admiration on the part of mother or nurse plays a decisive role; so does a hyperdevelopment of autoerotism in puberty, as well as an underdevelopment of the genital and sexual instincts, together with a preponderance of other sexual components (homosexuality).

DISCUSSION

TAUSK has not learned from the paper what narcissism is. The speaker adduced the patient's narcissism, but he has yet to prove it. Besides, on technical grounds it was impossible to follow the paper. It is true that narcissism was characterized as a conjoining of the sexual instincts with the ego instincts, but this was not demonstrated. The meaning of narcissism is the inability to achieve a transference. But that is unconscious; what we have heard about is conscious. Narcissism is the formula of identity by way of which the individual identifies with the sexuality of the species. That is why woman is basically narcissistic.

HITSCHMANN finds the presentation unsatisfactory from the medical-psychological point of view, as well as methodologically faulty. One ought not put any suggestive questions to the patient. It is a question whether the concept of narcissism should not be restricted to a certain period of life, while all the rest is regarded as fixation and residues thereof. Evidently, narcissism arises spontaneously and can merely be backed up by caresses and admiration. What was missing in the paper was the relation to pathology (paranoia, etc.). Does not a narcissism with a negative sign also exist—a kind of self-displeasure, which viewed psychologically, could be connected with repression?

RANK misses not only an explanation of narcissism, which cannot perhaps yet be given, but even a correct description of what we understand by narcissism. Where are the boundaries of what is pathological? Where does the general etiology (according to Sadger, admiration on the mother's part) go over into a specific one, etc.? Perhaps one should distinguish among degrees of narcissism. The derivation of narcissism in girls from the lack of a penis and from the wish to make up for that defect is quite reminiscent of Adler's "masculine protest"; it is, however, just as untenable as the latter, since there are a good many girls and women who are proud of *purely feminine* (real or imagined) merits. The very close relations between narcissism and exhibitionism would warrant exact definition and clarification. Some things in the character description seem well observed.

PROF. FREUD finds that Sadger has presented only individual traits, but not the fundamental traits on which the whole thing rests. The meaning of the problem has been pointed out by Tausk;

it is only that the biological element should not yet be placed in the foreground, nor should the problem be given a philosophical formulation. Narcissism is a borderline term in which the separation of sexual instincts from ego instincts is brought back to the underlying oneness of these. The derivation of narcissism from the presence or absence of a penis does not seem advisable for then it would have to arise in every case. The narcissism that arises in a woman by way of compensation is but one of its types. Narcissism is a normal phenomenon; it is only the fixations and the excessive forms that are to be regarded as pathological.

We can employ two methods of investigation for the study of narcissism: (1) starting from dementia praecox and paranoia; (2) starting from the third "actual neurosis"—that is, from hypochondria. A specific process seems to turn the narcissist into the hypochondriac: the libidinal cathexes appear to be changed into their opposite so that unpleasure is produced. For the state of hypochondria we have a normal model in the state of being ill and its concomitant psychic symptoms (the "egoism of the patient" to which Sadger referred). If we take these paths for the study of narcissism, starting from pathology, we draw away from the problem of neuroses and come closer to ego psychology. From our study of narcissism, however, we understand how regression to it has to interfere with the ego cathexes (in dementia).

199

SCIENTIFIC MEETING *on April 30, 1913*

Present: Dattner, Federn, Freud, Friedjung, Hitschmann, Jekels, Rank, Reik, Rosenstein, Sachs, Steiner, Tausk, K. Weiss.

BRIEF COMMUNICATIONS

SACHS brings to the Society's attention, as a counterpart to the symbolism of Mother Earth and the prevention of contiguity with her in the punitive ceremonial of patricide (Storfer[1]), another punitive ceremonial practiced among the Greeks and the Germans. This prescribes that during the passing of the sentence the criminal has to stand in such a position that the sun is shining in his face.

PROF. FREUD remarks to this that, as to the patient who discovered earth symbolism on his own, as a child, it was on the body of his mother that he had undertaken his first attempts to walk. Later, he became agoraphobic. Another neurotic boy conceives of volcanoes as the genital parts of the earth.

[1] A. J. Storfer: *Zur Sonderstellung des Vatermordes. Eine rechtsgeschichtliche und völkerpsychologische Studie.* [*On the Exceptional Position of Patricide: a Study in the History of Law and in Ethnopsychology.*] Leipzig, Wien: F. Deuticke, 1911. It was reviewed by Hanns Sachs in *Zb.* (1912), 2: 357–359.

SACHS, in corroboration of the connection between optimism and being preferred by one's mother, quotes an ancient proverb (which he got from Reinach): anyone toward whom his mother was not affectionate will not get far in life: he is not going to eat with the Gods, nor will he sleep with the goddesses.

Further, a place in the autobiography of Benvenuto Cellini that shows the connection of urine retention with money.

Finally, an observation that the anal character is also retentive of communications.

FRIEDJUNG: Remarks about the question of masturbation (case of an 11-year-old excessive masturbator).

REIK: Example of the unconscious rule of the omnipotence of thoughts in the life of the normal person.[2]

---

[2] The Minutes obviously are getting shorter and shorter. Rank takes less trouble with the recording, and seems satisfied with listing titles.

200

SCIENTIFIC MEETING *on May 7, 1913*

Present: Dattner, Federn, Freud, Friedjung, Hitschmann, Jekels, Marcus, Rank, Reik, Reitler, Rosenstein, Sachs, Sadger, Tausk, K. Weiss, Winterstein.

PRESENTATION

Education and Neurosis

SPEAKER: DR. KARL WEISS

DISCUSSION

DR. TAUSK finds the significance of intellectual influence upon the child to be overestimated; it is only by way of affects that one can exert influence here. The Oedipus complex has been represented from too one-sided a point of view; the child is also attached with a portion of his libido to the parent of his own sex. The child's feeling of having some (sexual) knowledge in common with his parents has been properly stressed by the speaker. Among his unenlightened peers, it is true, the child does get into a dangerous situation as a result.

195

PROF. FREUD finds that the speaker has adapted himself well to the framework of the discussion. It is only that the Oedipus complex has been represented too one-sidedly. The castration complex is perhaps not always to be derived from individual experience.[1] For the rest, the presentation might have been somewhat less optimistic, for the conflict between instinctual life and cultural life cannot be circumvented.

FRIEDJUNG, too, is of the opinion that the presentation is somewhat too optimistic. Moreover, too little importance has been attached to individual differences in the behavior of children. The child often wants merely to force his educator to concern himself with his [the child's] body. As to the dangers to which the child is exposed, mention is to be made, in addition, of overindulgence on the part of relatives, and of seduction by housemaids. It is preferable to speak of sexual "education" rather than "enlightenment."

SACHS joins in the praise expressed up to this point, and comments that the psychoanalytically trained educator is able to intervene even before the child has been ruined. In the definition of education as assimilation to the cultural milieu, the fact was neglected that education can also exert an influence on organic development. The value of arguments in education should not be underrated (Tausk); for the child, they smooth the way to sublimation.

REIK misses a comment on the question of from whom sexual enlightenment should come; he thinks psychoanalysis cannot regard school as the proper source.[2]

HITSCHMANN is inclined to view education as a *prophylacticum.* By way of regimented enlightenment in school, a monotonous uniformity would be spread among people and individuality would suffer.

FEDERN remarks that the main point in the question of sexual enlightenment is whether or not we bolster the child's sense of shame (reaction to the wish to show himself); for this protects the

---

[1] Later on, the castration complex was counted among the innate complexes.

[2] Nowadays, courses on biological sex development are included in the curriculum for 10- and 11-year-old students in many schools; but the controversy still rages about the fitness of school for the role of disseminator of sexual enlightenment.

child. In the process of enlightenment, any false information or half-truth, since it is harmful, is to be avoided. The reason for the sexual secretiveness of parents does not lie only in their sexual complex.

Normal children do not become neurotic, in any case. There is particular need for enlightenment in sadistic families; it protects the child against the transformation of his sexual instincts into sadism.

FRIEDJUNG is of the opinion that parents are for the most part incapable of providing enlightenment; yet, an enlightenment that is imparted in an awkward way is better than one that is given tactlessly [without regard for the child's feelings].

PROF. FREUD considers it expedient in some instances to leave to the oldest child the dissemination of enlightenment among his siblings. Education by way of the operation of affects could be stressed more strongly, because these serve to overcome the child's inclination toward defiance.

The "harmfulness" of infantile sexuality is entirely a product of civilization.

DATTNER makes the point that the vicissitudes of the libido have already been completed, before sexual enlightenment can set in. One has to differentiate between those children who show a spontaneous interest in enlightenment, and those who do not; as to these latter, in order for enlightenment to become effective, they would first have to be subjected to an analysis.[3]

---

[3] The idea of applying psychoanalysis to pedagogy was first advanced by Pfister, the author of *Psychoanalyse und Pädagogik* [Psychoanalysis and Pedagogy] in *Berner Seminarblätter* (1912), 6, and "Anwendungen der Psychoanalyse in der Pädagogik und Seelsorge" (Application of psychoanalysis in pedagogy and pastoral care), *Imago*, (1912), 1:56–82. In October 1926, Heinrich Meng, M.D., and Ernst Schneider, Ph.D., founded the *Zeitschrift für Psychoanalytische Pädagogik*, which continued to appear until 1938.

201

SCIENTIFIC MEETING *on May 14, 1913*

Present: Dattner, Federn, Freud, Friedjung, Hitschmann, Jekels, Marcus, Rank, Reik, Reitler, Sachs, Sadger, Silberer, Steiner, Tausk, K. Weiss, Winterstein.

Edoardo Weiss,[1] Krauss, Storfer[2] as guests.

PRESENTATION

A Contribution to the Mechanism of Name Forgetting

SPEAKER: STUD. MED. ED. WEISS (as a guest)

In spite of the tendency toward repression, there also exists a drive in us to come close to our repressed complexes. There is still need for a more precise explanation of how it is possible at one and the same time to go out of the way of the repressed complex and to draw closer to it. In the neuroses, it is the sexual

---

[1] This is the first time that mention is made of Dr. Edoardo Weiss of Trieste, who became the founder of the Italian Psychoanalytic Association and the translator of Freud's work into Italian. He subsequently lived and worked in Chicago.

[2] A. J. Storfer, 1888–1944, was the first director of the *Internationale Psychoanalytische Verlag.* He was a prolific and erudite writer, left Vienna under the Hitler regime, and died a lonely exile in Australia.

instinct that counteracts repression; this results in compromise formations. What is the corresponding drive in the process of forgetting?

The simple, free association invariably shows a tendency, a wish; if, then, the unconscious sends a name into consciousness, it is thereby expressing a wish. Substitute names, because of their tendentious nature, stand in certain relations to the repressed complex and owe their origin to the unconscious tendency to free oneself of the disturbing aspects of the complex; it is for this reason that we draw closer to the complexes. The repressed name corresponds, as it were, to the nonfulfillment of a wish. Tausk's discovery of the reward tendency elucidates this mechanism.[3]

The speaker is inclined to relate the cases of name forgetting to a single mechanism (the one described by Freud in the "aliquis" example[4])—namely, the inhibition of a thought by a contradiction coming out of the repression, or the reaction of the unconscious to the word that corresponds to the nonfulfillment of a wish. This is also evidenced by the affect that appears when one catches oneself forgetting something: one is impatient and annoyed, just as if things did not go as desired.

DISCUSSION

TAUSK comments that the speaker's conception, according to which the entire series of substitute names serves as a reward (and not only the last one before the forgotten name) appears to him a bit too generalized. In general it would have to be demonstrated that a reward appears in every case; this cannot yet by any means be asserted. As a rule, the first association (just as in treatment) comes closest to the forgotten (repressed) one. It is possible, however, for an idea to appear that is identical with the forgotten one, yet without its being recognized with regard to its identity and affect value. That is the mechanism of obsessional neurosis.

[3] V. Tausk, "Entwertung des Verdrängungsmotivs durch Rekompense" [Compensation as a Means of Discounting the Motive of Repression]. Z. (1913), 1: 230–239.
[4] Freud, The Psychopathology of Everyday Life (1901), S.E., 6.

FEDERN finds that the speaker has examined an insufficient number of examples, and, by way of the neurotic examples he has presented, has complicated matters. Whether the first association is nearest to the repressed is questionable; even more to be questioned is whether that is a "taking by surprise" of the resistance (Tausk). Another possible explanation lies in the fact that what is painful simply presses toward consciousness over and over again.

STORFER presents a clinical contribution: forgetting, with a substitute formation.

PROF. FREUD stresses that the cases of name forgetting represent *formes frustes* of neuroses, in which one can study everything. The speaker has a tendency toward generalizations; it is likely that more mechanisms of name forgetting exist than were enumerated in *The Psychopathology of Everyday Life.* Three mechanisms are there enumerated: 1. an inner contradiction; 2. a direct avoiding of the unpleasure that would result from evoking the name; 3. the name has an associative connection with ideas that arouse unpleasure. In a number of examples, the tendency toward recompense will not be able to assert itself. For the study of free associations, the mechanism of obsessional ideas mentioned by Tausk is of great importance. The first form in which the obsessional idea makes its appearance is undisguised. Here, the idea of "taking the resistance by surprise" cannot be rejected. It is just as true that the correct idea may come into consciousness without doing any good because the resistance has shifted from the amnesia to the association.[5] Even during treatment it often happens that the obsessional neurotic brings forth resolutions without being aware of it. As to recompense and similar mechanisms, one has to distinguish whether or not the substitute names actually lead to the recollection of the correct name. There are cases in which what is painful presses forward; melancholia, however, which Federn mentioned, is not a good example because what we see there is a repression substitute, for the sake of pleasure. The melancholic mood is an organic state.

[5] The mechanism of isolation, as described later.

200

RANK thinks one would obtain elucidation of the area of validity of the recompense mechanism, as well as of its nature, if one were to examine in addition, with reference to that mechanism, other cases of parapraxis. In two cases of losing, the loss entered consciousness only after solace and compensation for the sacrificed object had been hallucinated in a dream.

FEDERN adds that the (nosological) gain of forgetting lies in the fact that the person involved, instead of having to face the tormenting complex, merely feels anger (intellectual pain).

MARCUS expresses the opinion that the cases of losing adduced by Rank are not analogous to the process in name forgetting.

REIK calls attention to the connection existing between slips of the tongue and jokes, as well as to the similarity between unnoticed slips of the tongue and unintentional jokes.

HITSCHMANN refers to the concept of complex-readiness (Bleuler): the substitute names correspond to the repressed portion of the complex. Federn's "gain in forgetting" does not seem to be true.

SACHS points out that the speaker has left out of account the practical tendency of all these parapraxes.

SILBERER and FRIEDJUNG present examples that give rise to a lengthy discussion. Silberer calls attention to a source of error that lies in regarding the availability of the previously forgotten name as being the result of analytical elucidation. Analysis may also open up a mnemotechnical way by which one succeeds in remembering the word. (Friedjung, Storfer, and Freud each offers an objection to this.)

TAUSK remarks the parapraxes can also arise simply out of conflict. As to Rank's cases of losing, one cannot speak of a recompense in those instances; that can be demonstrated only where there are trains of associations. All the dream wants to do is to draw attention to the loss.

202

Present: Federn, Freud, Friedjung, Hitschmann, Jekels, Marcus, Rank, Reik, Reitler, Sachs, Sadger, Steiner, Tausk, Winterstein.

Guests: Jones, Krauss, Lorenz, Pollner, Mrs. Sachs, Mrs. Sperber, Storfer.

PRESENTATION

Fairytales

SPEAKER: RANK

[The minutes of this meeting are missing]

203

SCIENTIFIC MEETING *on May 31, 1913*

Present: No attendance list.

REPORTS

[The minutes of this meeting are missing]

204

SCIENTIFIC MEETING *on June 4, 1913*

Present: No attendance list.

PRESENTATION

Totem

SPEAKER: FREUD

[The minutes of this meeting are missing]
[This ends the working year 1912/1913]

205

SCIENTIFIC MEETING *on October 8, 1913*

Present: Dattner, Federn, Freud, Friedjung, Heller, Hitschmann, Hellmuth, Jekels, Rank, Reik, Reitler, Rosenstein, Sachs, Sadger, Silberer, Steiner, Tausk, E. Weiss, K. Weiss, Winterstein.
Guests: Dr. K. Landauer.[1]
General meeting.

CONGRESS REPORT [2]

SPEAKER: PROF. FREUD

[The minutes of this meeting are missing]

---

[1] This is the first appearance of the name of Dr. Landauer, who was to make important contributions to psychoanalysis. He met with a tragic death in a concentration camp toward the end of World War II.

[2] Congress in Munich, at which the break with Jung took place.

206

SCIENTIFIC MEETING *on October 15, 1913*

Present: Federn, Freud, Friedjung, Hitschmann, Hellmuth, Landauer, Rank, Reik, Reitler, Sachs, Sadger, Silberer, Steiner, Tausk, E. Weiss, K. Weiss, Winterstein.
Guest: Blum.

PRESENTATION

Unconscious effect . . . .[1]

[The minutes of this meeting are missing]

---

[1] The rest of the title is illegible.

207

Present: Federn, Freud, Friedjung, Hitschmann, Hellmuth, Jekels, Landauer, Rank, Reik, Reitler, Sachs, Sadger, Silberer, Steiner, Tausk, E. Weiss, K. Weiss, Winterstein.

DISCUSSION ON TOTEMISM

[The minutes of this meeting are missing]

208

SCIENTIFIC MEETING *on October 29, 1913*

Present: Federn, Freud, Friedjung, Hellmuth, Hitschmann, Jekels, Landauer,[1] Rank, Reitler, Sachs, Sadger, Steiner, K. Weiss, E. Weiss.

PRESENTATION

On Some Essays by Stanley Hall and His School,[2] *Seen from the Viewpoint of Psychoanalysis*

SPEAKER: DR. H. VON HUG-HELLMUTH

After first giving a brief comparative characterization of the two schools (Stanley Hall's and Freud's), their methods and conclusions, the speaker discusses from the psychoanalytic viewpoint an essay by Hall on "Rage," and a study by C. Ellis and Hall about "Dolls." (The paper is intended for publication in an American journal.)

[1] Actually present as a guest. Later on, he became a member of the German group, and then of the Dutch group.

[2] A Caswell Hills and G. Stanley Hall: A Study of Dolls. *The Pedagogical Seminary* (1896–1897), 4: 129–217.

Hug-Hellmuth's paper is not mentioned anywhere; it has probably not been published.

DISCUSSION

FRIEDJUNG advises caution in formulating statements that needlessly provoke the reader's opposition.

With regard to those attacks of rage in the first years of life that are described as "fainting away," it is for the most part a question of shortness of breath resulting from screaming, and a means for forcing the grownups to yield.

A fine observation concerning dolls is to be found in Ibsen's *Master Builder.*

HITSCHMANN is of the opinion that Hall's investigation of groups is overrated, as compared with analysis. Such an examination of rage should be preceded by a definition and a marking-off of closely related concepts (hate, sadism, narcissism, etc.). Some of these expressions of affect are the model for the hysterical symptom.

FEDERN thinks that Hall's exposition on the sexual sources of these psychic phenomena is indeed of historical value for us.

The idea that the bottle (in play with dolls) is a urethral-erotic symbol, Federn, counter to Friedjung's doubting, is able to confirm on the basis of a case. There seem to exist two sorts of playing with dolls: the narcissistic kind and the kind that has its source in the maternal instinct. To assume the existence, as the speaker did, of a specific drive for taking care of others is unjustified.

Through the absence of a definition, what is actually typical of rage has failed to become apparent: one of the characteristics of rage is a narrowing of consciousness, a complete lack of inhibition. Rage is a regression to the infantile; every fit of anger is a breakthrough of a suppressed affect (it is impossible for it to be a disguising of such an affect, as Hall thinks it is). Spitting in rage is not to be regarded as a urethral-erotic symbol; it is found even in the animal world.

To soothe a child's anger, it is useful to offer him a substitute: doing away with a punishment, not threatening it, removes the child's rage.

DR. LANDAUER shows, by way of an example, that ears that stick out have nothing to do with exhibitionism. Stripping oneself

209

in a state of rage nevertheless does play a large role. Mentally-ill persons spit in their rage and they uncover their buttocks.

E. WEISS thinks that, as far as the connection between sexuality and rage is concerned, the former may perhaps act merely as an ungratified need (just as any other need would).

DR. K. WEISS opposes Hitschmann's viewpoint—that Hall's material is too subjective. Then the discussant tries to establish an analogy between the symptoms of rage and various forms of sexual activity.

REITLER finds that in many instances Hall confuses the fleeting, temporary fit of rage with the more permanent hatred. Further, it is not true that it is only persons who are loved or hated that can provoke rage. One castrates bulls in order to make them docile and to soothe their rage.

Migraine seems to correspond to a suppressed fit of rage.

HITSCHMANN should like to see genuine migraine differentiated from pseudo- or hysterical migraine. Adler, too, has written about migraines that are simulated on the occasion of a fit of rage. The concept of neuralgia is now becoming more and more limited. So many psychogenic components have become apparent behind this concept that in the end all that will remain will be pseudoneuralgias.

RANK, too, finds incorrect the statement that it is only a loved or a hated person who can release rage. Since the affects that express themselves in rage are usually inadequate and have their source elsewhere, rage is often directed toward entirely indifferent persons or occasions; indeed, one might regard this precisely as a characteristic of rage.

Just like the beasts, man can be observed to fly into a rage easily if difficulties get into the way of his desire for love. The connection between alcoholism and rage, mentioned by Dr. Hug, plays an important role.

PROF. FREUD likewise comments that Hall seems to confuse rage with hatred; that, however, is due to the difficulties with the theory of affects in general. Playing allows the child to give vent to his instincts: in playing with dolls, he satisfies various sexual strivings.

209

SCIENTIFIC MEETING on *November 5, 1913*

Present: Dattner, Federn, Freud, Friedjung, Hellmuth, Hitsch-
mann, Jekels, Landauer, Rank, Reik, Reitler, Rosenstein, Sachs,
Sadger, Silberer, Steiner, Tausk, E. Weiss, Winterstein.
Dr. Hollos,[1] Dr. Zollschau and Mrs. Zollschau as guests.

CRITICAL REVIEWS

(*Jahrbuch V/1*)

DR. LANDAUER (on Itten, *Dementia praecox*) [2] first attempts
to prepare the way for a clarification of the contradictions resulting
from the terminologies of Freud, Bleuler, and the school of Kraepelin.

HITSCHMANN would consider such a clarification to be of great
merit.

---

[1] Istvan Hollos, 1872–?, was one of the pioneers of psychoanalysis in Hungary, where
in 1918 he became the first analyst to direct a State Hospital. He supported Federn,
whose disciple he was, when the latter analyzed psychotic patients with a modified
technique.

[2] W. Itten, Swiss psychiatrist, "Beiträge zur Psychologie der Dementia praecox" [Con-
tributions to the Psychology of Dementia Praecox]. *Jb.* (1913), 5: 1–54.

TAUSK finds that the reporter has not sufficiently differentiated between symptom and driving force. Dementia praecox is usually present as early as in the sixth to ninth year of age.

FEDERN can confirm this (he offers a case).

PROF. FREUD finds the discussion of these things sterile. The Zurich school concerns itself only with the contents of the symptoms of dementia praecox, not with their mechanism. They overlook the fact that the clinical picture is dominated by three aspects: (1) symptoms of regression or retrograde formation (hebephrenia and autoerotism); (2) residual phenomena; (3) process of recovery.[3]

HITSCHMANN (on Jones, *Obsessional Neurosis*) does not consider the cases to be typically obsessional-neurotic ones (Dr. Jekels shares this view); these are obsessions in the form of attacks. Jones groups the symptoms according to individual complexes. From the standpoint of a differential diagnosis, the paranoid relations of these patients to their environment are important.

JEKELS calls attention, in the second case, to what he has previously termed "cavity-erotism" (*Höhlenerotik*).

FEDERN draws into the discussion Jones's essay on hate and anal erotism in obsessional neurosis,[4] and comments, in relation to the question of marking off hate and sadism, that hate arises when the gratification of hostile impulses is impossible, whereas sadism unfolds itself precisely in that gratification.

As to anal erotism, one has to distinguish: (1) one portion of passive sensations which are pleasurable and linked with the mucous membrane of the anus; and (2) an active, hostile component. It is possible, however, that the anal zone is merely a means for the expression of infantile hate, and not its source.

Whether the omnipotence of thoughts has to do, as Jones would have it, with flatus is quite doubtful.

TAUSK, contradicting Federn, states that hate and sadism are two entirely different categories.

---

[3] Schizophrenia implies a detachment from reality (*Weltuntergang:* end of the world) which proceeds silently, whereas the process of recovery takes its course in clamorous symptoms.

[4] *Papers on Psychoanalysis*, Baltimore: Williams & Wilkins, 1948, pp. 553–561.

PROF. FREUD knows nothing about an origin of hate in thwarted anal erotism, as assumed by Jones.

HUG-HELLMUTH (on Pfister's *Kryptolalia*, etc.) [5]

SACHS: Pfister's "The Origin of Artistic Inspiration." [6] Review.

FEDERN (On Sadger's "Sadomasochism") [7] would wish for a sharper distinction between facts and conclusions. What is true is the assertion that sadism invariably goes back to childhood; it is not true, however, that submission to despotism has nothing to do with masochism. Tracing sadomasochism back to the erotism of skin, mucous membrane, and muscle means nothing at all, because there does not exist any other erotism. Nothing else is said, therefore, when one says this, but that sadomasochism goes back to abnormal sexuality. Moreover, Sadger has actually dealt only with algolagnia, and the gap in the elucidation of true sadism continues to exist.

SILBERER raises the question of whether the pleasure comes only from the increased intensity of the sensation, or is linked specifically with the feeling of pain; whether, therefore, the pain is a precondition or an accident.

PROF. FREUD likewise poses a question not answered by Sadger: how is it that these people experience as pleasurable what is painful to others? Increased skin- etc. erotism could just as well call forth an increased defense. It is a matter of the direction of the sensation, not of its intensity. In studying these phenomena, one should keep to the extremes only. In man's development, there exists a general physiological connection: along with any intense excitation, sexual excitation is brought on at the same time. It is from that point that fixation could take its start.

REITLER (on Bleuler, *Sexual resistance*[8]) will appear in print.

---

[5] O. Pfister: "Kryptolalie, Kryptographie und unbewusstes Vexierbild bei Normalen" [Kryptolalia, Kryptography and the Unconscious Picture-Puzzles as Used by Normal Persons]. *Jb.* (1913), 5: 117–156.

[6] O. Pfister: "Die Entstehung der künstlerischen Inspiration" [The Origin of Artistic Inspiration], *Imago* (1913), 2: 481–512.

[7] J. Sadger. "Über den sado-masochistischen Komplex" [On the Sado-masochistic Complex]. *Jb.* (1913), 5: 157–232.

[8] Reitler's review of Bleuler's *Der Sexualwiderstand* appeared in *Z.* (1914), 2: 67–71.

210

SCIENTIFIC MEETING *on November 12, 1913*

Present: Federn, Freud, Friedjung, Heller, Hitschmann, Hell-muth, Jekels, Landauer, Rank, Reik, Reitler, Sachs, Sadger, Silberer, Steiner, Tausk, E. Weiss, K. Weiss.
Guest: Peter Breithold.

PRESENTATION

Homunculus

SPEAKER: DR. SILBERER

[The minutes of this meeting are missing.]

211

Present: Federn, Freud, Friedjung, Heller, Hitschmann, Hellmuth, Jekels, Landauer, Nepallek, Rank, Reik, Reitler, Rosenstein, Sachs, Sadger, Silberer, Steiner, Tausk, E. Weiss, K. Weiss, Winterstein.
Guests: Mr. Breithold, Ferenczi, Dr. Meisels, Ing. and Mrs. Meitner, Dr. Moskowitcz, Dr. and Mrs. Fr. Alexander (Roth), Miss Zimmermann.

PRESENTATION

Experiments with Thought-Transference

SPEAKER: DR. FERENCZI

[The minutes of this meeting are missing.]

212

SCIENTIFIC MEETING *on November 26, 1913*

Present: Federn, Freud, Friedjung, Hitschmann, Hellmuth, Jekels, Landauer, Nepallek, Rank, Reik, Rosenstein, Sachs, Sadger, Silberer, Tausk, E. Weiss, K. Weiss, Winterstein.

CLINICAL COMMUNICATIONS

[The minutes of this meeting are missing.]

213

SCIENTIFIC MEETING *on December 3, 1913*

Present: Freud, Friedjung, Hitschmann, Hug, Landauer, Nepallek, Rank, Reik, Sachs, Sadger, Silberer, E. Weiss, K. Weiss.
Guests: Drs. Snyder and Smells, America; Eng. Friedmann.

CLINICAL COMMUNICATIONS AND REVIEWS

[The minutes of this meeting are missing.]

214

Present: Federn, Freud, Jekels, Landauer, Nepallek, Rank, Reik, Reitler, Sachs, Sadger, Steiner, Tausk, E. Weiss, K. Weiss, Winterstein.

PRESENTATION

On the Psychology of Schizophrenia

SPEAKER: DR. LANDAUER

Stimulated by Bleuler and Jung, the speaker has conducted psychoanalytic investigations of some cases of schizophrenia, and has also on occasion made attempts to explain individual minor symptoms dynamically, instead of considering them descriptively, as has been done until now. The speaker illustrates by way of a number of examples these attempts whose therapeutic hopelessness became evident. There is one single chance: to inflict a new wound. This can be done either by discharging the patient early, thus allowing him to go out into practical life, or through analysis; in both instances, however, the results for the most part have proven to be unpromising.[1]

DISCUSSION

HITSCHMANN thinks analyses of schizophrenics that would be convincing are feasible only under particularly favorable circumstances; we must have more extensive case histories and details on a larger scale.

FEDERN misses the application of Freud's viewpoint of the threefold root of the symptoms in dementia praecox. The speaker kept looking for the pathogenic complex, while the essential point is the degree to which the regression has taken place (Tausk and Abraham have tried to show this).[2] Therapeutically, it often proves effective to make good by way of other persons[3] the disappointment an individual has suffered in his infantile love objects.

FREUD cautions against regarding the complex that yields the symptom as being also the one that is pathogenic. What is obvious in dementia praecox is the withdrawal of libido from external objects; hence, too, the unfeasibility of transference therapy.[4] This withdrawal of libido is a partial one. On the basis of what we know about paranoia, one can figure out the mechanism of dementia praecox and consider the following to be probable:

[1] It might be of interest to note that Bleuler, upon seeing a large number of patients in catatonic stupor together in a ward, would remove them to a ward of excited patients (*Versetzungstherapie*, "removal-therapy"). The change of environment often acted as a shock, and pulled them out of their stupor.

Bleuler was of the opinion that patients who appeared to be on the way to recovery ought to be discharged, even "at the risk of a patient throwing himself into the lake." His method frequently had good results.

[2] Abraham: "An Approach to the Psychoanalytic Exploration and Treatment of Manic-depressive Derangement and of Similar States" (1912). In: *Selected Papers on Psycho-Analysis.* pp. 137–156.

Tausk: "Compensation as a Means of Discounting the Motive of Repression." *Internat. J. Psycho-Anal.* (1924), 5: 130–140.

[3] This is a first formulation of the therapy for psychoses that Federn developed thirty years later in his "Psychoanalysis of Psychosis" (in: *Ego Psychology and the Psychoses.* New York: Basic Books, 1955).

[4] This view is no longer maintained. Since in the schizophrenic withdrawal of libido is only partial, it is felt that treatment can be started by making use of the remaining portion of the libido.

(1) The etiology is the same as that of the other neuroses.

(2) The apparent similarity to other neuroses goes very far; patients react at first with the less severe methods of repression; the neuroses have an admixture of individual traits of dementia or paranoia.[5]

(3) What is characteristic is the withdrawal of the libido onto the ego.

(4) Grouping of symptoms according to three sources: regression and residual symptoms and those of healing.

[5] That is to say, schizophrenia may set in as hysteria or obsessional neurosis; later, on the way to recovery, it may heal with hysterical or obsessional neurotic symptoms.

215

SCIENTIFIC MEETING *on Dec. 17, 1913*

Present: Federn, Freud, Friedjung, Hitschmann, Hellmuth, Jekels, Landauer, Nepallek, Rank, Reik, Reitler, Sachs, Sadger, Steiner, E. Weiss, K. Weiss, Winterstein.
Guest: Eng. Friedmann.

CRITICAL REVIEWS

[The minutes of this meeting are missing.]

216

SCIENTIFIC MEETING *on January 7, 1914*

Present: Federn, Freud, Hitschmann, Hellmuth, Jekels, Landauer, Nepallek, Rank, Reik, Sachs, Sadger, Steiner, Tausk, E. Weiss, K. Weiss, Winterstein.

PRESENTATION

Molnar

SPEAKER: SACHS

[The minutes of this meeting are missing.]

217

SCIENTIFIC MEETING *on January 14, 1914*

Present: Federn, Freud, Friedjung, Hellmuth, Hitschmann, Jekels, Landauer, Nepallek, Rank, Reik, Reitler, Sachs, Steiner, Tausk, E. Weiss.

Reitler, jr., Eng. Singer, Eng. Friedmann as guests.

DR. TAUSK moves that the society officially offer an opportunity to learn psychoanalysis and that it declare the courses he has organized to be official.

The full assembly speaks unanimously in favor of giving official courses, entrusts Dr. Tausk with the conduct of these courses during the current year, and refers him to Dr. Steiner for arrangement of details (place, publicity, etc.)

CLINICAL COMMUNICATIONS

FEDERN reports on a three-and-a-half-year-old boy who identified each piece of feces with a person or a thing and then shifted that procedure from the excremental sphere.

DR. HUG states that glossolalia in children is closely connected with anal erotism.

TAUSK refers to swearing in expressions that have to do with the anal zone as being characteristic of certain peoples (in contrast to others who swear in genital terms). This is followed by a lengthy discussion (Hug, Steiner, Friedjung, Sachs).

FEDERN speaks about an attack of *pavor nocturnus* suffered by the same boy, which he interprets as the breakthrough of a compassion for flies that had been suppressed during the day.

TAUSK is of the opinion that it is a question here of the typical reaction, by way of repression, to a sadistic impulse.

REITLER is inclined to regard it as an (inherited) spermatozoon-fantasy (flies).

LANDAUER calls attention to the anal meaning of flies, as animals who eat of decaying flesh (*Aastiere*)—which would tally well with the first story about the boy.

HITSCHMANN would like to differentiate two sorts of *pavor*: the psychogenic anxiety attack (aftereffect of a fright that has been experienced during the course of the day), and hysterical *pavor*, which is produced by repression.

PROF. FREUD sees in the fear of small animals material capable of being utilized in the most varied ways. The anal meaning is the most plausible one (Scarabeus), but it is not the only one. Often, these animals symbolize small children (not spermatozoa), the wriggling being an analog to [the baby's] kicking.

FRIEDJUNG finds an indication of the anal meaning of these animals in the infantile notion that feces are creeping out.

FEDERN reports, as a supplement to his exposition about the inhibition dream whose psychoanalytic meaning (counterwill) he was able to corroborate experimentally, several dreams of partial inhibition, by which he tries to demonstrate that the sensation of being inhibited sets in when the execution of an act becomes involved with a prohibition ("I must not"). He points emphatically to the analogy between this state and that in catatonia.

DR. STEINER calls attention to the fact that inhibition dreams often signify impotence.

224

DR. LANDAUER remarks that Bleuler mentions the counter-commands in negativism, and that Ziehen,[1] too, laid great stress on counterimpulses.

PROF. FREUD does not think Federn has made a new contribution to the problem of the inhibition dream. The question of why the inhibition makes its appearance here precisely in regard to movement has remained as unexplained as ever. By contrast, he regards as an important *novum* the reference to the analogy with schizophrenia. Catatonia could, in fact, be viewed as the motor expression of negativism—that is, of ambivalence.

TAUSK lays claim to priority in that statement, on the basis of a remark made in Dr. Pötzl's course.

FEDERN disputes the value of that remark as the basis for a priority claim.

DR. LANDAUER reports some brief stories about children.

PROF. FREUD calls attention to a gap in the theory of sex: the transforming of pregenital cathexis into the later genital one.

To this also belongs the original meaning of feces as part of one's ego and as a gift of love (later, in repression, as cursing).

JEKELS, referring to the connection between hatred and anal erotism, raises the question of whether hatred as a means of repressing love is not a general mechanism.

DR. SACHS discusses Dostoevski's novel *The Husband*, calling special attention to the husband's love for his wife's seducer (together with the ambivalent impulse of hate) which is clearly expressed there—a love that Sachs has inferred analytically in Molnar's "Tale of the Wolf."

---

[1] A German psychiatrist and opponent of Freud.

225

218

SCIENTIFIC MEETING *on January 21, 1914*

Present: Federn, Freud, Friedjung, Heller, Hellmuth, Hitschmann, Jekels, Landauer, Nepallek, Rank, Reik, Sachs, Sadger, Steiner, Tausk, K. Weiss, Winterstein.

Balloting on Dresden. 17 yes votes.[1]

REVIEWS

[The minutes of this meeting are missing.]

[1] The intended congress in Dresden could not take place because of the outbreak of World War I.

219

SCIENTIFIC MEETING *on January 28, 1914*

Present: Federn, Freud, Friedjung, Hellmuth, Hitschmann, Jekels, Landauer, Nepallek, Rank, Reik, Sachs, Tausk, E. Weiss, K. Weiss, Winterstein.
Guest: Eng. Friedmann.

PRESENTATION

Narcissism

SPEAKER: TAUSK

[The minutes of this meeting are missing.]

220

SCIENTIFIC MEETING *on February 4, 1914*

Present: Dattner, Federn, Freud, Friedjung, Hellmuth, Hitschmann, Jekels, Landauer, Nepallek, Rank, Reik, Rosenstein, Sachs, Sadger, Tausk, K. Weiss, Winterstein.

REVIEWS

[The minutes of this meeting are missing.]

221

Present: Federn, Freud, Friedjung, Hitschmann, Hug [i.e., Hellmuth], Jekels, Landauer, Nepallek, Rank, Reik, Sachs, Sadger, Silberer, Steiner, Tausk, Dr. Weiss, Winterstein.
Guest: Miss Bloch.

PRESENTATION

Children's Games

SPEAKER: HUG [SIC]

[The minutes of this meeting are missing.]

222

SCIENTIFIC MEETING *on February 18, 1914*

Present: Federn, Freud, Friedjung, Hitschmann, Hellmuth, Jekels, Nepallek, Rank, Reik, Sachs, Sadger, Steiner, Dr. Weiss.
Guest: Krauss.

BRIEF COMMUNICATIONS

[The minutes of this meeting are missing.]

223

SCIENTIFIC MEETING *on February 25, 1914*

Present: Federn, Freud, Friedjung, Hitschmann, Hellmuth, Jekels, Nepallek, Rank, Reik, Sachs, Sadger, Steiner, Tausk, E. Weiss, K. Weiss, Winterstein, Landauer, Friedmann.

DISCUSSION ON THE INFANTILE OEDIPUS COMPLEX

PROF. FREUD opens the discussion by remarking that the point is to demonstrate the presence in the child of the Oedipus complex. One part of our opponents maintain that it does not exist at all, whereas others declare it to be merely a mode of expression in the adult, as well as in neurosis. The value of observing the Oedipus complex in the child lies in the fact that there it has only one meaning, and has the same significance for *infantile neurosis* [as it has for neurosis in adults]; consequently, the view [we have taken of the infantile Oedipus complex, in relation to the infantile neurosis] is also determining for the neurosis in the adult.

The complex is universal, that is true; but to a great extent it has been repressed or transformed, so that in many instances we have to be satisfied with indications; moreover, certain components of the Oedipus complex cannot at all be shown to exist in the child.

231

There are several sources at our disposal: (1) direct observation; (2) previous observations already known or published; and (3) appropriate biographies.

It will be the task of the discussion to consider critically the contributions, particularly from the viewpoint of whether the facts can be explained in Adler's sense, in terms of the striving for power or whether, in accordance with the Zurich view, the relationship which is no longer sexual is represented in these facts.

DISCUSSION[1]

HITSCHMANN sees a difficulty in the way of accepting these facts [i.e., the Oedipus complex] in that a substantial part of the opponents of them do no analysis; a further difficulty is presented in that at first only a crude schema was given, a schema that represents the theoretically ideal case, which cannot always be found in practice in its complete form: one forgets the repressed portion and the ambivalent impulses.

The distortion of the clear picture hinges also on the personality of the parents (which parent first showed the child affection, and to what extent); it is on that, in part, that the development in a homosexual direction depends. Up to now, only little consideration has been given to the "inverse" Oedipus complex connected with it.

A further difficulty lies in the fact that the opponents always think of an intercourse that is fully carried through; perverse impulses, let alone tender ones, they do not understand. There is also the question of whether and how far, once the child has learned to distinguish between father and mother, an instinctive attraction of the sexes is a contributing factor.

Hitschmann thinks the observation is, in terms of our topic, not sexual enough. Some things could also be interpreted differently: for instance, the little girl's wanting to be a mama as a wish to be grown up.

TAUSK considers the contribution, if placed in the right spot [in the publication], to be very appropriate.

[1] This discussion is on the remarks by Freud above. The later discussions in this meeting are not recorded. They may have been circulated in writing previously.

FEDERN comments that included among the evidences of the Oedipus complex is also cruder sexuality, which one finds in children side by side with tenderness. The desire to be grown-up is not the ruling factor in all children in the same way (there are also those who want to keep on being children); what determines this, in the individual case, is the child's total attitude on this question at the specific time.

LANDAUER thinks that in itself the contribution is not conclusive; the tenderness of children toward their parents is not indeed being denied.

PROF. FREUD finds hardly adequate the way in which the discussion is being carried on—that is, by rejecting or accepting a contribution in terms of its being conclusive or not conclusive. One observation cannot prove everything; the point is to judge how far its conclusiveness reaches.

In the girl's wish to put herself in the mother's place, the affection for the father is evident, to be sure; but the [mother's] power cannot be completely ruled out. It is interesting that, side by side with the manifest love for the mother, unconscious relations to the father come to light. The observation concerning the boy who is four years younger is clearer: he is tenderly in love with his mother and jealous of his father.

It is true, as Dr. Landauer remarked, that the tender relations are not being denied; for psychoanalysis, however, it is a question of finding evidence of the hostile impulses.

There is still the question of what expression of cruder erotism has been observed in the child. In the child, tenderness and sexuality are closely linked with each other: he relates his erotic inclinations to those persons toward whom he is affectionate.

DR. WEISS finds that there is apparently no agreement on the concept of sexuality, else one could not deny conclusiveness to his case. A striving to become grown-up seems to be out of the question in the light of that identification with the mother, because the child did not at that time express anything of the sort. The sexual note is for the most part clearly shown in the child's facial expression [and body language]. As to more obviously sexual occurrences, it

233

is to be mentioned that the boy, at the age of a little over a year, tried to unbutton the mother's blouse.

TAUSK relates about the same girl that she was once riding on his back, and when her mother came in she said with embarrassment: "That's not the thing to do."

HITSCHMANN, on the basis of these additions, takes back part of his objections. A great deal does depend on whether it is the father or the mother who is affectionate, which one of them does the punishing and in what way.

Jealousy also appears in animals (dog).

PROF. FREUD admonishes the discussants to take into consideration also the extent to which the Oedipus complex is a reflection of the sexual behavior of the parents.

FRIEDJUNG comments, in reference to [the boy's] unbuttoning the blouse, that that could be taken as a recollection of nursing. It is a question here of the entire ensemble, which is in most instances clearly erotic; besides, in Friedjung's experience, it occurs solely with boys.

PROF. FREUD discusses, in this connection, the trauma of weaning; as the prototype of being denied, it offers much that is of interest. The quite frequent later aversion to milk on the part of many people, and particularly to the skin on it, is probably connected with that instance of being denied. One should expect children, after they have been weaned, to have no interest in the breast for a while, and the interest mentioned by Weiss and Friedjung to be interpreted as a resurgence of sexuality and not as a recollection.

FRIEDJUNG relates a number of varied impressions of weaning which hinge on the way in which it was carried out and also on the time at which it was done. As to a latency period, in Freud's sense, he has seen nothing of it. On the other hand, even during the nursing period the infant uses the breast for fondling and playing.

FEDERN is able to confirm by way of one case that the child, having been suddenly weaned, no longer wanted the breast when he was offered it later on; but after some time he did show a sexual interest in it. Another child (a boy), who had been weaned gradually and easily, tried later with less intensity to uncover the mother's breast, but out of obviously sexual motives.

DR. WEISS, supplementing his report, relates that the boy was sexual only when the mother was present and when the father became affectionate toward her.

PROF. FREUD, too, stresses the influence on the child's behavior of the parents' presence or absence. A boy of four or five years is on very good terms with his father if the mother is not present.

LANDAUER is able on the basis of an analysis to trace the idiosyncrasy about milk back to the trauma of weaning: a child who had been suddenly weaned refused for two days any intake of food. It might also have some bearing whether it was the mother who had done the nursing, or a wet-nurse from the outside. In the case of a wet-nurse, the jealousy can be absent (as in the case mentioned), because one is the sole possessor of the love object.

FEDERN, too, stresses how significant parental behavior can be with regard to the Oedipus complex. If a great difference exists between the warmth of the father's love and that of the mother, this opens a direct pathway to homosexuality. As far as the jealousy of animals is concerned that Hitschmann mentioned, it is to be noted that the domestic animal takes on a relationship that follows along the lines of the Oedipus complex, which does not, after all, represent anything but the relationship of an animal, determined by the immature sexual instinct.

The presence or absence of one parent changes [the child's] behavior continually, and in a striking manner. Under such conditions, one cannot speak of a power complex.

E. WEISS, speaking with regard to parental behavior, relates the case of a three-year-old boy who was affectionate toward the father because the latter behaved in the same way [toward him].

FRIEDJUNG, on the matter of the child's reaching for the breast, raises the question of whether it has a sexual meaning or should be regarded as an expression of the eating-instinct; on the basis of his own observations of children, he would support the former. The speaker further calls attention to the often enormous difficulties that stand in the way of a relactation; it seems, therefore, that the pleasure-toned intake of food quickly disappears.

JEKELS comments that the parents' attitude is not of such significance after all; if this were so, it would hardly be compatible with [speaking about] the animal instinct.

HITSCHMANN, for the sake of verifying the connection between aversion to milk and weaning, would like to have observed children who have been brought up exclusively on the bottle.

A child's jealousy can be directed against any person who wants to contend with him for his mother, just as the bashfulness expressed to Tausk by the little girl, might indicate that it is vis-à-vis any man (not only the father) that she has sexual feelings.

PROF. FREUD calls attention to the fact that the circumstances supposed by Hitschmann would support the idea of an acquired component of the Oedipus complex.

SADGER mentions, on the basis of his researches on homosexuality, that during an early period of their life these men were being pampered more by father than by mother.

NEPALLEK relates the case of a lady who had been weaned as late as at two years of age and would then spit out any milk that was offered her in a glass; up to this day—she is now about thirty years old—she has continued to refuse milk. She has always known how to conceal her breasts carefully and with great skill, and she has also strictly seen to it that the same thing holds true for her mother.

DR. WEISS, countering Hitschmann's objection, asserts that the boy feels no jealousy toward his sister as far as the mother is concerned; on the contrary, he feels united with her and his mother against the father.

As to the relationship of the parents to the child, it is to be noted that the parents' caresses do not always make a difference, either; the feeling is present from the start.

PROF. FREUD can corroborate, by way of a case, Tausk's remark that the child's attitude toward his parents can reveal itself with less inhibition and therefore more clearly in relation to someone who is an outsider to the family. The case is that of a three-year-old boy who made a visitor he did not know feel the jealousy that was clearly meant for his father; the boy was indeed intensely in love with his mother. Such a visit can be used directly as a litmus for these relationships.

FRIEDJUNG tells, in this connection, of a little boy who regularly makes sarcastic remarks about male visitors—but never, however, about female ones. Occasionally, he dares to make such remarks even toward his own father.

PROF. FREUD states that this is clearly erotic and has nothing to do with other motives.

The more one delves into these relationships, the more it becomes apparent that the relationship between man and woman is a derivative of the father-mother series.

TAUSK tells about two boys who were in love with the same girl; she first favored the older boy, but then the father of the two of them. The hostility that the younger boy had felt toward his brother turned against the girl (not against the father), because she was now threatening to deprive him also of his father's love.

DR. WEISS thinks that in this case the homosexual factor is of particular importance.

HITSCHMANN traces the boy's aversion toward male visitors in general back to jealousy toward the mother. It is important to study the boy's passing over from the Oedipus complex to love for the father.

DISCUSSION ON THE FIRST REPORT BY HITSCHMANN

FEDERN: persons who are more strongly sexual in childhood have clearer memories of their early sexual attitudes and of the Oedipus complex.

Second Report by Hitschmann

PROF. FREUD finds the detail of the blinding conclusive.

TAUSK has the impression that this case does not have anything

237

to do with the Oedipus complex, but rather pertains to the early sexuality of the child in general.

FEDERN describes an analogous case of a child who had first been sleeping between his parents, then alongside his mother; there he would hold her in his embrace, with constant sexual excitement (later, he showed psychic impotence). He was careful not to let the mother feel the erection. It is immensely frequent among the "lower classes" for the boy to sleep alongside his mother.

Third Report by Hitschmann

PROF. FREUD thinks that in order for them to be effective, report I and II would have to be placed at a definite point [in the publication].

SACHS reports on a boy who, at the age of about seven to eight, acquired a stepmother who was, in every respect, outstanding. He never dared to kiss her, even though he was "head over heels" in love with her. Once, when a friend visited her while she was sick and, in parting, gave her a kiss, the sexual love became overpowering in the stepson, and he kissed the woman passionately.

DISCUSSION ON THE REPORT BY BARON WINTERSTEIN

DR. LANDAUER, in connection with the fact that, in this case, the childhood memories shut out the father, relates a memory from the seventh year of life: the father was absent for four months, and the son, before meeting with him again, asked for his photograph, because he thought he was not going to recognize his father.

In response to a remark by TAUSK, to the effect that this nonrecognition is a familiar phenomenon, the speaker emphasizes that what is involved here is the *fear* of that possibility.

224

SCIENTIFIC MEETING *on March 4, 1914*

Present: Federn, Freud, Hellmuth, Hitschmann, Jekels, Krauss, Landauer, Nepallek, Rank, Sachs, Sadger, Steiner, Tausk, E. Weiss.

PRESENTATION

On the Demarcation of the Reality Principle and the Pleasure Principle[1]

SPEAKER: FEDERN

Taking as his point of departure a sentence from a paper by Dr. Reik, "Cynicism is an offshoot of the reality principle," the speaker discusses the differences between Freud's views on this question and those of Bleuler and Jung, in order to stress the correctness of Freud's conception.

[1] On May 11, 1914, Federn presented a paper on this topic before the New York Psychoanalytic Society. It was published in *Z.* (1914), 2:492–505, under the title "Lustprinzip und Realitätsprinzip," as well as in English, in 1915, in the *Psychoanalytic Review*, 2:1–11 under the title "Some General Remarks on the Principles of Pain-pleasure and of Reality."

It is in accordance with the pleasure principle that a person is acting when he makes decisions on the basis of the degree of his affectivity at the moment: he either does something that gratifies the instinct—in which case pleasure is achieved—or, in the case of denial, he will express unpleasure, or else he will fulfill his instinct so as to avoid unpleasure.

The pleasure-unpleasure principle is, however, capable of development. The second stage is the one in which sublimated reactions have an inhibiting effect; the third is the one in which the individual does not wait for a feeling of unpleasure to be set into motion, but acts preventively.

The first stage might be termed that of the domination of instinct, its goal being the achievement of pleasure; the second, that of the rule of feelings, with the goal of [achieving] happiness; the third, that of morality, the goal being [the fulfillment of] duty. What they all have in common is that they take their course according to the affective need and that their goal is to gain pleasure and to avoid unpleasure. The factor of time is not taken into account; what is aimed at is momentary success. It is the reality principle that introduces logic (deliberation) and time (referring to the future).

The application to society of the reality principle, which (except for the affective factor) has been learned in the struggle with nature, is a cornerstone in the development of mankind—a cornerstone that is marked by Socrates. It was only after Socrates that cynicism became possible. Cynicism appears when we are bound affectively while another person overrides that and acts in accordance with reality. The cynic works momentarily without affect; it is only *in statu nascendi* that we have the impression of cynicism. Cynicism aims at a carrying through of the sober reality principle (FREUD: Cynicism is a socially useful brutality). This, however, holds true only with qualifications.

Even the cynic acknowledges the primary focus on pleasure; that is why cynicism is so often encountered in a witty form, etc. For psychological reasons, the cynic makes use of the old primitive sources of pleasure. The ancient Cynics turned against the primitive pleasure that was at that time still held in esteem. The cynic carries the reality principle through, as against the pleasure principle, but he does not care about the future; it is the infantile sort of reality principle. The narcissistic gratification gained from intellectual activity has the effect of forepleasure.

The opposite of the cynic is the sentimentalist who, on those occasions in which the normal person acts in accordance with the reality principle, reacts by way of the pleasure principle and takes narcissistic pleasure in his feelings. The sentimentalist is incapable of being witty.

The cynic and the sentimentalist represent actual and fleeting progress toward the reality principle or the pleasure principle, as the case may be. The stable condition with regard to the reality principle is represented by the skeptic and the natural scientist, while with regard to the pleasure principle it is represented by the naïve person.

DISCUSSION

HITSCHMANN thinks that a different moral height is necessary for the cynic. It does not have to be a matter of feelings; it can also be a matter of valuations. Kahane's definition of the *"Schmock"* (one who reacts to a situation with exaggerated affect) finds its counterpart in the cynic, who puts forth *less* affect than a situation calls for. There is no need to draw in the pleasure principle and the reality principle.

LANDAUER regards cynicism as a compromise between two opposite strivings.

SACHS finds that the two sections of the paper—that is, the general part about the two principles, and the specific application to the cynic—are to be viewed in different ways. As to the first, there has been a mistake, inasmuch as the speaker wanted to take the two principles concretely although they are meant to be taken in an entirely abstract sense. Besides, there always exist only compromises between the two. The development of the principles, one out of the other, is unclear; some conflict or other must have arisen.

Crude cynicism in and of itself is not noticed unless some ingredient is added (form, personality, situation) that reconciles one with it.[2] What was most convincing [in the presentation] was the contrasting of the cynic and the sentimentalist. The contrast between pleasure principle and reality principle, however, is not to be found in that.

TAUSK considers only topic and title to be of value; he cannot accord any recognition to the exposition. The reality principle and acting in accordance with it were frequently confounded; in other respects, too, vagueness in concepts and formulations was prevalent. The entire basis of the paper is erroneous; what was correct was the contrast of cynic and sentimentalist.

PROF. FREUD characterizes the paper as a valuable achievement, even if it is lacking in ultimate clarity. Two themes have been fused with one another—themes whose belonging together may be subject to doubt. It may be that the two principles do have some slight involvement with the theme of cynicism, but that they are at its root is quite doubtful. In any case, the investigation ought to start from the theme of cynicism. The view that it was intercourse with nature that taught men to turn away from the pleasure principle is also held by Frazer; but it is not completely convincing. Primitive men do not, indeed, yet have any discernment of inanimate nature.

The most significant part of the paper is the attempt to explain the passing over from the pleasure principle to the reality principle by way of the mechanisms of anxiety and defense (conscience)— that is, by way of the insertions that take the place of the instincts for us.

[2] This sentence is so condensed in the German that it is impossible to give it a meaningful translation.

225

SCIENTIFIC MEETING on *March 11, 1914*

Present: Federn, Freud, Friedjung, Hellmuth, Hitschmann, Jekels, Landauer, Nepallek, Rank, Sachs, Sadger, Silberer, Steiner, Tausk, E. Weiss, K. Weiss.
Guests: Friedmann, Krauss.

PRESENTATION

A Case of Foot Fetishism[1]

SPEAKER: PROF. S. FREUD

The case in question is that of a 47-year-old foot fetishist with psychic impotence who was treated for a short time but without success. His peculiar traits made it possible to cast a new light onto the genesis of this perversion, and to point out the constitutional and

---

[1] Freud had presented a paper on the genesis of fetishism at an earlier meeting (see Volume II, Minutes 89, pp. 338–352). In 1927 he published a paper, "On Fetishism" (*S.E.*, 21:149–157).

accidental preconditions of this attitude. These are at the bottom of Binet's "childhood trauma," which shows the perversion already fixated.

From the case history and the analytic reconstruction of the patient's sexual development, the following overall standpoints emerge with regard to the origin of a perversion and particularly of foot fetishism:

Probably an excessive stress on the erotogenicity of the foot, and a correspondingly early abnormal sexual stimulation (which in this case most likely came from the mother, who was herself sexually quite abnormal), which seems to have taken the foot as object.

Then a regression during the course of sexual development, as a consequence of sexual intimidation—that is, one such as occurs in childhood and disturbs the development, and one in puberty that calls forth the fixation. The childhood disturbance is, in the case of our patient, produced by castration threats on the part of the father and by the sight of the sister's genitals (childhood recollection, in which he is lying with his head between the legs of his naked sister); because of rickets, this sister wore leg splints, and it is from this that the narrow, straight foot-ideal that is exciting to him is derived.

In the "traumatic" scene of his sixth year of life, in which the patient was intensely interested in the foot of his English governess, the perversion appears to be already fixated. To begin with, however, it remains latent up to the time of puberty, when the second powerful frightening-away from the female genitals (sexual intercourse) took place by way of his tutor (a repetition of the father's threats). To this is added the symbolic meaning of the foot, which replaces the penis that is missing in the woman (as a result of castration). (Patient dreams that his wife possesses a penis.) Shortly after this intimidation in puberty, the impotence set in that has lasted to this day. His very early interest in the foot (creeping on the floor as if he were a dog; keeping himself under the table) is explained by his wanting to see the genitals from below upwards. The great trauma concerning the sister, however, produces an inhibition of his sexual curiosity; it is from here that his regression begins: his interest is thrown back to the starting point of his sexual investigation—that is, the foot. Another precondition is accordingly created—predominance of the drive to look, and fixation by way of topical or "geographical" regression.

Lastly, foot fetishism appertains as a subspecies to masochism, which is connected with the relationship to man and woman. The most significant factor, however, is the child's attitude to sexual intimidation: on the one hand, he will struggle and defend his penis; on the other hand, he will accept castration and reconcile himself to the female role. It seems to depend on the primary bisexual *Anlage* whether he turns to activity or to passivity; this is determining for whether the outcome is a neurosis or a perversion. Someone who has been intimidated early by a man has a tendency to be masochistic toward women, and the other way around. The briefest formula for the foot fetishist would be: a masochistic secret voyeur.

DISCUSSION

TAUSK tries, by means of an example of his own, to supplement a detail of the analysis, from which it follows that the homosexual searches quite explicitly for himself.

It is not necessarily a matter of becoming reconciled to the female role. Man has in general two modalities for having done with the problem of the mother whom he has wooed in vain: (1) by turning toward the man; and (2) by over and over again representing (as a symptom) the relationship one has had to the mother, whereby one comes into contact with her, after all.

STEINER misses in this case the urge to smell, which is generally so significant in the foot fetishist. A masochistic attitude on the part of the patient usually warrants an unfavorable prognosis.

HITSCHMANN calls attention to the negligible conclusiveness of the "corroborating" dreams, which are occupied with the material of the latest session.

FEDERN points out as one of the preconditions for becoming a foot fetishist that the sexual instinct must have been roused at a time when the child is still crawling. The fact that the patient as a child lay between his sister's thighs also seems to have been not without bearing on his later oral perversion. The constitutional pre-

245

condition is tantamount to the question of at what age the individual components of the sexual instinct come to be stressed, and of how far they are inhibited by the outside world, or how far they are able to manifest themselves in action. A masochistic attitude is produced, not only by the threat of castration, but by any inhibition directed toward the functioning of the male membrum. Present in every masochist is also a marked female constitution. It is worth mentioning that manual masturbation is—as in this case—shunned by most masochists.

RANK points to a possible confirmation to be found in paranoia of the role of sexual intimidation that has been described; there, this entire portion of development seems to be repeated in pathological distortion. According to Freud's expositions, the later homosexuals would have experienced sexual intimidation at the hands of a woman, and would then adopt a masochistic homosexual attitude toward men. With this would tally very well the fact that, not infrequently, the *outbreak* of paranoia is characterized by sexual persecution (masochistic) on the part of a woman, whereas later on, quite logically, the turning toward the man (in the form of defense), and finally erotomania (as an attempt at a cure), would reveal the attitude toward the woman in the form in which it was originally desired.

PROF. FREUD, in his closing words, first reacts to Tausk's remarks, by referring to the fact that the homosexual's infatuation with himself had already been set forth explicitly by Sadger, as well as by himself. As to the completion of the interpretation with regard to the one point, he is in agreement; but he cannot accept the idea that the patient only incidentally places himself in the female role. The two mechanisms of masochism, as reaction and as adaptation, contain too much construction, just as do Federn's remarks on the same theme (identification of masochism with passive instincts).

It is true that the urge to smell plays no role in this case; it may be that this urge was replaced by voyeurism. The unfavorable prognosis in cases of masochism seems at present to give way, after all, to more favorable chances.[2]

[2] According to my experiences, it seems that foot fetishism stands on the borderline to schizophrenia—that is, the fetishist attempts to sustain the relation to the object by means of the fetish (as a symbol of the object). Thereby a split of the ego is brought on, since the role of the fetish is both accepted and denied.

226

Present: Federn, Freud, Hitschmann, Hug, Jekels, Nepallek, Rank, Sachs, Sadger, Silberer, Tausk, E. Weiss, K. Weiss, Landauer.

Discussion on the Infantile Oedipus Complex
(Discussion on Rank: Biographical Material)

LANDAUER mentions that Stendhal, in "The Cenci," has dealt with an incest relationship between father and daughter. Also, it is striking that in his love scenes the hero tries to win over his beloved by infantile means (lamentation, illness).

SACHS finds a counterpart to Baudelaire in the characteristic motif of Thackeray, who identifies in his works with his stepfather.

HITSCHMANN sees a factor supporting the Oedipus complex in those cases in which the father is younger and the mother older. With regard to girls, the neglected mother plays an important role.

An eight-year-old girl who falls ill with an obsessional neurosis betrays in her dreams her death wish directed against the mother. A 12-year-old girl who is suffering from an obsessional- and anxiety-neurosis shows clearly that she is in love with her father—a feeling

247

he returns. The anxiety fails to appear, or it disappears when the child is allowed to get into her father's bed with him. This habit goes back to her earliest childhood (second to third year). Consciously, she has expressed the wish from her seventh year on. She has had typical oedipal dreams at earlier times as well. Aversion toward her mother is not manifest because her parents' marriage is a happy one.

In cases such as these, it becomes apparent that the Oedipus complex is the content of the childhood neurosis. Children's poetry also often reveals the Oedipus complex. Later, the oedipal attitude is often rendered unclear by an aversion toward the entire family. Of interest are the later reaction formations to the oedipal attitude— as, for instance, the assertion that the mother is so old and ugly that erotic love for her is quite impossible.

PROF. FREUD finds the first example very well suited for the pathological series. It would be better to avoid the term "Electra complex" (Jung), because of the complexities of the relationships in the Electra story.

TAUSK confirms the important role played [in girls] by the neglected mother. It belongs among those things that persist: they reach far into life and also supply artistic motifs. This does not, however, belong among the earliest motives, for the original attitude is brought about by the fact that the *child* is being neglected.

FEDERN raises the question of the extent to which girls are active in their oedipal attitude. At the start, the girl has exactly the same attitude as the boy—that is, she is jealous of her father. It is only later that the female Oedipus complex appears; often it appears in girls when a new child arrives—which means an intensive disappointment inflicted on her by the mother.[1]

SACHS finds in accord with this the fact that during their earliest childhood years girls are also active in other ways.

---

[1] A most pertinent remark, which was only much later elaborated in detail by Freud, in "Einige psychische Folgen des anatomischen Geschlechtsunterschieds" [Some Psychological Consequences of the Anatomical Distinction between the Sexes], 1925; *S.E.*, 19: 243–258; and "Über die weibliche Sexualität" [Female Sexuality], 1931; *S.E.*, 21: 223–243.

248

PROF. FREUD adds to Federn's exposition the question of just when the Oedipus complex is formed. We have to expect certain prestages. The point is, under what conditions and at what stage of development does it arise? The initially uniform attitude [on the part of both boy and girl] toward the mother is certainly significant.

FEDERN tells about a little three-and-a-half-year-old boy who in his play with animals simply ignores the male (father-animal): "That one, there is no need for," he says.

WEISS sees in the two children he has observed a great difference as to the time of development of the Oedipus complex. The girl's positive attitude toward her father had been latently present for a long time before it became manifest—which happened when he began to occupy himself more intimately with the child. The girl showed an interest in sexual matters, and the father enlightened her about them. The boy, on the other hand, had from the beginning a negative attitude toward the father. It is only recently (at what age?) that a certain degree of latency has begun to set in; even though rarely, he is friendly toward the father. In the girl, it seems to be a matter of an "even-handed" attitude toward both parents. That may perhaps be connected with the fact that during the very earliest period of life the ego drives (feeding) play the chief role, whereas the sexual instincts do not yet have any psychic significance for the child.

JEKELS recalls that with dream interpretation, as well as with symptom interpretation, the homosexual attitude is invariably to be found at the deepest stratum. From this, one should conclude that the homosexual attitude is the primary one. There remains then the question of whether the heterosexual attitude comes about by way of reaction or as a consequence of having been attracted by the other sex.

PROF. FREUD replies that this psychological stratification does not repeat the chronological order [of appearance of these attitudes], and he points to the negligible significance the difference between the sexes has for the child. That fact is sufficient in itself to rule out any attempt to deal with the entire problem of neuroticism from the standpoint of the differences between the sexes.

249

DR. HUG supplements Federn's report about the little boy with the animals by adding that the same boy also asserted, in reference to plants, that they have no father: they need only a mother.

HITSCHMANN calls attention to the fact that the complex stressed by Adler, "I want to be a boy, or masculine," hinges on the Oedipus complex. A girl who is in love with her father does not, of course, have that attitude, and the girl who has been referred to as an example has indeed given assurances to that effect, being quite content with her feminine role. It is only where the mother is not esteemed at home in terms of her being female, and the daughter does not wish to play the role of the despised mother—only there can this [attitude] make its appearance. The transformation of the boy who loves his mother into a somewhat *more* masculine person probably takes place at a time when the Oedipus complex is receding to some extent. This latency is once again interrupted at puberty.

RANK confirms the significance of the neglected mother, even with regard to the Oedipus complex of the boy. The mother who is really ill-treated converts into reality those fantasies that are typically directed toward the mother's ill-treatment by the father, and that is why they are as persistent as Tausk thought.

FEDERN reports on a little girl who very early expressed the wish to be a boy. That was since her second year, when she saw her brother's genital and said that she too wanted to have that. Soon, however, she did become reconciled to the feminine role—namely, when she succeeded in identifying with her *pregnant* mother. In contrast to the boy's attitude toward his father, as Weiss has described it, the speaker mentions a boy who initially loved his father more, because the latter would carry him around a lot; this predilection came to an end, however, when the father began to tell him what to do and what not to do.

PROF. FREUD comments that the child's object choice is guided by all his other needs. One should trace under what influences changes in the Oedipus complex come about. Reactions set in in conjunction with the accidental ego-gratifications that children experience.

TAUSK adds a typical fantasy in reference to the neglected mother; it is also found in fairy tales. The fantasy is of the beloved little old mother whom the son at the height of his life tends and waits upon; the father is missing, and the son makes amends to the mother for her earlier neglect.

LANDAUER mentions in this connection a scene from *Gil Blas*, when the protagonist returns to his parents as a nobleman, just as his father is dying. In the same novel, there is an analogue to the story of Ninon.

FEDERN refers to the Oedipus complex as the cause of either bachelorhood or of marriage after the mother's death. In the latter case, the wife is clearly turned into a mother substitute.

HITSCHMANN has doubts about a "dear-little-old mother" complex on the part of the child; for him, the mother is always young and beautiful. ("Dear little old mother" might perhaps signify the grandmother.)

FEDERN thinks the youngest child might have this complex (the mother is now older).

PROF. FREUD stresses that for the child, age plays no role. Grandparents serve merely as parent substitutes.

The material [when it is prepared for publication] could be arranged in four categories: (1) direct observations of normal children and (2) of pathological children; (3) memories uncovered in analysis; and (4) biographical data.

251

227

SCIENTIFIC MEETING on *April 1, 1914*

Present: Federn, Freud, Friedjung, Hitschmann, Jekels, Landauer, Nepallek, Rank, Sachs, Sadger, Silberer, Steiner, Tausk, E. Weiss, K. Weiss, Winterstein.
Guests: Miss Bloch, Eng. Friedmann, H. Jones, Krauss.

PRESENTATION

The Double[1]

SPEAKER: RANK

[The minutes of this meeting are missing.]

---

[1] "Der Doppelgänger; eine psychoanalytische Studie" [The Double; a Psychoanalytic Study] was published in *Imago* (1914), 3: 97–164.

228

SCIENTIFIC MEETING *on April 8, 1914*

Present: Federn, Freud, Heller, Hitschmann, Hug, Jekels, Nepallek, Rank, Sachs, Sadger, Silberer, Steiner, Tausk, E. Weiss, K. Weiss, Winterstein.

Sokolnicka as guest.

Discussion on the Infantile Oedipus Complex:
On Federn's Contribution

DR. WEISS considers the conclusions arrived at incorrect. The crudely sexual Oedipus complex does not belong among the rarities. The fact that the boy [in Federn's case] does not want to grow any bigger indicates that this wish is not the rule. The fear of flies does not seem so easy to understand.

SACHS agrees with Weiss' exposition in that he finds the Oedipus complex in Federn's material obvious.

HITSCHMANN thinks a narcissistic child will want to stay small.

JEKELS finds there has been too much schematization: there is not only hatred for the father, but also love for him: it is out of identification [with him] that the child wants to grow up.

TAUSK remarks, in reference to the fear of flies, that flies in a dream signify something other than they do in the waking state. It is not in the least astounding that the repression [in this case] proceeds so rapidly.

FEDERN tends to concur with Hitschmann in the matter of wanting to grow up or to stay small. In many cases, the Oedipus complex is not grossly obvious; there are some things—even in childhood—that only psychoanalysis is able to bring to light.

PROF. FREUD finds the Oedipus complex in Federn's case obvious enough. It is our task to establish that the behavior has only sexual motives. Narcissism can have been present long before its manifestation is brought about by an actual occasion (as happens, in this instance, at the age of three-and-a-half). Children select what they tell their parents; they do not tell them everything they tell to their siblings, for instance, to servants, or to others. This concern with the censorship on the part of those around them comes into play very early: the child reads in their facial expression (just as the patient wants to do in treatment) what is agreeable to his parents. The wish of children to stay small or to grow up changes, as Jekels has correctly noted: the child wants to settle down at the point at which he gains pleasure.

On Tausk's Contribution:

FEDERN: Sleeping in mother's bed is of importance to the Oedipus complex. A strongly sexual child will always want to sleep with his mother. Of importance also is the parents' behavior: it is Laius who exposes Oedipus.

HITSCHMANN: The prohibition against masturbation plays an important part if it comes from the parent of the same sex.

PROF. FREUD would like to support this view emphatically. Everything that restrains the sexuality of the small child—this generally comes from the father—will preform the child's behavior and throws some light on the nature of object love. It is in this sense that the Oedipus complex, which renders a normal love-choice secure, becomes a foundation of society. Tausk's case belongs close to the pathological series. Discord between the parents has an exciting effect on the child's sexuality.

229

SCIENTIFIC MEETING on *April 22, 1914*

Present: Dattner, Federn, Friedjung, Hitschmann, Hellmuth, Jekels, Landauer, Nepallek, Rank, Sachs, Sadger, Steiner, K. Weiss, Winterstein.

Guests: H. Jones, Loe [Lou?], Kaum [Krauss?], MacCurdy, Sokolnicka.

PRESENTATION

Napoleon[1]

SPEAKER: JEKELS

[The minutes of this meeting are missing.]

---

[1] "Der Wendepunkt im Leben Napoleons I" [The Turning Point in the Life of Napoleon I] (In Author's *Selected Papers*). New York: International Universities Press, 1952, pp. 1–73.

230

SCIENTIFIC MEETING *on April 29, 1914*

Present: Freud, Hitschmann, Hug, Jekels, Landauer, Nepallek, Rank, Sachs, Sadger, Steiner, Tausk, Weiss.
Guests: Friedmann, Krauss, Sokolnicka.

REVIEWS

[The minutes of this meeting are missing.]

231

SCIENTIFIC MEETING *on May 6, 1914*

Present: Freud, Friedjung, Hitschmann, Jekels, Landauer, Nepallek, Rank, Sadger, Steiner, Tausk, E. Weiss, Winterstein.
Guests: Mr. Joliasch, Krauss, Sokolnicka.

PRESENTATION

Psychosis

SPEAKER: LANDAUER

[The minutes of this meeting are missing.]

232

SCIENTIFIC MEETING *on May 20, 1914*

Present: Freud, Friedjung, Hitschmann, Hug-Hellmuth, Jekels, Nepallek, Rank, Sadger, Steiner, Tausk, E. Weiss, K. Weiss, Landauer.
Guests: Krauss, Sokolnicka.

DISCUSSION ON THE INFANTILE OEDIPUS COMPLEX:

Comments on Landauer's First Contribution

TAUSK mentions, as a counterpart to coquetry, the utterance of a six-and-a-half-year-old boy: upon seeing a very striking lady's hairdo, he says, "Mother does not wear anything like that (as disgusting); if she did, then every man would spit on her."

JEKELS asks about the reason why children who have already been enlightened (as in Landauer's case) show a tendency to forget all over again what they were told.

DR. WEISS thinks that this is because what they were told was incomplete and insincere.

E. WEISS reports about a two-and-a-half-year-old boy whose father comes out to the country [where the boy is staying] only on Saturdays. On those evenings, the boy wakes up from his sleep and cannot be calmed down. He screams that he wants to get into another bed; finally he says that he wants to go to Mommy, in her bed. When the father says, "Mother does not need you," the little one replies, "Oh yes, she does—for loving."

Comments on Landauer's Second Contribution

FRIEDJUNG has found that it is only boys who unbutton the mother's blouse, and so has DR. WEISS.

LANDAUER has seen it also in an eight-year-old girl, which

RANK would be inclined to view as an act of aggression (malice).

FRIEDJUNG comments that at that age one is no longer dealing with a purely infantile case.

FREUD singles out as typical (in Landauer's case) the fact that the boy undresses his mother in the presence of the man of whom he is jealous—something an adult would never do.

DR. WEISS regards that as an act of taking possession.

TAUSK tells of the opposite behavior on the part of a boy who likes to uncover his mother's foot in the presence of his aunt, but covers it up when the father comes in.

Comments on Landauer's Third Contribution

FREUD regards this as merely an example of the child's early object choice. One does, indeed, observe cases in which the popular [notion of] "attraction between the sexes" seems to be operative. Observation of a girl nine-months-old, whose behavior toward men differs from that toward women.

HITSCHMANN finds that cases such as this are often seen among hypersexual children who have developed early. It may, however, be caused after all by an early "seduction."

FRIEDJUNG has observed an object choice that was not directed toward the parents taking place even at an early age. Parents of children nine months to a year old (girls) can often be heard to say: "The child likes men very much." These are not always men who resemble the father. Little boys, too (of three years, for instance), are aggressive toward the mother and toward household help.

TAUSK comments, in reference to [the idea of] "attraction," that we have indeed always presupposed a sexual constitution, and that the influences of both sexes are always present.

FREUD replies that the conditions of seduction are not always the same. The adults force upon the child his sexual role. Intimidation of sexuality also has the effect of pushing the child toward the opposite sex. Children with one parent missing (it does not matter which one) become, as a rule, homosexual (the relative weakness of one parent leads to the same result).

Landauer IV

HITSCHMANN thinks an objection might be found [on the part of future readers] in the fact that the observations were made by psychoanalysts.

RANK believes, for similar reasons [out of regard for the reader], that the time at which enlightenment occurred has to be distinguished in the material.

HITSCHMANN: *Report on the "Reversed" (Negative) Oedipus Complex*

(Case of a male homosexual, with an etiologically significant scene of being beaten by the mother in childhood. Dreams containing death wishes directed against the mother. Notion that the defloration of the woman is linked with pain for the man.)

TAUSK reports about three homosexuals, only two of whom had an energetic mother and an easygoing father; in the third case, the constellation was reversed. Some childhood recollections are only subsequently endowed with the quality [Qualität] they later have.

DR. WEISS believes that such an experience (dream of being beaten) cannot be of decisive significance; it merely arouses a constitutional *Anlage*. The determining factor is the disappointment inflicted by the mother.

FREUD comments, with reference to Tausk's remark, that it has long been known that childhood recollections are produced later on —that is to say, picked out for a definite purpose and distorted (screen memories). At the start of treatment, one has to examine the intent. This is not true, however, of scenes that are remembered during the course of the treatment itself; these are spontaneous childhood recollections. The scene mentioned by Hitschmann is important. It is precisely such dreams that are sexual intimidations in the same way as seductions are; that scene is a screen memory for a sexual intimidation.

LANDAUER raises the question of why it is that children occasionally forget their sexual knowledge all over again.

TAUSK thinks that it has not really been repressed; for a certain situation, it is necessary not to know something.

HUG (like Dr. Weiss before her): Incompleteness of the enlightenment: the child is told only the role that the mother plays.

DR. WEISS (adding to what he had already said earlier): Often the child represses what he knows about the origin of children, perhaps in order not to have to deny himself his aggression against another child.

KRAUSS remarks that among other peoples the child is clear about the father's role.

FRIEDJUNG believes that the child accepts only what he can master intellectually. Besides, those who take part in his education, over and over again inculcate in him the incorrect ideas which are more productive in terms of his fantasy life.

RANK thinks that children normally do not repress what they themselves have observed (animal coition, etc.). Nor do they repress what has been imparted to them; they simply do not believe their parents if they have noted insincerity in one point or another (in most instances, precisely on the basis of their own observation). Perhaps it is also true that the child has to go through the phylogenetic myths of procreation and birth.

FREUD finds that the child behaves like a patient: while he is in negative transference, he simply does not believe what he is told. (In Landauer's case, the child is angry with his parents because they have gotten a new child.) [1]

---

[1] This discussion, like the debates on suicide and on masturbation, does not, it is true, bring forth anything definitely new. Yet, like the two other debates, it does produce considerable clarification, as well as offering much stimulation and posing some new questions. It is regrettable, however, that the discussions were recorded in such a cursory manner.

233

SCIENTIFIC MEETING *on May 27, 1914*

Present: Freud, Hitschmann, Hug, Jekels, Landauer, Nepallek, Rank, Sadger, Steiner, Tausk, E. Weiss, K. Weiss, Winterstein. Guests: Emden, Krauss, Sokolnicka.

REVIEWS

[The minutes of this meeting are missing.]

234

SCIENTIFIC MEETING *on June 3, 1914*

Present: Emden, Freud, Friedjung, Heller, Hitschmann, Hug, Jekels, Landauer, Nepallek, Rank, Sachs, Sadger, Steiner, Tausk, E. Weiss, Winterstein.
Guests: Mrs. Emden, F. Krauss, Lampl, Präger, Sokolnicka.

PRESENTATION

Narcissism[1]

SPEAKER: FREUD

[The minutes of this meeting are missing.]
[This is the last meeting of the working year 1913/1914]

---

[1] "Zur Einführung des Narzissmus" [On Narcissism: an Introduction] (1914), *S.E.*, 14: 69–102.

265

235

SCIENTIFIC MEETING *on October 7, 1914*

Present: Federn, Freud, Friedjung, Hitschmann, Hug, Jekels, Nepallek, Rank, Reitler, Sachs, Sadger, Silberer, Steiner, Tausk, Dr. Weiss.

Guests: Dubrovicz, Ferenczi, Krauss, Nunberg.

General Assembly.

BRIEF COMMUNICATIONS

[The minutes of this meeting are missing.]

236

SCIENTIFIC MEETING *on October 21, 1914*

Present: Federn, Freud, Friedjung, Hitschmann, Hug, Nepallek,
Rank, Reik, Sachs, Sadger, Silberer, Steiner, Tausk.
Guests: Ferenczi, Kaplan, Krauss, Nunberg, Mrs. Reik, Sokolnicka.

BRIEF COMMUNICATIONS

[The minutes of this meeting are missing.]

237

SCIENTIFIC MEETING *on November 4, 1914*

Present: Federn, Freud, Friedjung, Hug, Jekels, Sachs, Sadger, Steiner, Tausk, Weiss.
Guests: Dubrovicz, Kaplan, F. S. Krauss.

DISCUSSION ON NARCISSISM

FEDERN, TAUSK

[The minutes of this meeting are missing.]

238

SCIENTIFIC MEETING *on November 18, 1914*

Present: Federn, Freud, Friedjung, Hitschmann, Hug, Jekels, Rank, Reik, Sachs, Sadger, Steiner, Tausk.
Guests: Kaplan, Krauss, Nunberg, Sokolnicka.

PRESENTATION

London Impressions

SPEAKER: SACHS

[The minutes of this meeting are missing.]

239

SCIENTIFIC MEETING *on December 2, 1914*

Present: Federn, Freud, Hitschmann, Hug, Jekels, Nepallek, Rank, Reik, Sachs, Sadger, Steiner, Tausk, Winterstein.
Guests: Kaplan, F. S. Krauss, Nunberg, Dr. (Mrs.) Sokolnicka.

[No title of presentation or discussion given.
The minutes of this meeting are missing.]

240

SCIENTIFIC MEETING *on December 16, 1914*

Present: Freud, Friedjung, Hitschmann, Hug, Jekels, Nepallek, Rank, Reik, Sadger, Steiner, Tausk.
Guests: Nunberg, Sokolnicka.

PRESENTATION

Puberty Rites

SPEAKER: REIK

[The minutes of this meeting are missing.]

241

Present: Freud, Hitschmann, Hug, Jekels, Rank, Reik, Sachs, Tausk.

PRESENTATION

Contributions to a Psychoanalytic Exposition of Melancholia

SPEAKER: DR. VICTOR TAUSK

To begin with, the speaker refers to two of Freud's ideas that stimulated his own view: Mania as a substitute for a mood, and the thesis about libido detachment. His topic is the relationship of melancholia to mania, and melancholia as a problem of libido detachment.

The relationship between melancholia and mania can best be characterized in the following way: the unconscious seems to be free to decide, at a certain point, in favor of one or the other; the utterances themselves are unchanged, it is only that they are rendered in a different mood. Mood is a function of libidinal cathexis

—that is to say, cathexis of objects and of the patient's own person —the point being from what stage of development the libidinal cathexis makes its appearance in the illness (whether from the narcissistic or the autoerotic stage).

The speaker then describes, on the basis of two cases, the things that are to be observed at the onset of the illness. The first case, a woman painter, became deeply melancholic after her father's death, and again 18 years later, upon the death of her sister. Of interest is the fact that in place of the manic phase this patient showed malice, spite, aggression.

All the anamneses of these patients are narcissistic insofar as they show grandiose self-esteem, although in the form of self-contempt. True ideas of grandeur, not ideas arrived at *ex contrasto,* also make their appearance. In addition, there is a fear of excessive punishments, which betrays connections with sadomasochism; it seems to be a matter of infantile fantasies that were active at an earlier period.

Relations to dementia praecox. The nihilistic delusional ideas of melancholia, which are connected with the subject's own body, have their analogue in the patent mechanism of dementia—to represent figures of speech by way of an organ. In melancholia, hallucinations that have to do with stomach, intestines, and smell are prevalent.

The fear of melancholics is not about the entire person as such; it is a fear about the body (ideas of being endangered). It is this autoerotic libido position, which fastens itself onto individual organs and thus becomes conscious, that leads, in this way, also to dementia praecox [organ speech].

The difference lies in the fact that in dementia praecox the ego endeavors to adapt itself to this autoerotic libido position and, as a result of the intellectual regression, attempts to reach that stage of the libido; whereas melancholia, in which the intellect remains intact, does not attempt to make that adaptation. As a consequence, self-accusation comes into being. Thus, in both cases autoerotic libido (at an organ) becomes conscious: in one instance, regression occurs onto the organ; in the other, condemnation from a portion of the narcissistic libido position that has been preserved. It is in accordance with this that the narcissistic constitution is predominantly sadomasochistic and anal erotic. The tendency to self-punishment derives from the damming-up of autoerotic libido.

Mania shows everything of which melancholia accuses itself; it is the flight from the unbearable situation of self-accusation, carrying with it insults, aggressions, etc. In mania, there is no such thing as judgment, since it permits itself everything. These people are autoerotic and narcissistic, which is why they have no contact with the physician.

Indeed, such people have actually loved—but unconsciously. They fall ill when love objects are being given up. The absence of awareness leads also to a lack of personality formation. It is, therefore, a matter of a libido that has not become sufficiently conscious and is being detached. The different outcome of the melancholia of old age is explained by the fact that younger persons still have the capacity for object love and restitution.

DISCUSSION

RANK calls attention to Abraham's investigations,[1] which have shown melancholia and mania to be expressions of the same complexes.

The patients' apparent self-accusation following the loss of persons close to them—"I have never loved!"—would be better understood as an attempt to deal with their sorrow (something of the sort: "If only I had not loved that person so much!"). The melancholic's fear for his own body could perhaps be subsumed under the concept of the fear of death—which, it is true, would first have to be elucidated. (Also, the connection with narcissism.)

HITSCHMANN thinks that explanations could be obtained sooner by way of less severe cases. The feeling of not having loved often goes together with inferiority and ugliness. In most instances, it is a matter of an earlier attachment. The fact that mania and melancholia are the outcome of one and the same complex has always been known to us.

[1] "Ansätze zur psychoanalytischen Erforschung und Behandlung des manisch-depressiven Irreseins und verwandter Zustände." [Notes on the Psychoanalytic Investigation and Treatment of Manic-depressive Insanity and Allied Conditions. In: author's *Selected Papers*. New York: Basic Books, 1953, pp. 137–156.]

NUNBERG again raises the question touched upon by the speaker, in connection with Kraepelin—the question of whether it is melancholia as such that is being referred to, or the melancholia that appears during the course of other illnesses. The manic handwriting of melancholic patients could rather be a result of dementia praecox.

JEKELS, like Hitschmann, finds missing from the presentation the demarcation from certain forms of hysteria. As to clinical objections, he singles out the fact that the refusal of nourishment is generally accounted for by ideas of unworthiness. It is also questionable whether the fear concerns only the patient's own body.

PROF. FREUD finds in the presentation some new things, and some that are not new at all. The actual criterion according to which a distinction is to be made between the symptoms which in practice never appear in their pure form and the forms of illness—is the mechanism. Observation of light cases offers, as Hitschmann mentioned, the only possibility for marking off the limits of the pure picture. If that is so, there is only one *single* melancholia, which has the same mechanism, one that would have to be curable by psychoanalysis.

Mention is made of two cases that have been treated successfully. Technique: treatment during intervals between the attacks; only during the initial stage was it successful. It is well known that melancholia and mania are only two stages of the same illness; this situation is, by the way, similar in the other neuroses (for instance, anxiety/phobia; compulsion/secondary defensive struggle; dementia/recovery process). Melancholia is an attempt that has completely failed; mania is then a secondary attempt. The self-reproaches of melancholia are aimed at other persons and are merely turned onto one's own person.

A case of spontaneous recovery, as proof of the fact that the occasion determines everything. The physiological model of melancholia is the affect of mourning; its precondition is the loss of a loved person. One cannot bring the mourning to an end, perhaps because it is really an unconscious love (which has already been described). Mania comes about by way of contradiction: "I have not loved at all."

The question is whether one succeeds in carrying through that contradiction. That depends—and herein lies what is new in the presentation—on whether the individual succeeds in annihilating his conscience. If he does not, and can still measure himself against his previous being, he stays melancholic. It is correct to group melancholia with the narcissistic neuroses; the analogy with dementia praecox is explained in terms of this characteristic.

The specifically melancholic anxiety is at bottom organ anxiety. Narcissistic anxiety derives, of course, from the castration complex; moreover, ego anxiety produces severe trophic symptoms, while hysteric anxiety, by contrast, does not. Melancholic women are characteristically anaesthetic (libido deflection).

The organic process that may go on behind melancholia is not our concern. In psychoses, we are faced with a disturbance of the entire libido; in neuroses, only with disturbances of object libido; at the borderline stands paranoia, with its struggle against object choice, a struggle that stems from narcissism. Disturbances of libido may be secondary; an ego disturbance does not, however, come about without object disturbance. This is what entitles us to characterize as libidinal the disturbances within the ego.[2]

[2] Freud elaborated the ideas he expressed in this discussion in his paper "Mourning and Melancholia" (1917), S. E., 14:239–258.

242

Present: Freud, Hitschmann, Kaplan, Rank, Reik, Sachs, Sadger, Silberer, Steiner, Sokolnicka.

CASE MATERIAL AND REPORTS

REIK: Pronouncement of Louis the XIVth on Anal Erotism

> The Talmud on an Infantile Trauma.
> Nietzsche on Forgetting
> On Mourning Ceremonials
> On the Castration Complex
> Dumas' Father Complex
> On Jung's Conception of Rebirth-Fantasies

HITSCHMANN: A case of obsessional neurosis, apparently psychosis (with a religious tinge), in a young girl who has conscious thoughts of hate and murder directed against her mother. Her first idea [of this sort] at the age of four or five: mother should die. Originally, she had loved her mother tenderly; the first basis for her hatred was sympathy with her father. Later on, the mother was felt to be a disturbance of her love [life]. (She had an affair with an older man and a child by a young man.) Out of her enormous feeling of guilt arose a profound need for atonement, which she, who was originally Jewish, hoped to find in Christianity. At present, she also has blasphemous ideas. Some of her traits are reminiscent of dementia praecox (hearing voices). Yet the transference is as obvious as it can only be in a transference neurosis.

RANK has the impression that the importunate hatred of the mother is not a genuine one stemming from the Oedipus complex, but a "paranoiac" one which has its source in defense against the love for the mother. There is ample evidence for her sexual inclination toward her mother. On the basis of this interpretation, some details of the case that have remained unintelligible should be capable of being explained.

REIK argues against this, saying that the paranoiac mechanism is encountered not only in the paranoiac clinical picture. Defense against homosexuality is evident also in obsessional neurosis.

PROF. FREUD finds that from the psychiatric angle the case presents difficulties. It gives the impression of being an obsessional neurosis and must, indeed, at one time have been a pure obsessional neurosis. It is not a rare occurrence, however, for an obsessional neurosis to turn into an obsessional psychosis [paranoia], in which case it shows loss of the critical faculty. The patient feels the obsessional impulses to be identical with her, and what has hitherto been rejected wins the upper hand, while nothing changes as far as the contents are concerned. The situation is similar to those cases that are initially hysterias and later on turn into dementias, as soon as the hysteric mechanism of defense is no longer able to do its job. (It then seems as if, by removing the hysteria, one has been promoting dementia.) Dementia makes only a partial appearance—namely, at those points at which neurosis is no longer sufficient, as well as for the purpose of warding off other object cathexes.

Against the mother, who is the exquisite love object, the patient has retained the obsessional neurotic defense (ambivalence). Choosing the father as object is, in dementia, replaced by identifying with him. A transference nevertheless takes place, so long as the process is still fluid. The dementia may, however, also have set in in connection with the mother relationship, because few reaction formations are shown here.

Dementia is not to be mistaken for paranoia: that is directed against the homosexual object choice that arises out of narcissism, whereas dementia may be turned against any sort of object choice. The case is interesting in that, by way of the process of dementia the unconscious of the obsessional neurosis is uncovered.

SILBERER: On "mediumistic art" (Review of the book of that title by Freimark as well as of Flournoy's "Seer of Geneva.") (Will be published as a review).

243

SCIENTIFIC MEETING *on February 3, 1915*

Present: Federn, Freud, Hitschmann, Jekels, Nepallek, Rank, Sachs, Sadger, Steiner, Tausk, Weiss.
Kaplan, Sokolnicka as guests.

BRIEF COMMUNICATIONS AND REVIEWS

REIK: On rape-murder: Rapist-murderers, who murder after coition: side by side with the infantile-sadistic conception of intercourse, intercourse here serves as forepleasure to the end-pleasure achieved in murder. This view is supported by ethnological material.

TAUSK finds in this two entirely different mechanisms which work together only by way of the fact that the man wants to have intercourse with a living woman, and does not want to commit a necrophilic act.

FEDERN believes that just as sexuality in general is a bit of infantilism, so in the rapist-murderer a bit of infantile sadism is reactivated, in the same way as in the normal person a bit of infantile affection is reactivated.

HITSCHMANN is not inclined to attribute to intercourse in this case the role of forepleasure.

SACHS, by contrast, tends to agree with Reik's view.

PROF. FREUD, in support of Reik's view, calls back to mind those patients who, after intercourse, have to masturbate; for them, intercourse actually corresponds merely to a forepleasure, since they have to discharge their excitation by the old accustomed path. However, an objection arises out of the most frequent form of rape-murder—disemboweling, which does not belong among the infantile sexual theories, but only in later years has to do with the birth of children. The phenomenon seems to be of a more complex nature, and not explicable in such simple terms.

SACHS: example of a symptomatic act that has the function of self-reassurance (appears in print) (Z. [1915] 3: 43).

Review of Stekel's *Zentralblatt*, latest issue, and *Journal of Abnormal Psychology*.

TAUSK: supplement to melancholia. Account of the love story that had been missing in the case of a young girl (Rank). Her betrayal of her superior, which was the apparent precipitating cause of her illness, finds its counterpart in her lover's betrayal of her when he married someone else; when he left the shop her depression began.

FEDERN finds characteristic of melancholia the fact that it does not break out all at once, but has its prestages. At the outset, one is generally successful in mastering depression by way of shifting the libido. The persons involved are unsatisfied people, who even in their youth were already reacting to masturbation with depression.

PROF. FREUD can confirm that melancholias do have prestages, which are, however, actually already full melancholias; the first ones occur as early as in childhood. The key to the case related by Tausk is the love story with the betrayer: this melancholia produces its symptoms by way of an identification (that is how her love manifests itself), in which she disparages herself: this is the condemnation of her lover. What is involved here is a mishap in love that, by way of identification, is thrown upon the person's own ego. Thus, the role played by the libidinal disturbance proves to be greater than one thinks. The narcissistic disturbance is nothing but the regressive result of the love disturbance, and shows the complete dependence of the former on object choice.[1]

FEDERN mentions, in connection with the topic of identification, the cases of frigid women who satisfied themselves by way of identification with the man.

FREUD comments that frigid women are indeed those who are unable to satisfy themselves narcissistically (for the gratification achieved in cohabitation is essentially a narcissistic one).

HITSCHMANN: Report on Friedmann and Kohnstamm: "Curing of a Basedow, Accompanied by some Critical Remarks on Psychoanalysis" (being published).[2]

---

[1] The synthesis, as it were, of the discussions on melancholia is presented in Freud's "Mourning and Melancholia" (*S.E.*, 14: 239–258).

[2] "Zur Pathogenese und Psychotherapie bei Basedowscher Krankheit, Zugleich ein Beitrag zur Kritik der psychoanalytischen Forschungsrichtung" *Ztschr. für die gesamte Neurologie und Psychiatrie* (1914), 23. (On the Pathogenesis and Psychotherapy of Basedow's Disease; At the Same Time a Contribution to the Criticism of the Psychoanalytic Trend of Investigation.)
This is a report of a successful psychotherapy of a case of Basedow's disease. Hitschmann appreciates the courage shown by the authors in applying psychoanalysis in some aspects and defending it, and he expresses his hope that they are soon going to overcome the numerous misunderstandings and the ignorance encountered.

244

SCIENTIFIC MEETING *on February 17, 1915*

Present: Federn, Freud, Hitschmann, Hug, Nepallek, Rank, Reik, Sadger, Silberer, Steiner, Tausk.
Guests: Kaplan, Nunberg, Sokolnicka.

CASE MATERIAL AND REVIEWS

[The minutes of this meeting are missing.]

245

SCIENTIFIC MEETING *on March 3, 1915*

Present: Federn, Freud, Friedjung, Hitschmann, Hug, Jekels, Nepallek, Rank, Reik, Sachs, Sadger, Steiner, Tausk.
Guests: Kaplan, Krauss, Nunberg.

PRESENTATION

A Case History

SPEAKER: FREUD

[The minutes of this meeting are missing.]

246

Present: Federn, Freud, Friedjung, Hitschmann, Jekels, Nepallek, Rank, Reik, Sachs, Sadger, Steiner, Tausk.
Guests: Kaplan, F. S. Krauss, Nunberg.

A Case History[1]

PROF. FREUD

DISCUSSION

HITSCHMANN: raises the question of how it is that a neurosis comes into being if these primal fantasies are general.

PROF. FREUD comments that it is precisely against this typical fantasy, which has become intolerable, that repression is directed.

NUNBERG is of the opinion that if a person does not react to these typical fantasies, but simply allows them to go on, a dementia praecox could result.

---

[1] Only the discussion is recorded. "From the Case History of an Infantile Neurosis" was published in 1918 (*S.E.*, 17:3–122).

PROF. FREUD thinks that these hitherto repressed fantasies re-emerge in dementia praecox; prior to that, the individual may have reacted to them just as the neurotic does.

TAUSK doubts whether one can regard so complex a fantasy as something inherited. It is enough to assume that man's capacities for reaction are inherited; what is given, in addition to these, is man's surroundings and his instincts. From these factors, together with the mechanics of the psyche, those uniform fantasies have of necessity to follow. For an understanding of these fantasies, one need not look farther than the ontogenesis. For instance, the little boy already experiences the castration threat (prohibition and pleasure) in connection with the anal zone. As to the parents' coition, the child instinctively guesses about it at a very early stage; conditions are similar with regard to the ontogenetic origin of other primal fantasies.

With regard to the difference between fantasy and experience in terms of their import for neurosis, the speaker is inclined to see this as lying in the fact that the traumatic experience causes other formations to come about. (For instance, it seems that melancholic depression can be traced back to experience, not to fantasy.)

FEDERN objects, as does Hitschmann, to the standpoint taken by Tausk, who regards the instinct as being sufficient to give the child an idea, yet does not explain why it is that that idea invariably goes in the same direction. Heredity is often specific to an astonishing degree. (It may be that in the mother's-womb fantasy an element of cannibalism also has an effect.)

It is also worth noting that in a dream of as early as the fourth year of life, the whole technique of reversal is employed, and that the human backside plays a prominent role in the story. With regard to the question of whether the child actually has to interpret sexual intercourse (*a posteriori*), as castration, the speaker is not convinced; earlier, the sexual impression was sufficient per se to generate anxiety in the child.

FRIEDJUNG thinks that one tends to resist a thesis of such significance, so long as another explanation is still possible. This seems to him not to be the case only with regard to the mother's-womb fantasy; he is not convinced with regard to the other fantasies. The seduction fantasy in particular can be explained very well in terms of ontogenetic experiences alone.

RANK calls attention to the fact that Freud's conception of the primal fantasies finds support in the psychological consideration of myth formation: he gives an example of a condition for loving (washing laundry) that is meaningful to a patient. The ontogenetic explanation brought forward by Tausk merely explains the mechanism of fantasy formation as we have always understood it; it does not explain what is precisely the point here: the origin of the core content, which always remains constant.

PROF. FREUD comments that Tausk, even though he is an exponent of the psychoanalytic view that we have held until now, is nevertheless fighting for a lost cause: in the realm of symbolism, a decision has long since been reached in favor of primal fantasies. However, the view that fantasies are inherited as such—that is to say, as complexes—he himself has never sought to advocate.

As Rank remarked when he spoke against Tausk, the contents of the castration complex are not to be explained on the basis of anal erotism. In general, one can say that fantasy plays a greater role than experience in the formation of neurosis (this is also true of melancholia). The meaning of castration fear is to be supported, against Federn's doubt about it, in light of the fact that, between the observation of animals (coition) and his dream, the child discovered the female genital.

SACHS tries to turn back Tausk's objections by pointing to the fact that instinct and traces of experience are simply not enough to bring about the formation of primal fantasies.

FEDERN thinks the fact that it is the behavior of the ego, and not the impression as such, that is depicted in the dream argues in favor of the fantastic nature of the primal scene.

JEKELS recalls the criterion that he, together with Rank, had stressed—namely, whether or not the patient in later life tried to turn the fantasy into reality.

287

247

SCIENTIFIC MEETING *on March 31, 1915*

Present: Federn, Freud, Hitschmann, Hug, Jekels, Nepallek, Rank, Sachs, Sadger, Silberer, Tausk.
Guests: Kaplan, Nunberg, Sokolnicka.

COMMUNICATIONS AND REVIEWS

PRESENTATION

On the Psychology of Alcoholic Occupational Delirium[1]

SPEAKER: DR. TAUSK

For an understanding of the contents of the occupational delirium, reference is made to typical occupational dreams which have to do with "not-getting-finished"; in analysis, these prove to be dreams of the fear of impotence. If it is true that the occupational delirium is analogous to these dreams, then it has to be an anxiety delirium; in fact, in six cases (two women and four men), it was learned

[1] "Zur Psychologie des alkoholischen Beschäftingungsdelirs." Z. (1915), 3: 204–226.

that the patients were in fear of not getting through with something. The typical "bursting out into a sweat" could be of perspiration that had been caused by anxiety.

As to the further question of which instincts are dammed up here and transformed into anxiety, a number of traits point to homosexuality: the persons concerned are social drinkers (this is also true of women; in most instances, they are mother and daughter); all the men have broken up with their wives and generally also develop a paranoia.

DISCUSSION

HITSCHMANN recalls that, in relation to Rosegger's dream, he had earlier drawn attention to the occupation-impotence dream. The relationship between impotence and frequent visits to restaurants is likewise familiar to us. Recently, he heard such an occupation dream from an old man who was incapable of performing *immissio*.

SACHS mentions an occupation dream of Gottfried Keller, who was impotent and an alcoholic. These dreams are not to be interpreted only in terms of impotence, but also of the lack of sexual satisfaction; in women, for instance, they signify the impotence of the men.

It was Juliusburger who was the first to treat of the relationship of alcoholism and homosexuality from the psychoanalytic viewpoint, and after him Abraham; Bleuler and Ferenczi both had discussions about this.

FEDERN would like to define the term "impotence-anxiety dream" more precisely as "fear of impotence." It is common knowledge that alcoholics have both a stronger libido and a weaker potency. The significance of the homosexual component is beyond doubt. In alcoholic delirium, it may be a portion of the general anxiety of the manic mechanism of defense that is operative. (During the transition from one phase to another, fear arises that the defense is not going to be successful.)

289

TAUSK denies emphatically that mania feels anxiety: that is true only at the moment of the sudden change into the opposite, and at that point it is already melancholic.

As to the fear of impotence, Tausk is inclined to interpret it in the case of the woman in the same way as he interprets it in the man—namely, as a feeling of congestion (minus, of course, the erection).

The dream of "running after and not being able to catch up with" (mentioned by Silberer) does not belong in this context. It is not an impotence-anxiety dream but rather a defense against libido that is bursting forth: a dream of not *wanting* to get finished (in the delirium, not *being able* to).

FEDERN understands the dream of "not getting finished with something," in Freud's sense, as *ejaculatio praecox*. Dreams of "running after, etc." and those of "not getting finished" mean the same thing: the common factor lies in the failure to achieve end-pleasure. The question is why it is that in alcoholism this is transferred onto work.

PROF. FREUD calls attention to an attempt made by Meynert to explain the alcoholic occupation-delirium. The alcoholic who is reproached for being averse to work shows in his delirium that he does not deserve the reproach. As to Tausk's explanation, the essential point seems to be correctly taken: these patients rush themselves because they are afraid they are not going to finish. This is true whether or not their anxiety becomes manifest; the anxiety is merely an expression of the fact that one has not succeeded in something, and under these circumstances any instinctual impulse can pass over into anxiety.[1] By contrast, where something has succeeded, anxiety finds no room; one example is mania.

Anxiety is merely the outcome of the inhibition tendency; by analogy with the inhibition dream, it signifies a conflict that may be, in this case, a conflict between homosexuality and heterosexuality. It is from this conflict that impotence results. The "rushing" is in fact a running away from something; what he is running away

---

[1] Later on this statement becomes the basis of Freud's new theory of anxiety (see "Inhibitions, Symptoms and Anxiety" [1926]. *S.E.*, 20: 77–174).

from is his homosexual libido. The impotence explains only the contents of the delirium; it does not explain its mechanism. The impotence is a consequence of the homosexuality.

The reason why it is precisely *working* [that constitutes the delirium] of these people is to be explained, to begin with, in terms of the ancient symbolic interpretation of this word, which has been passed on in the history of language: he is demonstrating how proficient he is in (hetero-) sexual matters; he has to do this continuously, in order to prove that he is always concerned with the woman; and it is in his own line of work that he has to do all that much work, because it alone can provide him with evidence of his proficiency. "Not getting through with a job" is a mythical motif (Sisyphus; Danaïdes), which makes its appearance in fairy tales in the form of an otherwise insoluble task; supernatural helpers assist in completing it.

To the question, raised by Federn, as to why the delirious person offers such resistance to homosexuality by laying such stress on heterosexuality, Prof. Freud replies that he comes to the delirium only for the purpose of gratifying a wish: he feels himself to be at the mercy of homosexuality, and it is for that reason that he produces the delirium. As to Meynert's conception, this much is correct: he did pick up the manifest reproach about shirking work; behind that, however, stands the latent reproach of neglecting the woman.

* * * * * * *

HITSCHMANN: *Anxiety and Obsession*

In the obsessive fear that something may happen to a relative, anxiety and obsession come together, without its being possible to mark them off from one another by way of clinical observation. Case of a woman, 25 years of age, who has attacks of rage and death wishes directed against her husband (and her child); these have to do with an exquisite father-fixation and an ambivalent attitude toward him. Husband is a frequent visitor to inns, and impotent. The woman has an anxiety neurosis, with obsessive fears directed against her husband (and the parent of the same sex: the father).

291

DISCUSSION

FEDERN formulates the following question: is the obsessive fear an obsessional neurosis or is it an anxiety neurosis? He thinks he should answer the question the first way. Even though every neurotic symptom makes its appearance in an obsessive manner, nevertheless, in the case of the obsessional neurosis it is a matter of a specific sensation. During the course of an analysis, it sometimes happens that what were earlier obsessive fears later become hysterical impulses.

TAUSK comments that obsessive fears differ appreciably from the hysterical fear that something may happen to someone. In obsessional fear, what is involved is a sort of two-sidedness; part of the obsessional formula remains unconscious.

SACHS sees the difference between anxiety hysteria and obsessional fear in that a patient with the former finds some reason for the anxiety, whereas the patient with obsessive fear knows that it is irrational.

PROF. FREUD believes this problem cannot be solved. The case is of an anxiety hysteria, with an admixture, however, of obsessional neurosis: the phobic mechanism is to be found in both these neuroses. In general, cases that put together parts of the mechanisms of various neuroses, arouse the suspicion that they are merely temporary ''solutions'' of a conflict that is going to provide itself with other solutions (psychosis).

SACHS: Review of Schrötter, *Beginnings of Art in the Animal World and in Dwarf Tribes.*

On Hauptmann: *The Bow of Odysseus.*

RANK: Review of Adolf Paul: *Strindberg. Memories and Letters.*

248

Present: Federn, Freud, Hitschmann, Rank, Sachs, Sadger, Steiner, Tausk, Weiss.
Guest: Dr. Kaplan.

PRESENTATION

On the Genesis of the Primal Phantasy that has a Traumatic Effect

SPEAKER: DR. KAPLAN

[The minutes of this meeting are missing.]

249

SCIENTIFIC MEETING *on April 28, 1915*

Present: Federn, Freud, Hitschmann, Hug, Jekels, Nepallek, Rank, Reik, Sachs, Sadger, Silberer, Steiner, Tausk, Kaplan. Guests: Miss Bernays, F. S. Krauss, Nunberg.

Vote Kaplan.

[No topic is noted.
The minutes of this meeting are missing.]

250

SCIENTIFIC MEETING on *May 12, 1915*

Present: Federn, Freud, Friedjung, Kaplan, Nepallek, Sachs, Sadger, Steiner, Tausk.

Guests: Bernfeld,[1] Krauss.

[This is the end of the attendance book. The minutes of this meeting are missing. Attendance lists and Agenda are the only entries for the next three years. A single protocol is in existence, that of the meeting on November 19, 1918, one week after the end of World War I.]

---

[1] Bernfeld's name appears here for the first time.

SCIENTIFIC MEETING *on November 19, 1918*

Present: Dr. Deutsch (Mrs.), Dr. Ferriere (Geneva), Dr. Fogschaner, Dr. Friedjung, Prof. Freud, Dr. Freund (Budapest), Dr. (Mrs.) Hug-Hellmuth, Dr. Hitschmann, Dozent Dr. Pötzl, Dr. Rank, Dr. Sokolnicka, Dr. Steiner, Dr. Tausk, Dr. Weiss.

Guests: Dr. Bernfeld, Mrs. Bernfeld, Medical student Fenichel, Dr. Karl Frank, Miss Anna Freud, Mrs. Pötzl.

PROF. FREUD welcomes the guests; DR. RANK announces the moving of the Library; DR. REIK reports on new acquisitions of the library.

DR. BERNFELD presents a paper on
Poetic Writing by Youth

The speaker has collected a vast amount of factual material. He distinguishes two types of youthful poets: in the first, it is only at times that there is the urge to write poems, dramas, etc., while the other produces unceasingly during the period from his 13th to his 19th year of life. These youthful poets keep diaries, and they have critics and an audience, at least among friends; they concern themselves with the process of their production and regard themselves as poets.

296

The speaker has examined analytically the work of a youth stemming from the period from his 13th to his 19th year of life. At first he had chosen his material from school and his reading, dealing with it in ballads and dramas. In the 11th month of his 14th year, there is a distinct break in his creative writing. From the scholastic, narrative form, he makes a switch to lyric poetry. He writes short lyric poems, which deal not with material from elsewhere, but with his own moods. In his 16th year there is another distinct break toward objectivity and the artistic outlook. His major themes are either invented by the poet himself or substantially modified.

The differences between the three periods are the following: During the first, what prevails is the compulsive urge to create poetic works, although often there is a lack of subject matter. When he does have it, he reflects upon form and meter and takes great pains to carry out a plan in a scholastic manner. In the second period, lyric poetry emerges as an emotional release; it is only the act of writing poetry that is felt as subjectively valuable, not the product. During the first period, the poetic works are carefully written out; from the 15th year onward, however, much less care is taken. While previously he placed great store by judgment on his production, it is now a matter of indifference to him.

The objective period is characterized by his relative lack of choice in the selection of subject matter. In contrast to earlier periods, he readily succeeds in carrying out what he attempts; often, the conviction forces itself upon him that he is a great poet. The difference between this and the previous period: in type and range, his production approaches the artistic. The decision to publish his poetic writings becomes plain; they are no longer entered into copy books, but instead made ready for printing.

The wish to be a poet preceded his actual production in all periods. The speaker discusses the relationship between writing and daydreaming. All young poets characterize themselves as daydreamers. At the bottom of the lyric poem, however, lies not a daydream, but a mood. Yet many young poets want to express a thought. The elements of poetry writing can be derived from daydreams, moods, and obsessive thoughts. Youth composes more poetry than do people of any other age. Puberty is favorable for daydreaming. Most often, it is mood that is at the bottom of poetry; it is the symptom of an affect displacement. The poetry of moods has the tendency to enable a mood to continue; in terms of time, to spread the affect; to keep it fixated by means of the word. Poetry arising out of daydreams consists essentially in communications of daydreams. The poetry of moods is traceable to heterosexual experiences; it is being refused that brings about the experiencing of moods; but the poetry writing that has its origin in daydreams is not complete either, without an appreciation of the fact that there has been an actual renunciation. If the loved one denies you, that is to be compensated for by the acquisition of love of another sort (glory, honor, etc.). As one example of this, first novelettes by youths are referred to; all of them are structured along the lines of a single scheme: the author stands at the center. It is clearly his wish to have someone else represent him in this manner; in his novel, he depicts his future as he imagines or desires it to be. What is particularly revealing is the dedications in the creative writing of the young. In the first novels or sketches, they are addressed to the father or the loved one. In every instance, the narcissistic cathexis is obvious. The speaker calls attention to the process of sublimation in these poems, and explains its mechanisms. In the poetry, one sees the triumph of a narcissistic component over sexual components of another kind.

DISCUSSION

DR. WEISS refers to his paper Refrain and Rhyme [see This Volume, Minutes 190], which contains several points of agreement [with what has been said].

DR. TAUSK criticizes the fact that contents and forms of poetic writing were not clearly separated in Dr. Bernfeld's paper. He thinks that drama represents a higher development than narrative, since it is, in poetry, a more advanced stage in the overcoming of narcissism. It is true that the poetic creation is compensation for renunciation; by means of the work, the ego is enlarged. Burning one's poems means removing the evidences of an old period. Tausk presents the example of a poet who counted 17 periods and after each of these burned his poems. Poetry of moods consists of getting through with the affect by binding it to the word.

DR. HITSCHMANN does not consider it a matter of indifference whether it is great poets or minor ones who are examined analytically. More emphasis should be put on the Oedipus complex. What does it mean when young people say they want to be or to become poets? That is an essential question.

MR. FENICHEL expresses the opinion that mood and daydream do not have different attitudes toward reality. He discusses three possible ways of objectifying daydreams, and likens youth's reflections upon form, and their requirements with regard to it, to obsessional neurotic traits.

DR. REIK calls attention to the fact that the speaker interprets the concept of sublimation differently from the way psychoanalysis generally does; the latter places its stress on the social element— that is, on what is of higher value in this process. The poetry of youth is interesting because of the elements that are later on made use of for other purposes.

DR. RANK: The aspect of the poetic creation by youth of value for psychoanalytic investigation is that all those primitive complexes which in the distinguished poet have to be painstakingly sought for are here clear enough to be seen. Examples: A youth writes a play for his father's birthday, in which he, who is fixated on the father, plays the father. A sculptor, who later on was to become famous, first of all succeeded in making his primitive complexes disappear. The drama of an 11-year-old girl deals with her mother's death. All poets begin by imitating. Hebbel's confessions.

Poetry is not only the means, but also the result of repression. Arousing compassion is often the motive of a poem.

DR. FEDERN considers it of great value that Dr. Bernfeld has shown the poetic creation to be a compromise aimed as much at fixating a mood as at getting rid of it. The poet has a narcissistic attitude toward his own moods. For writing poetry one needs greater constitutional strength of instinct than is usual. Every artist, in spite of his extensive adaptations to reality, also has an atavistic instinctual life. To this belongs narcissism—which means, in this context, the

299

art of creating that is based on the fixation onto narcissism; it is through the means of object libido that narcissism achieves gratification. Artists have, in addition, an increased capacity for sense reception. Besides, there is self-censorship, just as if it were not their own work that is involved. Creative artists as well as psychologists emphasize that an integral part of the great artist is his bisexual *Anlage*. His attitude toward his work may become an extremely feminine one. In the artist, stress is placed on the narcissistic libido and the narcissistically borne object love.

DR. RANK adds: the great poet also has everything that youthful poets have; it is only that he has a bit more besides.

DR. FRIEDJUNG traces the conscious intention of youths, "I want to be a poet," back to imitation.

An 11-year-old boy writes poetry after hearing his mother's lyric poems; another one writes dramas after a visit to the theatre. There are two types of poets: one is finished with his affects as soon as his work is finished, while the other cannot gain inner freedom from them through the completion of his work.

DR. TAUSK, in connection with the factor of imitation in the psychogenesis of the poet, relates the following: in the case of a boy of three years, an enema he received became the motive for imitating his doctor. Tausk stresses the relationship to anal erotism —a poet's relationship to his work as being determined by the degree to which anal erotism has been overcome; the child's attitude toward the [text missing in original] has great bearing on this.

PROF. FREUD: The chief merit of Bernfeld's paper lies in the fact that it was with knowledge of psychoanalysis yet without bias that he approached his material; as a result, he saw unexpected confirmation of psychoanalytic findings. Prof. Freud relates the associations that have come to light during the presentation on classification of poets. Essentially, the problem falls into three parts. The motives for, the technique used in, and the effects achieved by writing poetry are to be investigated. As to motives, one may probably distinguish five types:

(1) Motivation by illusion: this poetic activity produces wish ful-

fillment; it arises out of daydreams. Its product: idealistic poetry.

(2) What matters to the second type is: to describe. The motive is an exhibitionistic one—that is, the poet wants to show what he is able to produce. This type comes close to

(3) the third one, who is someone who knows because he looks. The poet wants to make a showing of what he has seen. The situation is similar to the one at school, in which one child displays what are "secrets" to another, inexperienced, child. Product: realistic writing.

(4) Psychological writing seeks to uncover what is concealed—for instance, Dostoievski.

(5) The poet, moved by instinctual drive, solicits compassion, sympathy, love; lyrics are typical of that sort of thing.

In writing, two points of view are to be distinguished: whether the social motif was there from the beginning or became added on only later. It is there from the beginning, for instance, in writing that is based on illusion as well as in writing that stems from the need to explore.

2nd viewpoint: whether the ego is providing only the motive, or the contents of the poetic work as well. Lyrics and writing arising out of illusion take their contents from the ego, while the content of psychological writing is taken from the hidden parts of the ego.

DR. BERNFELD offers his thanks for the comments and explains that he did not deal with the determination of complexes or with the mechanics of writing poetry because they are known. Narrative is older than drama. The burning of one's poems signifies a struggle —that is, a struggle against continuing on the narcissistic path. What distinguishes the great poet from the minor one is not the quantity of talent. In the great poet, too, the narcissistic attitude is central. Works of major size are denied the writing of youth; their novels contain no more than six or eight pages. A person's wish to be a poet, which is there before he begins to produce anything, can be explored only in individual cases. A codeterminant is the high valuation of the poet, the social esteem that he enjoys. Side by side with the part played by imitation, the part played by differentiation has to be taken into consideration. The killing of the father often stands at the center of poetic writing by youth.

[Protocols are preserved of the working years 1931/1932 and 1932/1933. They contain mainly reports of general business, attendance lists, and topics of presentations and discussions, without giving any details.]

MEETING

In the small meeting room of the Vienna Psychoanalytic Society on March 20, 1938, there appeared the commissioner appointed by the NSDAP [Nazi Party], Dr. Anton Sauerwald.

[*Present:*] Dr. Ernest Jones, as President of the International Psychoanalytic Association.

Marie, Princess of Greece, as a Vice President of the International Psychoanalytic Association and Deputy Chairman of the Vienna Psychoanalytic Society.

Miss Anna Freud, as a Vice President of the International Psychoanalytic Association, and Deputy Chairman of the Vienna Psychoanalytic Society.

Dr. Carl Müller-Braunschweig as Secretary of the German Psychoanalytic Society and as a member of the administrative council of the German Institute for Psychological Research and Psychotherapy, Berlin.

In an advisory capacity for the support of Dr. C. Braunschweig, Mr. August Beranek, Berlin.

Of the Vienna Psychoanalytic Society, Deputy Chairman, Dr. Paul Federn.

As members of the Board of Directors, Dr. Eduard Hitschmann, Dr. Edw. Bibring, Dr. H. Hartmann, Dr. E. Kris, Dr. Robert Waelder, Dr. W. Hoffer.

Of the *Internationaler Psychoanalytischer Verlag*, Mrs. Berta Steiner, Dr. Martin J. Freud.

303

After prolonged consultation, the assembled members of the board of directors of the International Psychoanalytic Association agree on the following propositions:

The chairman of the Vienna Psychoanalytic Society, Prof. Dr. Sigm. Freud, should ask of Dr. Müller-Braunschweig as the representative of the German Psychoanalytic Society that this society take over as trustee the rights and obligations of the Vienna Psychoanalytic Society and at the same time also its assets.

Prof. Dr. Sigm. Freud accepts this proposition.

Dr. Müller-Braunschweig, after a conversation by telephone with Prof. Dr. Goering, declares that the German Psychoanalytic Society is prepared to take on the role of trustee.

The members and members of the board of directors of the Vienna Psychoanalytic Society named in this protocol as present in person take affirmative cognizance of the state of affairs.

Vienna, March 20, 1938.

APPENDIX

The Attendance Book

The attendance book was, of course, never intended for publication. It contains notes on the meetings from 1909/1910 to the end of 1914/1915. As can be gathered from the dates of the individual minutes, the meetings were held bi-weekly in 1914–1915.

The list for 1914/1915 differs from those for the preceding years; no longer is a full page devoted to each meeting; attendance lists and topics of papers for three or four meetings are written on a single page. There is no roll of members, although it would appear that Rank had intended to write one, for the name and address of Ludwig Binswanger appear at the top of a page that has remained otherwise empty.

The names marked with an asterisk were crossed out on the original list in the attendance book.

NINTH YEAR OF THE SOCIETY
1910/1911

Role of current members: 40
Dr. Alf. Adler*
Dr. Guido Brecher
Dr. Paul Federn
Dr. S. Ferenczi
Dr. S. FREUD
Dr. Josef K. Friedjung

Dr. Carl Furtmüller*
Dr. Max Graf
Hugo Heller
Dr. Hilferding*
Dr. Eduard Hitschmann
Dr. Edw. Hollerung
Dr. Franz v. Hye*
Dr. Ludwik Jekels
Dr. Albert Joachim
Dr. Stefan Maday*
Dr. Richard Nepallek
Dr. D. E. Oppenheim*
Dr. Otto Rank
Dr. Rudolf Reitler
Dr. Oskar Rie
Dr. I. Sadger
Dr. Maxim Steiner
Dr. Wilh. Stekel
Dr. Viktor Tausk
Dr. Rudolf Urbantschitsch
Dr. Fritz Wittels*
Dr. D. J. Bach*
Doz. Dr. G. Holzknecht
Gustav Grüner*
Paul Klemperer*
General-Director Leopold Rechnitzer
Dr. Hanns Sachs
Herbert Silberer
Richard Wagner
Alfred Freih. v. Winterstein
Franz Grüner*
Gaston Rosenstein
Erwin Wechsberg*
Dr. Leonide Drosnés
Dr. jur. Bernhard Dattner
Dr. M. Wulff (Odessa)
Dr. Josef Reinhold

TENTH YEAR OF THE SOCIETY
1911/12

Roll of current members: 34
Dr. Guido Brecher
Bernhard Dattner
Dr. Leonide Drosnés
Dr. J. E. G. van Emden
Dr. Paul Federn
Dr. S. Ferenczi
Prof. Dr. S. Freud
Dr. Josef K. Friedjung
Dr. Max Graf
Hugo Heller
Dr. Eduard Hitschmann
Dr. Edwin Hollerung
Doc. Dr. Guido Holzknecht
Dr. Ludwik Jekels
Dr. Albert Joachim
Dr. Richard Nepallek
Otto Rank
Leopold Rechnitzer
Dr. Rudolf Reitler
Dr. Josef Reinhold
Dr. Oskar Rie
Gaston Rosenstein
Dr. Hanns Sachs
Dr. I. Sadger
Herbert Silberer
Dr. S. Spielrein [Mrs.]
Dr. August Stärcke
Dr. Maxim Steiner
Dr. Wilhelm Stekel
Dr. Viktor Tausk
Dr. Rudolf Urbantschitsch
Richard Wagner

APPENDIX

Dr. Alfr. Frh. von Winterstein
Dr. M. Wulff
Theodor Reik
Sanitätsrat Gerster
  [member of the board of health]
Dr. Tatjana Rosenthal [Miss]
Dr. Karl Weiss
Dr. Friedr. L. Krauss
Doz. Dr. Hans Kelsen

ELEVENTH YEAR OF THE SOCIETY
1912/13

[Roll of members:]
Dr. Guido Brecher
Dr. Bernhard Dattner
Dr. Leonide Drosnés
Dr. Jan van Emden
Dr. Paul Federn
Dr. S. Ferenczi
Prof. S. Freud
Dr. Josef K. Friedjung
Sanitätsrat Gerster*
Dr. Max Graf
Hugo Heller
Dr. Eduard Hitschmann
Dr. Edwin Hollerung
Doz. Dr. Guido Holzknecht
Dr. Ludwik Jekels
Dr. Albert Joachim
Dr. Richard Nepallek
Dr. Otto Rank
Leopold Rechnitzer
Dr. Theodor Reik
Dr. Tatjana Rosenthal
Dr. Rudolf Reitler
Dr. Josef Reinhold

308

Dr. Oskar Rie
Gaston Rosenstein
Dr. Hanns Sachs
Dr. I. Sadger
Herbert Silberer
Dr. S. Spielrein-Scheftel [Mrs.]
Dr. August Stärcke
Dr. Maxim Steiner
Dr. Wilhelm Stekel*
Dr. Viktor Tausk
Dr. Rudolf Urbantschitsch
Dr. Richard Wagner
Dr. Karl Weiss
Dr. Alfr. Frh. v. Winterstein
Dr. M. Wulff
Dr. Ernst Marcus
Dr. Tatjana Rosenthal*
cand. med/Ed. Weiss
Dr. Hermine Hug v. Hugenstein
   [usually listed as Hug-Hellmuth]

TWELFTH YEAR OF THE SOCIETY
1913/14

[Roll of current members]
Dr. Ludwig Binswanger
Dr. Guido Brecher
Dr. Bernhard Dattner*
Dr. Leonide Drosnés
Dr. Jan van Emden
Dr. Paul Federn
Prof. Dr. S. Freud
Dr. Josef K. Friedjung
Dr. Max Graf*
Hugo Heller
Dr. Eduard Hitschmann
Dr. Edwin Hollerung*

Doz. Dr. Gustav Holzknecht
Dr. H. v. Hug-Hellmuth
Dr. Ludwig Jekels
Dr. Albert Joachim*
Dr. Richard Nepallek
Dr. Otto Rank
Leopold Rechnitzer*
Dr. Theodor Reik
Dr. Tatjana Rosenthal
Dr. Rudolf Reitler
Dr. Josef Reinhold*
Dr. Oskar Rie
Gaston Rosenstein*
Dr. Hanns Sachs
Dr. I. Sadger
Herbert Silberer*
Dr. S. Spielrein-Scheftel
Dr. August Stärcke
Dr. Maxim Steiner
Dr. Viktor Tausk
Dr. Rudolf Urbantschitsch*
Dr. Richard Wagner*
Dr. Karl Weiss
med. stud. Ed. Weiss
Dr. Alfr. Frh. v. Winterstein
Dr. M. Wulff
Dr. Karl Landauer

[Following the roll of members in the attendance book are several names in smaller handwriting: Ferenczi, Marcus, Joachim, Wagner, Hug, E. Weiss, Dr. F. S. Krauss, Dr. A. Deutsch. At the bottom of the page, in pencil, appear the names: Kaplan and Nunberg.]

ADDENDA

to Volume III

Footnotes

on p. 17, with reference to "Frischauf as guest":
Herman Frischauf, M.D., 1879–1942, assistant at the clinic Wagner–Jauregg, was a leading psychiatrist at Vienna's juvenile court and *Dozent* for Forensic Psychiatry at the University of Vienna. After April 1910 he was an extraordinarily frequent guest at the meetings of the Society, but did not become a member.

on p. 59, with reference to "Doctor of Law Bienenfeld":
Franz Rudolf Bienenfeld, LL.D., b. 1886, a highly respected attorney in Vienna, kept up his close contact with Freud and psychoanalysis, although he was not a member of the Society. In 1937 he published, under the pen name Anton von Miller the book *Deustsche und Juden*, which appeared in English in 1939 as *The Germans and the Jews*.

ERRATA

Volume I

Page xxxiii, last line of first paragraph should read, "Rowena Ansbacher."

Page 24, footnote 23: the explanation in brackets following *"Nährpflicht"* is incorrect.

Page 26, footnote 30 should read, "Grillparzer was staying in London."

Page 43, footnote 9 should read, "Freud may refer here to what was later called etiological 'complemental series,' which means that constitution and external experiences complement each other."

Page 62, footnote 4 should read, "Eduard Castle (1875–1959)."

Page 82, footnote 2 should read, *"Zöglings Törless."*

Page 132, footnote 11 should read, *"Schmidts Jahrbücher."*

Page 198, footnote 6 should read, "Well-known Viennese surgeon."

Page 214, footnote 3 should read, "Emil Raimann."

Page 226, footnote 1 should read, "Willy Hellpach."

Page 334, footnote 6 should read, "Siegmund."

Page 339, footnote 3 should read, "Oswald Bumke (1877–1950)."

Page 339, footnote 5 should read, "Theodor Ziehen (1862–1950)."

Page 351, footnote 7 should read, "Gomperz's."

Page 398, footnote 1 should read, "See Minutes 43, fn. 5 and Minutes 46, fn. 7."

Page 399, footnote 4 should read, "Ernst, Freiherr von Feuchtersleben."

Volume II

Page v, the presentation for the meeting on October 21, 1908 was by Sadger.

Page 2, opening lines of presentation should read, "Stekel introduces his presentation by stating that anything of value we knew about dreams before Freud was said by poets."

Page 13: the speaker was Dr. Sadger.

Page 78: footnote 11 should have been omitted.

Page 130: the Hermann referred to on line 11 was Joseph Herman (1817–1902). Chief physician at the Wiedener Spital in Vienna, he was opposed to the mercury treatment of syphillis.

Page 300, line 9 from bottom should read, "Adler has made a highly promising beginning."

Page 348, line 13 should read, *"[verhüllen]."*

Page 359, footnote 5 refers to "Formulations on the Two Principles of Mental Functioning."

312

Page 384, line 14 from the bottom should read, "Julius Bauer."

Volume III

Page XV, Paul Klemperer was not a refugee from the Nazis; he arrived in the United States in 1921 and worked for many years in New York, a highly esteemed representative of his profession.

Page 67, footnote 2: The outrageous date of 1774 for the death of Le Sage should read 1747.

Page 74, footnote 2: The article mentioned is a later work on the same subject. The title of the paper mentioned at this meeting is "Versuch zur Begründung einer Wissenschaftlichen Experimentalmagie."

Page 82, footnote 2: An addendum is in order here. The affair had to do with the publication of Wittels' novel *Ezekiel der Zugereiste* (Berlin, 1910), which caricatured Karl Kraus and implied that he was impotent. (C. W. M. Johnston [1972], *The Austrian Mind.* University of California Press, page 250.)

Page 140, footnote 1: The year 1922 is incorrect. The essay appeared in 1914.

Page 180, line 2 should read, James Putnam.

Page 206, footnotes 1 and 2: Read "literally" for "literature."

Page 238, footnote 1 should read, Dr. Wulff left Russia in 1927 to work in the Simmel Sanitarium in Tegel near Berlin. When the Nazis came to power, he emigrated to Israel.

Page 306, first line of final paragraph, should read, "Groos."

Page 353, paragraph 4 refers to a review of Spitzer's book. The title of this book is *Die Wortbildung als Stilistisches Mittel, Exemplifiziert an Rabelais* (1910) [Word-formation as a Means of Style, as Exemplified by Rabelais], Halle a.S.: Max Niemayer. Sachs' paper appeared in the Zentralblatt, I:237–242.

CUMULATIVE INDEX

VOLUMES I–IV

NAME INDEX

Abels, H., I, 202, 204, 212, 218, 220, 224, 226, 238

Abraham, K., I, 248, 252, 270, 272, 273, 390; II, 51; III, 81, 274, 337; IV, 99, 289

"An Approach to the Psychoanalytic Exploration and Treatment of Manic-depressive Derangement and of Similar States," IV, 219, 274

"Dreams and Myth: A Study in Folk-Psychology," II, 68n

"The Psychological Relations between Sexuality and Alcoholism," II, 35–37, 39

"The Significance of Intermarriage Between Close Relations in the Psychology of the Neuroses," II, 76

Adler, A., I, xxii, xxiv, xxvi, xxxiii, xxxv, 1, 6–7, 11–12, 14, 16, 17, 18–19, 30, 32, 33–34, 36, 47, 48, 52, 59–60, 62, 67–68, 69, 71, 81, 82, 89, 92, 95–96, 103, 105, 106, 107, 109, 111, 114, 115, 117–118, 119, 128, 130, 131, 135, 138–140, 141, 142, 143, 144–145, 146, 149, 153, 157, 158, 159, 162–163, 164, 166, 167, 171, 172, 175, 179, 180, 183, 187–188, 190, 191–192, 195, 200–201, 202, 203, 207, 208, 210, 212, 217, 218, 221–222, 226, 234, 235, 237, 242, 245, 248, 259, 265, 266, 270, 274, 281, 286, 288, 298, 299, 302, 303, 306–307, 308, 311, 313, 315, 316, 317, 318–319, 321, 322–323, 324, 336–337, 338–339, 340, 342, 343, 345, 347, 352, 353, 355, 358, 360, 361, 362, 368, 372, 375, 390, 392, 394, 395, 396, 397, 399, 400, 401, 402, 403, 404; II, 1, 2, 11–12, 13, 20, 23, 25, 33, 34, 36, 38, 42, 57, 65, 66–67, 69, 82, 91, 93, 97–98, 106, 108, 112–113, 117, 120–121, 145, 146, 147, 150–151, 163, 164, 168–169, 170–171, 172, 195, 204–205, 207, 211, 237, 246–249, 250, 251, 255, 257, 259, 275–276, 278–280, 282, 288–289, 290, 301, 303, 308–310, 315, 320–321, 322, 328, 333–334, 338, 349–350, 353, 356, 358, 360, 363, 382, 388–389, 394–396, 404, 410–411, 413, 419, 445, 447–448, 452–454, 457–458, 463–471, 472–478, 479–481, 491, 497, 498–499, 503–504, 507–508, 510, 513, 517–518, 519, 526, 527, 530, 535–541, 542, 545, 549, 550, 553, 557, 559–560, 564, 566–571, 573–574, 577, 579–581; III, xiv, xvi, 1–3, 7, 8–10, 12, 14, 26, 33–34, 35, 37, 45–46, 50, 52–53, 56–57, 58–59, 61–63, 64–66, 68–73, 74–75, 78–79, 81, 82, 84–86, 87–89, 91–92, 93, 98–99, 101–111, 112–113, 120–122, 124–125, 126, 131–132, 133–135, 139, 140–151, 152–158, 159, 168–177, 188, 190, 194, 206, 208, 217, 221, 233, 236, 238, 250, 256–259, 262–263, 267–268, 275, 277–278, 366; IV, 40, 71, 78, 99, 109–111, 129–130, 185, 191, 210, 232, 250, 305

317

on aggression, II, 138, 143, 169, 173, 177–178, 260–264, 425; III, 18, 33, 56, 61

"The Aggressive Drive in Life and in Neurosis," I, 406–410; II, 120, 121; III, 45

on anxiety, II, 403, 536; III, 16, 158

on bisexuality, II, 423–434; III, 174; *see also* Adler, A., on psychic hermaphroditism

on choice of neuroses, II, 262–264, 269

"Concerning Neurotic Disposition. At the Same Time a Contribution to the Etiology and to the Question of the Choice of Neurosis," II, 125–144

on doubt, II, 403, 428, 535; III, 46, 109

on dreams, II, 422–428; III, 86, 103, 172–174

on ego, III, 142

on erotogenic zones, III, 104

"A Fabricated Dream; a Contribution to the Mechanism of Lying in Neurosis," III, 17–25

on femininity, I, xxv; II, 423–434; III, 109, 111, 170

on "feminine protest," III, 25

on flight into illness, III, 157

on instincts, I, 406–410; II, 173–174, 260–263, 269; III, 104, 158

on libido, II, 454; III, 102–105, 107–108, 157

"Male Attitudes in Female Neurotics," III, 121

on Marxism, II, 172–178

on masculine protest, II, 426–427, 447, 458, 503–504, 567, 579; III, 18–19, 24–25, 33, 46, 56, 61, 71, 103, 108–109, 111, 140–144, 149–150

on masculinity, I, xxv; II, 423–434; III, 109, 111, 131, 170

on neuroses, I, 407n; II, 38, 125–126, 143–144, 178, 259–274, 321, 403, 424–434, 503, 518; III, 46, 68–73, 102–105, 107, 109, 140–144, 149–150, 176

on Oedipus complex, III, 145

On the [Organic] Bases of the Neuroses, I, 36–47

on organ inferiority, I, 36–41, 406n–407n; II, 147, 260–264, 321, 503–504, 567; III, 33, 46, 56, 61, 68–73, 104, 132, 142–143, 157

on oversensitivity, II, 247, 261–262, 268, 273, 349

on psychic hermaphroditism, II, 423–434, 447

"The Psychic Treatment of Trigeminus Neuralgia," III, 108, 154–155

on psychoanalysis, II, 426

"The Psychology of the Class Struggle," II, 97–98

on repression, I, 410; II, 264; III, 103, 140–144, 149–150, 157–158

on safeguarding tendency, III, 98–99, 102–104, 111, 125, 132, 142, 144, 157–158

on sexuality, II, 143–144; III, 104–105, 108, 149–150

"Study on the Inferiority of Organs," III, 157

on sublimation, II, 141

on symptoms, II, 321; III, 107

on transference, III, 103–104, 143

on unconscious, III, 25, 103

Adler, O., IV, 159

Albrecht, P., I, 339

Altenberg, P., II, 101, 386, 389, 392; III, 364

Amrein, K., III, 325–326

Anaximander, I, 147

Andreas-Salome, L., I, xxvi, 366; II, 28; IV, 107, 108, 113, 126, 133, 138, 147, 150, 154, 163, 167, 172, 176, 181, 183, 185, 256

Anzengruber, L., I, 23

Arend, I, 390

Aristotle, I, 358; II, 328–329

Arnim, L., IV, 151

Artemidorus, IV, 139

Aschaffenburg, G., I, 62, 166, 338

Auerbach, I, 338

Auersperg, G. von, I, 65, 65n

Avenarius, R., I, 322

on infanticide, III, 119

on infantile hysteria, II, 323–324

on infantile sexual theory, II, 341, 426, 581; III, 90, 147, 275; IV, 156; *see also* Freud, S., on children

on infantile sexuality, II, 48–50, 215; III, 119; IV, 24–25, 39, 161, 197, 233, 254–255, 260–261

on inferiority (feeling of), IV, 110, 130, 184

on instincts, I, xxii, xxviii, 87–88, 99n, 122–123, 135, 135n, 137, 396, 408; II, 160, 174, 266; III, 28, 308, 318, 335, 349, 352–353, 355, 367; IV, 72, 85–86, 88, 104–105, 112, 196, 210; *see also sub* aggression, sex, etc.

on interpretation, III, 203–204, 250–251

Interpretation of Dreams, I, xxvii, 221, 371; II, 79–80, 218–219; III, 3–4, 86, 130, 180–187, 288, 307; IV, 44, 136

on introversion, IV, 175

on jealousy, II, 37, 194; IV, 98

on jokes, III, 81

on Judaism, III, 273; IV, 42

on judgment, I, 35, 35n; III, 28

on latency, II, 217, 546; IV, 77–78, 88

"Leonardo da Vinci and a Memory of His Childhood," II, 340–352

on libido, I, xxviii, 86–87, 351, 408; II, 100, 115, 124, 268, 432–433, 494, 505, 538–539, 560; III, 148–149, 151, 173, 246, 352; IV, 5, 86

on love, I, 66, 86–87, 108–109, 216; II, 90, 237–249, 250–258, 447, 495; III, 81, 248; IV, 4, 53, 171, 175, 254

on lying, II, 516, 518; III, 22–23

on mania, I, 59; II, 182; IV, 99–100, 272, 275, 290

on marriage, III, 14; IV, 189

on masculine protest, III, 73, 145; IV, 109–110

on masculine–feminine, II, 432; III, 262–263

on masochism, I, 114, 232n; II, 249, 449; IV, 114–115, 119, 186, 213, 245–246

on masturbation, I, 56, 239–240, 283, 403; II, 38, 51, 61, 203–204, 224–225, 229, 242, 301–302, 371, 441–442, 542, 544, 552, 556–558, 560–564, 568–569, 572; III, 206–207, 321, 324, 327–328, 339, 345–346, 360–361, 363; IV, 22, 24, 25, 27, 39, 41, 60–61, 92–96, 281

on mathematics and sexuality, II, 217

on matriarchy, III, 63, 334

on megalomania, I, 55–56, 295; II, 538, 541; III, 13

on melancholia, I, 279; II, 182, 505, 538; III, 91; IV, 200, 275–276, 281–282, 287

on memory, I, 50–51; II, 216–217; III, 28, 307

on menstruation, IV, 124, 155

on metaphysics, I, 149

on methodology, I, 10–11, 136–137, 156, 171–172, 180, 227, 237, 249–250, 257, 265–266, 279–280, 335–336; II, 9–10, 19, 35, 41–42, 115–116, 175, 180, 203, 213, 280, 284–287, 301, 324, 359, 371, 379–381, 417, 442–443, 447, 453–454, 493; III, 48–49, 62, 83–84, 95–96, 118, 146–148, 151, 166–167, 187, 204, 236, 335, 339, 352; IV, 24, 39, 60, 85, 152, 180, 185–186, 192, 219, 232–233, 275

on moral insanity, II, 516

on morality, II, 31, 175

on morphine, I, 223

on mother–child relation, III, 118–120; IV, 53, 186

on mother–daughter relation, III, 122; IV, 110

on mother–etiology, I, 172; II, 71, 239–240, 242, 312, 462

on mother–son relation, I, 66, 193; *see also* Freud, S., on mother–etiology

on mourning, I, 278; II, 182, 538; III, 91, 318; IV, 275

250–251, 252, 253–254, 256, 257, 258, 259–261, 264, 265, 266, 267, 269, 270, 271, 272, 274–275, 277–278, 280–282, 283, 284, 285–286, 288–289, 291–292, 293, 294, 296, 299, 303, 306–309
"Schopenhauer, an Attempted Psycho-analysis of the Philosopher," IV, 101–102
Hoche, A., I, 340
Hochwart, R. von, I, 65n
Hock, S., II, 457
Hoffer, W., IV, 303
Hoffman, E., I, 23; II, 62, 349; III, 75; IV, 151
Hoffman, R., II, 421
Höfler, M., I, 367
Hofmannstal, H. von, II, 193; IV, 151
Hollerung, E., I, xxxv, 1, 14, 15, 30, 34, 36, 45, 48, 51, 69, 81, 90, 92, 93, 119, 126, 138, 143, 159, 163, 183, 201n, 202, 204, 226, 259, 270, 286, 298, 318, 355, 362, 372, 391, 397, 399, 401, 402, 406, 407; II, 1, 13, 19, 25, 30, 53, 65, 82, 101, 117, 121, 163, 179, 182, 195, 207, 237, 275–281; IV, 306–309
Hollos, I., IV, 211
Holzknecht, G., III, xv, 2, 8, 17, 35, 74, 159, 178; IV, 108, 306–308, 310
Hug–Hellmuth, H. von, IV, 205, 206, 207, 208–210, 211, 213, 214, 215, 216, 217, 221, 222, 223–224, 226, 227, 228, 229, 230, 231, 239, 243, 247, 250, 253, 256, 257, 259, 262, 264, 265, 266, 267, 268, 269, 270, 271, 272, 283, 284, 288, 294, 296, 309–310
Hume, D., II, 328–330
Hye, F. von, II, 275, 498–499, 507, 519; III, xv, 35, 279, 281; IV, 306

Ibsen, H., I, 22, 53, 127; II, 194, 543; III, 118; IV, 209
Immermann, K., IV, 151
Itten, W., IV, 211

Janet, P., II, 40, 531, 539

Jaszny, A., III, 141
Jekels, L., I, 391; II, 275, 290, 299, 303, 315, 327, 328, 338, 346, 353, 365, 376–377, 382, 394, 423, 423n, 431, 439–440, 463, 473, 476, 479–480, 498–499; III, xv–xvii, 8, 17, 26, 35, 50, 58, 64, 74, 82, 87, 93, 101, 107, 113, 126, 133, 140, 152, 159, 168, 188, 194, 201, 293, 299; IV, 75, 82, 107, 108, 113, 117, 121, 126, 128, 133, 135, 138, 141, 149, 150, 154, 158, 162, 163, 167, 176, 181, 185, 187–188, 190, 193, 195, 198, 202, 205, 207, 208, 211–212, 214, 215, 216, 218, 222, 223, 225, 226, 227, 228, 229, 230, 231, 236, 239, 243, 247, 249, 252, 253–254, 256, 257, 258, 259, 264, 265, 266, 268, 269, 270, 271, 272, 275, 280, 284, 285, 287, 288, 294, 306–308, 310
Jensen, W., I, 112–113, 195, 243, 246–247; III, 212
Jerusalem, W., III, 305
Joachim, A., I, xxxv, 204, 288, 306, 318–323, 324, 338, 347, 353, 362, 368, 372, 375, 376, 397, 401, 406; II, 1, 2, 11, 13, 18, 21, 25, 38, 43, 47–48, 51, 52, 53, 59–60, 65, 73, 82, 93, 101, 104, 125, 156, 158, 163, 172, 176, 195, 214, 217, 227, 237, 250, 252–253, 257, 259, 275–276, 282, 328, 365, 368, 371–372, 374, 382, 389, 435, 452, 472, 476, 478, 519, 525, 542, 573; III, 50; IV, 306–308, 310
Johns, I, 341
Joire, P., II, 149
Jokl, IV, 43
Joliasch, IV, 258
Jones, E., I, xxvi, 18n, 389, 391, 392, 394; II, 456–458; III, 180; IV, 30, 148, 202, 212–213, 303
Jones, Mrs. E., IV, 147, 183
Jones, H., IV, 252, 256
Juliusberger, O., II, 147; IV, 99, 107, 289
Jung, C., I, xxv–xxvi, 30, 62, 72, 101, 103–110, 138, 144, 166, 180, 254, 325, 327, 330–335, 340, 365, 367, 390,

117, 145, 147, 163, 164, 168, 170–
171, 172, 176–177, 178, 185, 193–
194, 195, 207, 211, 213, 214, 217,
219, 220, 227–228, 233, 237, 245,
259, 275–276, 282, 284, 290, 297,
299, 315, 328, 338, 347–348, 349,
382, 394, 404, 411–412, 423, 423n,
431, 435, 438–439, 445, 448, 452,
463, 468–470, 472–476, 479–480,
498–499, 507–508, 519, 530, 553,
557–558, 561, 563–564, 566, 573–
574, 580, 582; III, 1, 8–9, 17, 20,
26–27, 35, 58, 60–62, 74–75, 79,
93, 126, 133, 140, 152, 168, 175–
176, 178–179, 184, 188, 194, 201,
208, 212–213, 217, 233, 238, 250,
260, 279–282, 284, 293, 299, 320,
329, 336, 347, 357; IV, 7, 13, 20,
26–27, 28, 35, 42, 50, 57–61, 63, 68,
70, 75, 82, 92, 97, 101, 104, 113,
117, 128, 133, 141, 147, 150, 154,
156, 172, 181, 183, 185, 187, 193,
198, 202, 205, 206, 207, 208, 211,
214, 215, 218, 221, 222, 223–224,
226, 229, 230, 231, 239, 243, 245,
252, 253, 256, 257, 258, 259, 264,
265, 266, 267, 268, 269, 270, 271,
277, 280, 283, 284, 285, 293, 295–
296, 306–307, 309–310

Stekel, W., I, xx, xxxvi, 6, 14, 18, 19, 25,
26, 30, 34, 35, 36, 45, 52, 54, 62,
66–67, 69, 73, 81, 82, 83, 85, 92,
95, 96–97, 103–105, 106, 107, 108,
109, 110, 119, 125–126, 128, 130,
134, 138, 141–142, 144, 146, 153,
157, 158, 159, 162, 165, 166, 170,
175–178, 179, 180, 181, 182, 183,
187, 190, 195n, 201n, 202, 204–211,
212, 218, 226, 232, 233, 234, 235,
238, 239, 241, 242–247, 248–253,
254, 255–256, 257, 259, 270, 274,
276–280, 281–282, 285, 288, 296,
297, 298, 299–300, 302–303, 318,
321–322, 323, 324, 335, 336, 338,
340–342, 343, 344, 347, 350, 355,
361, 362, 363, 370, 372, 390–391,
397, 398, 401–402, 403, 405, 406,

407; II, 1, 2–12, 13, 25, 34, 38, 39–
40, 41, 42, 53, 59, 60, 61, 65, 71,
73, 76, 77, 82, 93, 101–105, 106,
109–111, 112, 117, 124, 145, 146,
147, 148, 150, 156, 157, 159, 161,
163, 172, 179, 180, 181–182, 185–
194, 195, 200, 202, 203, 206, 207,
212, 220–221, 225–226, 227, 232,
233, 237, 243–245, 246, 248, 249,
250, 251, 254, 256, 257, 259, 270–
271, 273, 275–277, 282, 287–288,
290, 315, 326–327, 328, 338, 348–
349, 353, 363–364, 365, 368–372,
376–378, 380, 382, 390–391, 404,
412, 415–419, 422, 423, 433–434,
435, 438–441, 445, 450, 452, 454,
456, 458, 463, 466–467, 470–471,
472, 475, 479–480, 497, 498–502,
504–506, 507–511, 513–514, 517,
519, 523–524, 526, 529, 530–541,
542, 547, 549, 551–552, 553–560,
563–564, 566, 568–569, 572, 573–
574, 581; III, 1, 3, 8–9, 14, 17, 19,
21–22, 24–25, 26, 31–34, 35–49,
50–57, 58–61, 63, 64–65, 67, 70–
73, 74, 76, 80–81, 82–83, 85–86, 87,
101, 126, 133, 138, 140, 150–151,
152, 159–162, 165, 168, 172–173,
177, 178–179, 183–184, 187, 188,
194, 201, 203–204, 206–207, 208,
211, 217, 219–224, 229–231, 233–
237, 238, 250–251, 258–259, 260–
263, 267, 269–274, 277, 279–282,
284, 290–292, 293, 297–298, 299–
300, 306–307, 309, 310, 317–318,
320, 322–323, 328, 329, 333, 336,
338–339, 345, 347, 357, 359–360,
362–363, 365–366; IV, 1–3, 5–6, 7,
9, 11, 13, 15, 20, 22–23, 25–27, 30,
33, 35–40, 42, 43, 45, 48–49, 50,
54–55, 57, 59, 61, 63–64, 75, 78,
80–81, 82, 85–88, 92–93, 95–96,
97–98, 101, 103, 104, 107, 117, 173,
281, 306–307, 309

*Analysis of a Case of Hysterical Pseudo-
epilepsy*, II, 13–24

"Doubt," II, 394–403

SUBJECT INDEX

in children, II, 44

mass, see Group psychology

and masturbation, II, 557, 564; IV, 94

repression in, II, 215; IV, 145–146

and sexual anesthesia, I, 304–305

stigmata of, II, 111; III, 239, 242, 245, 249

treatment of, II, 42

Hysterical attacks, II, 376–381

Illness

flight into, III, 157

see also Pathology

Imbecility, I, 185

Impotence, I, 212–217, 241, 251, 392–396, 400; II, 41, 75n, 76n, 241, 349, 415, 544

fear of, IV, 288–291

and masturbation, III, 337, 344; IV, 95

psychic, III, 5, 12–13, 206; IV, 188

and sexual enlightenment, II, 310

somatic, III, 344

and suicide, II, 501

Incest, I, 17, 19–29; II, 75n, 232, 434; III, 15, 234; IV, 11

fantasies, II, 248–249, 273; III, 103–104, 366; IV, 42

in history, IV, 177–180

and impotence, I, 393–394; II, 76n

in literature, I, 7–13, 15–17, 194; II, 9

and suicide, II, 494, 501

Infanticide, III, 114, 117, 119, 121–122

Infantile sexuality, II, 43–52, 215; III, 119, 360, 364, 545–547; IV, 24–25, 39–40, 75, 158–161, 197, 231–238, 254–255, 260–261

Inferiority

feeling of, IV, 110–111, 129–130, 184, 188

organ, see Organ inferiority

Inhibition, IV, 72–74

of creativity, I, 17, 25, 28; IV, 126–127, 131

sexual, II, 75n; III, 342

Insanity

and genius, I, 9n; II, 427

Instinct(s), I, xxviii, 31–32, 84, 99n, 122–123, 130–131, 133–137, 177–179;

II, 83, 84, 87, 91, 160, 173–174, 177, 260–263, 266, 269, 272, 328, 331–332; III, 104–105, 108, 110, 153, 158, 287, 317–319, 331–335, 352, 355, 359; IV, 112, 196, 286–287

aggressive, I, 356, 407n, 406–410; II, 260–261, 425; III, 37, 51; see also Libido

ambivalence of, IV, 104–106

condensation of, IV, 69–72

of destruction, IV, 86

ego, III, 28, 31, 51, 54; III, 365–366; IV, 83, 85, 88–89

life, III, 333

maternal, IV, 87, 209

and neurosis, I, 394–396; II, 262–263, 272

nutritional, I, 85–91; III, 51, 354; IV, 87–88, 106

overdetermination of, IV, 70

polygamous, IV, 188–189

reproductive, I, 83–88; II, 84, 87; III, 330

of self-preservation, III, 33; IV, 83

sex, I, 394, 395, 407n, 409; II, 332, 358, 399, 425; III, 28, 31, 33, 248–249, 316, 318, 329–330, 335, 348–350, 353–354, 367; IV, 82–89, 104–106, 158–159; see also Libido

International Psycho-Analytic Association, I, xxvi, xxix; II, 553, 573–574; III, 179–180, 201, 208–209, 218, 260, 280; IV, 226, 303–304

Interpretation, III, 203–204, 250–251, 261

Introversion, IV, 175

Jealousy, II, 396; IV, 51, 98–99, 234–236

paranoid, II, 37; IV, 98

and sadism, II, 188, 191, 193–194

Jesuits, II, 57, 121

Jews, I, 94, 98, 214, 283–284; II, 44–47, 387; III, 272–273, 313; IV, 66, 178–179

Jokes, III, 81, 213, 353

Judaism, III, 272–273; IV, 42

see also Religion

Kleptomania, II, 39–40, 200; III, 24, 48
  and masturbation, III, 358, 360; IV, 79–80
Knowledge, theory of, II, 328–337

Language, I, 349; II, 8, 169
  and symbolism, I, 319, 322–323
  see also Words
Latency, I, 305; II, 217, 545–546; IV, 75–78, 88, 234
Libido, I, xxviii, 85–91, 349, 351, 408–409; II, 100, 115, 124, 268–269, 399, 432–434, 512, 560; III, 102–108, 144, 148–149, 151, 153, 157, 169, 173, 175, 243, 245–247, 256, 314, 317; IV, 197
  displacement of, IV, 141–146
  and estrangement, II, 538–539
  and suicide, II, 494, 500, 505
  see also Sexuality, *sub* Instincts
Literature
  incest in, I, 7–12, 15–17, 19–29
  see also Art, Myth
Little Hans, II, 103, 202, 229–235, 286, 371, 387, 395, 414, 437, 581; III, 111
Logic, II, 329–331
Love, I, 66, 85–87, 108–109, 214, 216–217, 349; II, 55, 62, 83, 86, 87, 90, 90n, 92, 237–249, 250–258, 431, 447–448; III, 81, 248, 321, 334; IV, 4, 6, 53–55, 106, 144, 171, 175, 188, 254
  and estrangement, II, 534–535
  maternal, III, 113–125
  and suicide, II, 492–493, 495, 501
  see also Libido
Lying, II, 195–206, 215–216, 511, 516–518, 551
  neurotic, III, 17–25

Madness
  religious, II, 40
Magic, I, 10n; III, 74, 126–132, 307
  primitive, III, 351, 354; IV, 10–12, 137, 149, 242
Mania, I, 59; II, 182; IV, 99–100, 272–275, 290

Marriage, II, 88, 98; III, 14; IV, 187–189
  and neurosis, *see* Neurosis and marriage
Masculine protest, I, xxv, 9n; II, 426–427, 447, 458, 503–504, 567, 569, 579; III, 18–19, 21, 33, 46, 53, 56, 61, 71–73, 103, 107–109, 111, 135, 140–151, 152–158, 168–177, 258, 276; IV, 78, 109–111, 250
Masculinity, I, xxv; II, 423–434; III, 107, 109–111, 169–170
Masochism, I, 114, 117, 141, 143, 409–410; II, 22, 57, 59, 61–62, 249, 445–451; III, 130, 251–259, 314; IV, 87, 113–115, 120, 186, 213, 245–246
  anlage of, IV, 245–246
Masturbation, I, 68, 71, 84, 239–240, 281–284, 402; II, 44, 47, 51, 55–57, 59, 61–62, 109–110, 217, 221–222, 224–225, 228–229, 232, 234, 313, 362–364, 371, 433, 510, 512, 542–552, 554–565, 567–572; III, 19, 53, 75, 81, 83, 90–91, 93–94, 121, 203–204, 206–207, 228–229, 320–328, 336–346, 357–367; IV, 20–27, 35–42, 57–62, 68–74, 75–81, 92–96
  anlage of, III, 322–324, 327, 337, 339, 343; IV, 35, 57, 60, 76
  and anxiety neurosis, II, 298–299, 301–302; III, 352
  childhood, II, 436–443, 559; III, 344, 360, 363–364; IV, 20–26, 36, 42, 58–59, 93–94
  effects of, III, 326–328, 336–343, 361–362; IV, 26–27, 41–42, 58–59, 68–72, 76, 92–96
  and erythrophobia, I, 403; III, 327–328
  and fantasy, III, 321, 322, 328, 336–337, 344; IV, 21–25, 37, 42, 77, 80, 94
  and guilt, III, 338, 345, 357, 359, 363, 366; IV, 37–42, 59–61, 79, 94–95
  and impotence, IV, 95
  interrupted, II, 37–38
  and kleptomania, *see sub* Kleptomania
  and lying, II, 197–206, 215–216; III, 21–23, 324–325, 360–362, 367
  and masochism, II, 447–448, 451

preconditions for, III, 321, 323, 327, 339–340; IV, 21–22
prohibition against, IV, 254
prophylaxis, III, 337–338
psychic, IV, 76–77, 79
and redemption fantasy, II, 241–242
and sexual anesthesia, II, 62, 306, 313; III, 337–339, 344
and suicide, II, 501, 504; III, 359
symbols for, *see sub* Symbols
symptoms of, III, 321–327, 357–362, 365
therapy for, III, 321, 323–325, 327, 337–338; IV, 58
of women, IV, 25, 69–71, 78–80
Mathematics and sexuality, II, 217
Matriarchy, III, 63; IV, 176, 178
Matricide
and incest, I, 24
Mechanical therapy, II, 24
Megalomania, I, 52–57, 60, 291, 295, 295n; II, 538, 540; III, 13
Melancholia, I, 64, 277–279, 321–322; II, 182, 258, 538; III, 90–91, 93–94; IV, 52, 200, 272–276, 286–287
and dementia praecox, IV, 273, 275–276
and masturbation, IV, 41
and suicide, II, 485, 492, 505
see also Depression
Memory, I, 49–51; II, 216–217; III, 28, 307
see also sub Childhood, Screen memories
Menopause, II, 107, 109–110
Menstruation, I, 347–348, 353; II, 571; III, 185–186; IV, 118, 155
Methodology, I, 83–84, 180, 185, 189, 192, 227, 227n, 232, 234, 237, 249–250, 253, 255–258, 259–269, 335–337, 368; II, 9–11, 19, 21, 22, 35, 41–42, 111, 113, 115–116, 203, 206, 280, 283–284, 286, 324, 326–327, 376–378, 454, 493; III, 48–49, 52–53, 75, 80–81, 83–85, 95–97, 118, 138–139, 160–163, 165–167, 185–187, 191, 203–204, 227, 230–232, 235–237, 252, 258, 261, 265, 303, 335,

339, 352, 354; IV, 2–4, 12, 24, 36, 39–40, 60, 74, 85, 87, 111, 152, 178–180, 191–192, 218–219, 233, 274–275, 299
Freud's, I, 7–9, 77–80, 136–137, 156, 171–172, 180, 227, 227n, 237, 279–280; II, 175, 180, 324, 359, 416–417, 435, 442–443, 447, 453
Migraine, IV, 210
Misogyny, II, 255; III, 174
Monogamy, II, 94–95, 98
Moral insanity, II, 516–518
Morphine, I, 219–220, 223, 224
Mother, II, 257, 431; III, 137
-child relation, III, 113–125; III, 52, 186
complex, III, 22, 228–229
-daughter relation, IV, 110
motif of "dear-little-old," IV, 251
motif of neglected, IV, 247–248, 250
and perversions, II, 62
as prostitute, I, 396; II, 244, 246
in rescue fantasy, II, 242, 254
-son relation, I, 9, 12, 66, 171, 193; III, 4–5, 10
"Mother etiology," symbols for; *see sub* Symbols I, 172; II, 71, 239–240, 307, 310–312, 314, 462
Motility, II, 458–459
Mourning, I, 318; IV, 275
see also Melancholia
Muco-membraneous colitis, III, 240, 243
Music, III, 53, 55; IV, 67, 79–80
Mysticism, I, 146–148, 151–152; III, 303; IV, 134
Myth(s), I, 341–345; II, 10, 65–72, 121–122, 233, 253, 410–411, 457, 459–460, 579; III, 29, 122–125, 127, 214–216, 330–332, 335, 348; IV, 80–81, 174
of hero, IV, 123
incest in, I, 7–13

Narcissism, I, 61n; II, 307, 311–312, 541; III, 5, 13, 270–271, 351–354; IV, 86, 116, 135, 148–149, 173–174, 178, 184, 190–192, 253–254, 273–274, 276

162, 303, 307; IV, 77, 148, 299
of incest, I, 23, 24
Succubus, II, 458
Sucking, IV, 165
Suggestion, I, 32, 34; II, 78n, 316; III, 161
Suicide, I, 114, 192–194; II, 183, 200,
226, 456, 479–497, 499–506
among children, II, 479–497, 499–506,
510; III, 3–4
Superstition, III, 136
Suppression, I, 15n, 19n, 21, 200, 200n,
408; II, 89–90
Swaddling, IV, 118–120
Symbol, I, 7–13, 14, 161–165, 291, 295,
318–323, 363, 368, 399, 403–404,
404n; II, 121–122, 367–370, 374,
568; III, 23–24, 62–63, 64–68, 74–
77, 79–81, 84, 128–130, 132, 225–
226, 250–251, 260–263, 265, 276;
IV, 66–67, 136–137, 139, 151–153,
209, 287
autumn as, I, 291, 296
bisexuality of, III, 220–222, 234–235
of bisexuality, II, 380
biting as, I, 11
body as, IV, 7–10
for children, III, 67–68; IV, 224
choice of, IV, 123
cravat as, III, 180–181, 184–187
crowds as, IV, 9, 11, 32
for death, III, 38, 66
in dreams, II, 219, 311; III, 38, 180–
187, 333; IV, 7–12, 26, 156–157, 254;
see also sub Dreams
drowned body as, II, 243
dying together as, II, 225–226; III, 315
earth as, II, 460–461
eye as, IV, 123
for father, II, 460–461; III, 53, 76; IV,
122–123
finger, as, I, 11
flies as, IV, 224, 253–254
formation, IV, 123
geographical, II, 219
goblins as, I, 123
head as, I, 112, 114, 116–118; II, 410–
412; III, 95
horse as, I, 250

house as, I, 29, 363
landscape as, IV, 7–10
map as, II, 371
for masturbation, IV, 26–27
moon as, I, 403–404
for mother, I, 29; II, 243, 341–342, 460–
461; III, 77
in myth, II, 67–72, 311, 410–411; III,
215–216, 330–331, 335
nose as, I, 12
paired organs as, III, 251, 260–261
for penis, I, 11, 161–165, 296, 404; II,
121, 123, 348, 410–412; III, 62, 65–
67, 79, 84, 180–181, 184–187, 215–
216; IV, 118, 157
and psychoanalysis, I, 323n
serpent as, I, 11; III, 215–216, 220–
222, 225–226, 266
soldiers as, I, 291, 295–296
spider as, III, 64–67
stairs as, II, 219; IV, 32
in suicide, II, 183
sun as, II, 460–461
for vagina, I, 29; III, 62; IV, 151–153
vehicles as, II, 415–416, 418
violin as, I, 66–67
white as, I, 116
wind as, III, 89–90
for women, II, 311; III, 181, 183–187
women as, *see* Women, as symbols
wood as, III, 181, 183–187
Symptom(s), I, 145, 149, 186, 407; II, 272,
297, 321, 401–402, 450, 453, 528;
III, 106–107, 203; IV, 169, 249
and actual neurosis, II, 417
bipolarity of, III, 80
and bisexuality, II, 427, 431, 434; IV,
98
and childhood defects, II, 510
of dementia praecox, *see sub* Dementia
Praecox
inversion of, II, 151
Synthesis, IV, 73–74
Syphilis, I, 238–241, 399; III, 311
and erythrophobia, I, 403

Temperance movement, II, 36; *see also* Social movements

Testicles, II, 304–305, 311–312
Thanatos, III, 312
Thought, II, 164–170; III, 28, 76–77, 79,
    130; IV, 148
  omnipotence of, IV, 173–175, 212
Tickling, III, 239, 242, 248
Tragedy, III, 137, 139; *see also* Art
Transference, I, 60, 96–97, 101–102, 180;
    II, 149, 249, 359, 443, 496; III, 20,
    61–62, 103–104, 143, 153, 204, 242–
    243; IV, 169, 219
  bisexuality in, II, 287
  negative, IV, 263
Transformation, III, 329–335
Trauma, I, 234, 234n, 252; II, 142, 232
  in paranoia, I, 289, 292, 296, 297
  sexual, I, 270–275
Traumatic neurosis, I, 336–337; II, 107,
    110, 115, 353; III, 239–240, 242–243

Unconscious, I, xxviii, 8n, 9, 12, 122–126,
    131–137, 232, 266, 268, 320; II, 164–
    170, 174, 209, 216, 245, 279–281,
    331, 377, 432; III, 24, 32–33, 76–77,
    80, 103, 274–275, 291–292, 295–
    296; IV, 136
  and Devil, II, 122
  and estrangement, II, 533
  and repression, I, 26
  and time, III, 299–309
United States, III, 14, 40, 199, 249; IV, 64,
    86
Urination, II, 217
Urticaria, III, 6, 239, 242

Vagabondage, I, 103–110; III, 77, 270; IV,
    170
Vagina
  fear of, I, 396
  symbols for, *see pub* Symbols
Vagoneurosis, III, 91–92
Vampires, II, 457; III, 312
Vegetarianism, I, 399; III, 364
Venereal disease, I, 238–241; II, 84, 86, 94,
    99; *see also* Gonorrhea, Syphilis
Vertigo, IV, 29–31
Vienna Psychoanalytic Society, I, xvii–xx,
    xxiii–xxiv, xxix–xxx, xxxvii, 7n, 373;

II, 553, 573–574; III, xi, 7, 50, 57,
    82, 101; IV, 12, 102, 103
  organization of, I, 298–303, 313–317;
    II, 463–471, 472–478, 479–481,
    498–499, 507–509, 519; III, 1–3,
    8–9, 17, 26, 58–59, 93, 112–113,
    126, 159, 167, 177, 178–179, 201,
    208–210, 218, 279–283; IV, 158,
    223, 303–310
  see also Psychological Wednesday Society
Virginity
  history of, IV, 177, 179–180
Vomiting, II, 218; III, 203–204; IV, 131–
    132
Voyeurism, III, 243

Weaning, II, 324–327; IV, 234–236
Witch trials, II, 119–123, 458
Wolfman case, IV, 285–287
Women, I, 193–201, 211, 216–217, 310n,
    347–354; II, 36n, 36–37, 40, 57, 60,
    83, 85–86, 88, 90–92, 98–99, 217,
    296–297, 301, 411, 454; IV, 14, 53–
    54, 56, 140, 156, 249, 262–263, 323;
    IV, 53–55, 118, 129, 136, 170
  aesthetic ideal of, III, 195–200
  emancipation of, III, 343–344
  fantasies of, IV, 70–71, 80–81
  madonna type of, IV, 51–53
  and masturbation, II, 562–564, 571–
    572; IV, 25, 69–71, 78–80
  narcissism of, IV, 174–175, 191
  and Oedipus complex, *see* Oedipus com-
    plex and women
  and religion, IV, 8–10
  sex life of, II, 87, 160
  and suicide, II, 183, 504
  as symbols, I, 63
  and transference, I, 20
  with-a-penis, III, 143–144
  see also sub Symbols
Word(s), I, 61, 148, 150, 320, 335; II, 164–
    170, 568; IV, 148
Word-association experiments, II, 454; IV,
    48
Work, I, 196
  and neurosis, IV, 167–191

357